To Michael R. Greasley, who turned a racing spectator into a rally enthusiast . . .

ISBN 0 85429 410 4

A FOULIS Motoring Book

First published 1984

Published by:
Haynes Publishing Group
Sparkford, Yeovil, Somerset
BA22 7JJ, England.

Distributed in North America by:
Haynes Publications Inc.
861 Lawrence Drive, Newbury Park,
California 91320 USA

Editor: Rod Grainger
Page layout: Tim Rose
Printed, in England, by: J.H. Haynes
& Co. Ltd.

Audi quattro

the development & competition history

or

'quattrophenia'

by jeremy walton

Foulis

Haynes

Foreword
by Hannu Mikkola

I can remember sharing a hotel room in Scotland with Jeremy Walton. At the time I was driving the Ford Escort. I had to go from the very last place, after I had made a mistake early in the rally, and finished second. This was very difficult for me, but not as hard as the party during the next night and morning with Roger Clark in our room!

Now I have driven Audi Quattro for three seasons and it has brought me a World Championship — and one for Audi at Ingolstadt too. I have enjoyed driving Audis very much — and I look forward to driving the new short Quattro later in 1984.

I wish Jeremy good luck with this book, just so long as he does not use my room for his parties anymore!

Contents

Author's introduction

To understand the Quattro itself, and the competition and road derivatives it inspired, a great deal of technical help was needed. Audi Sport's Roland Gumpert supplied most of the competition development history but the central reasoning behind the car's existence was supplied by the man who fathered the project, Jorg Bensinger. His Research & Development colleagues filled in the specialist areas − such as transmission, suspension and engine − but it was thanks to Jorg Bensinger's enthusiasm that much of the basic knowledge was acquired, enriching the early chapters particularly.

R&D Audi chief Ferdinand Piech gave his usual dryly perceptive insight into the Quattro tale too, and I relied heavily on an old friend from my European Touring Car Championship reporting days, Dr Fritz Indra. Fritz moved to Audi in a senior engines engineering role in 1979 and we can now see why he was excited about the prospect with powerplants such as the new DOHC 20-valve five for the Quattro Sport. Another old friend, this time from Ford Competitions in Cologne, had also moved to Audi when this was written. I owe Thomas Ammerschläger a considerable vote of thanks for ensuring that the manuscript was checked, and for details that added much to the overall picture of this fascinating 4-WD concept.

Of the Quattro drivers I relied most on Hannu Mikkola, who has literally been with the Quattro project from its earliest competition steps in the Audi 80 body. Yet I would not have talked to Mr Mikkola at all, or been conveyed in such fabulous style during pre-1981 RAC Rally testing, if it had not been for Michael Greasley. Then editing *Motoring News*, Mike has always tried to instil in me a proper respect for rallying's often muddy ways, and the considerable enjoyment − which I hope is transmitted textually − that I gain from watching top crews' master machines like the Quattro, comes largely from MRG's shrewd guidance over the years.

quattro

Although the German factory and sports departments took the brunt of my questioning — and I'd like to thank their PR Department under Rolf Urban (factory) and Dieter Scharnagl (sport) for their hospitality and readily supplied high quality illustrations — it remains a fact that I would not have visited Germany at all if it had not been for the efforts of Tony Hill, Laura Warren and Don Hume at VW-Audi UK. My thanks to their managing director, Michael Heelas, for supplying an interesting commercial insight into the Quattro's UK rallying and commercial role with an interview given at short notice.

Also in Britain my personal thanks, for help given, to David Sutton, Terry Hoyle and David Bignold. The three of them supplied a lot of information in a very little time.

Photographically I did my best to lose all Audi's best shots on the morning this manuscript was delivered, but enough survive to show how well the company document their "Progress through Technology". Of the private photographic sources used LAT and Kathy Ager supplied by far the most material, including the excellent cover shots by Maurice Selden. Very high quality work at short notice came from Colin Taylor Productions. David Bryant at VAG in Milton Keynes supplied most of the British road and rally Quattro pictures. The copious technical drawings are from factory sources, but Norman Hodson of *Cars & Car Conversions* supplied the 1983 technical pictures of the works team cars at Ingolstadt. Rod Grainger at Haynes had the nervous breakdown whilst we replaced the missing pictures, but managed to patiently edit my manuscript once more.

Where performance figures are quoted they are always courtesy of *Autocar*, unless otherwise stated. German facts and figures were drawn mostly from *Auto Motor und Sport*, particularly prices. The conversions from metric to imperial are nearly all via my own Casio, rather than just accepting a turbocharged capacity or wheelbase from another printed source. Thus the mistakes are my own . . . A situation which applies throughout!

Finally my domestic thanks to my wife Patricia, who once again trudged through the manuscript teaching me some basic spelling that will doubtless be forgotten before the next tome.

Jeremy Walton
Henley-on-Thames

Chapter 1

Who are Audi ?

How Mercedes, VW, Auto Union, NSU and others were involved in the creation of today's technology-loving Audi at Ingolstadt, Upper Bavaria.

Globules of rain from an early Spring shower race uncertainly across the flush-fitted glass beside me, tracing their progress in dotted arcs as the world rushes by at over 120mph. Ahead *autobahn* unreels, bordered by fields and occasional architectural reminders of Bavaria's other role as a picture postcard tourist attraction. The shimmering metallic silver Audi "Car of the Year" 100 saloon had picked me up at Munich airport, and transported me away with much of the effortless high speed displayed by the Lufthansa Boeing that I had recently vacated.

Naturally we turned away from *Olympiapark* and its adjacent BMW 'four-cylinder' building, heading due north up the A3 *autobahn* for Ingolstadt at an average pace well beyond Britain's overall 70mph limit. While strange sounding, to English ears, place names such as Pfaffenhofen and Wolnzach swept past on the large blue and white signs; I reflected that the engineers in the muddle of companies that spawned Audi, before Volkswagen ownership, would not have been that surprised by the existence, in the eighties, of such technically innovative Audis as the slippery 100 and the permanent four-wheel-drive (4-WD) Quattros. For Audi's history is full of men and companies subscribing to the present company slogan: *Vorsprung durch Technik*, or "Progress through Technology" in literal translation.

The old town section of Ingolstadt is fascinating for tourists and historians alike, but my base, in sharp contrast, would be an eighties Holiday Inn —

quattro

The globule-gatherer at rest and at speed. Audi's 100 — winner of the 1983 Car of the Year award — started my journey into a past full of Wanderers, Horchs and the more familiar names of today. In 1982 Audi sold 88,000 of the old 100 model; in 1983 sales of the sleeker, current 100, reached 162,000 and Audi built a record 390,000 cars.

complete with every Mod Con and hideous green "grass carpet" to wave its fronds in the air-conditioned atmosphere. However the Inn of the eighties faded away rapidly on this and subsequent visits as I appreciated excellent food while absorbing the astonishing tale that lies behind Audi and the Quattros.

Because the official company name today incorporates both NSU and Auto Union, Audi history goes back to the 1873 foundation of NSU at Neckarsulm, a town that houses part of Audi's manufacturing capability today. However the most logical start for the Audi researcher is with a gentleman called August Horch. In November 1899 the enterprising Horch was already in business with patented parts for Bosch magneto ignition. By 1900 he had developed a two-cylinder car with 10bhp and his own carburettor patents.

In 1901 Horch and his 15 workers had test run their car prototype up to 32km/h (19mph), which may be cause for merriment today but was 19mph faster than most people would then have dared go on a mechanical contraption!

By 1904 Horch had 90 employees and a fledgling auto works at Zwickau making a small four-cylinder Horch with 80×120mm bore and stroke. The company were confident enough to enter competitions from 1907, and were regular competitors in pre-WW1 races. Typical of the period was their 1910 *Typ* 35/40, powered by four-cylinders displacing 6395cc: enough to provide 55bhp at a serene 1400rpm and 90km/h (56mph). Today's 1.1-litre Polo of 40bhp travels close to 90mph, so some of that much vaunted technological progress *is* getting through to the customers . . .

In the early 1900s this is the kind of thing Audi's ancestors were constructing. The wire-wheeled wonder is a 4/5HP Horch with shaft drive and a twin cylinder engine. Aspirant automotive historians qualify for further points by identifying, with christian names, the occupants . . .

August Horch divided up his original company in 1909, founding a new company to build cars under his own name with more partners. However there was naturally confusion with two companies using Horch in their titles and

quattro

eventually an awful pun helped them out of the dilemma. In German *horch* means "hark", so *audi* for "to hear" was an obvious rejoinder! Well, that is one story they tell today, and in the words of that old journalistic cliche, "why spoil the story with facts?" However Audi state that their name came simply from the translation of Horch's name into Latin.

Which ever way the name was acquired, "Audi Automobilwerke GmbH" was registered as the company name in 1910. Despite the fact that Horch remained interested in motor sport, and cars bearing his and the Audi name were to be seen in frequent action, the Audis on sale from 1910 were in the main very upright black carriages and not at all sporting in appearance.

Remembering that at one stage, prior to the outbreak of WWII, Germany had over 200 registered car makers — and that West Germany currently has just seven motor manufacturers — it is easy to see that any of the surviving manufacturers is liable to have a history full of amalgamations. Add in the fact that the Germany of the twenties went broke in the most inflationary manner seen outside South America, and you find that companies from the turn of the century such as Horch, Wanderer, NSU, or even Wartburg, wander in and out of the most famous lineage particularly as an after-effect of two World Wars and the partition of Germany.

Test track fever! The roof-tops made a convenient proving ground for the first NSU motorcycles, which had belt drive from the engine, as well as chain-driven pedal power for reverting to the bi-cycle basics of the plot. By 1904 NSU were making over 2200 machines a year.

Sports Past

Alpine rallies were a feature even of pre-WW1 motor sport, and Audis were an integral facet of events like the Alpenfahrt — winning 14 prizes and the team award by 1913 with their soft-topped, wire-wheeled machines — a useful reminder of the 10/28 horsepower sports Audis sold between 1913-14.

World War 1 involved all the engineering resources and car companies that could be mustered but, as with so many other German engineering-based concerns, the twenties swiftly saw Audi in financial trouble: Horch himself leaving the board in 1920. By 1925 Audi were so deep in the red that investment in the production and development of their six-cylinder range was bleeding the company's capital so rapidly that talks with the original Horch factory commenced about possible avenues of salvation.

Audi rally victories can be traced back to at least 1912, when this machine was part of a team that took first and second on the Alpine Rally, winning a silver medal as well.

Audi managed to procure injections of capital in 1927 and 1929 that kept them in the car-making business. However, as so often has happened in automobile history, one finds that Audi were making the most luxurious products at a time of deepest financial woe! Thus, in 1929, they had acquired the licence to build the Rickenbacker 90 bhp V8; a model of Detroit origin. The price of this deal was their independence, for famous motorcycle builders DKW had taken over both the Rickenbacker rights and Audi during a hectic period of acquisitions.

However 1929 brought yet more trouble. October 24, "Black Friday" produced the infamous Wall Street Crash. Then, as now, when America sneezed the poor men of Europe were likely to catch pneumonia; and in those days, Germany was just such a poor man. The effect on NSU, car and motorcycle makers, was immediate: they handed over their car manufacturing activities to Fiat.

The First Union

In 1932 some of Germany's leading manufacturers anticipated the kind of super-grouping that would characterise the European motor business in the sixties and seventies. As with Peugeot-Citröen-Talbot (née Chrysler) or British Leyland, the "Big is Beautiful" policy carried the day.

DKW, who had 15,000 workers by 1927, found that the effort of absorbing 16 other companies in that growth to substantial size had left them with yearly losses, and bank debts of over 2.3 million Reichmarks. The banks had their say,

quattro

In 1923 an outing to Avus' banked track for the works NSU team — seen here in front of the works — brought a 1-2-3 result at an average of some 75mph. At the time NSU had 3500 employees making a bicycle every five minutes, a motorcycle every 20 minutes and motor cars at the rate of one every two hours. Audi archives recall that a large beer cost 21 *million* Marks by the end of 1923, owing to the chronic inflation that struck Germany in the wake of the First World War . . . and you thought the *Dog and Badger* overcharged today!

as banks will, and DKW became part of a new, 20,000-strong, car company called Auto Union AG. This alliance of Horch, Audi, Wanderer and DKW was headed by Dr Ing Carl Hahn and was symbolised by the four silver interlinked circles that are so prominently displayed on the grilles of·Audis today.

As in any other amalgamation it took time for the effects to reach the products — and all concerned kept their individuality to a far greater extent than was normal in the bad old days of BMC badge-engineering. In the year of alliance Audi seemed most indicative of the way things could go with a 5/30 model which had a Peugeot 1115cc motor but a transmission and chassis developed by DKW. Incidentally you will find that Audi today frequently refer to over 50 years of front-wheel-drive experience and this dates back to the 1931 Berlin motor show at which DKW displayed their first production car *"mit frontantrieb"*. Disciples of Citroen's *traction avant* school may care to note that it was 1934 before the French came to market with the front-wheel-drive system that is now almost universal amongst European small cars. However, neither Audi/DKW nor Citröen pre-dated the British, who had a 12/75 Alvis sports model with all independent suspension and front drive in limited production in 1928.

In the years after Auto Union was formed, it was that company name and its familiar four-ring badge which became famous all over the world owing to its motor racing exploits with such fearsome devices as the V16 mid-engined

The four manufacturers and their individual logos, prior to the birth of Auto Union AG. Audi's original number 1 is above a picture of their victorious Typ C Alpine Rally winner, capable of 62mph. Next are DKW with an illustration of their first front drive mass production design, DKW F1. Horch's symbol and plump Pullman 12 Cabriolet 600 are displayed alongside the Wanderer emblem and their popular light car design, nicknamed *"Puppchen."*

The 1932 conglomerate called Auto Union with its quadruple rings logo, still used on today's Quattros, fused together DKW, Horch, Audi and Wanderer under Auto Union's leadership.

GP machine of 1933 onward. Yet the subsidiary companies were very much alive and well, with Audi making a particularly nice 2-litre six with front drive. DKW continued to enjoy strong motorcycle sales and racing success whilst developing the two-stroke technology that would be a feature of post-war two-stroke three-cylinder engines: potent little smokers that would propel DKWs and SAABs to victories in racing and rallying until the early sixties.

Wanderer were left with the job of serving the working middle classes via such stolid saloon designs as their 1.8-litre W24, while NSU had something really world-beating brewing away in their corner of the quad circle car co. NSU at Neckarsulm worked with Professor Porsche on the construction of three *Typ 32* prototypes — only a glance at the lines of these cars is necessary to identify the early ancestors of the VW Beetle. Small World . . .

Another Ferdinand Porsche-Auto Union project of the thirties was the construction of three prototypes as part of the preliminaries to the legendary VW Beetle. These date from 1934 and were coded Typ 32.

quattro

The genius of Dr Ferdinand Porsche lay behind the Auto Union racers too. In 1933 the initial 16-cylinder car was rated at 295bhp and a maximum of 280km/h (174mph), but their best racing year in the face of the consistent rivalry from Mercedes-Benz in this state-funded internal war to produce the best racing goods for Germany, was 1936. By then a 6-litre version of the V16 was rated at 520bhp and, on the crossply racing covers of the thirties, it could be fairly said that the job of racing such machines around a track like the 14 mile Nurburgring was best left to heroes such as Bernd Rosemeyer, Achille Varzi or Hans Stuck's equally famous father.

In 1934 Auto Union scored the first ever victory for a rear-engined Grand Prix car. That Typ A was designed by Ferdinand Porsche and driven by Hans Stuck snr; here we show the awesome V16 Typ C development, both in 1936 racing trim and as it has been preserved into the eighties. Its 6-litres produced 520bhp at 5000rpm during 1936, enough to provide 211mph according to Audi archives! Three such cars were seen at Donington in Britain during 1937 and one, driven by Bernd Rosemeyer, defeated the rival Mercedes team in a display of tail-sliding majesty that any present day rally driver would envy.

Rosemeyer also had the task of record-breaking for the honour of Auto Union, a streamlined body and that tumultuous power of 1937 providing 405km/h (251mph). As European Racing Champion, in an Auto Union, Rosemeyer certainly gave the company their money's worth. Auto Union and their divisions, such as NSU, were competing in Motor Sport until the outbreak of war in 1939; NSU already running the supercharged 350cc bikes that foretold of their brief, but nevertheless completely effective, postwar motorcycle racing achievements.

Meanwhile Wanderer were producing eleven production models, Audi offered a 3.2-litre in saloon and convertible bodies. Horch continued their tradition of eight-cylinder motivation with magnificent machines such as a 3.8-litre V8 in seven derivatives, a 5-litre motor in five models and a 3.5-litre layout to underpin ambulances. There was certainly variety in the group for, in 1938, some 3500 NSU employees made 136,000 bicycles, besides 63,000 motorcycles and 142,000 brake hubs! Perhaps it is relevant to note at this point that NSU's chief designer was a Briton from 1929 to 1939! His name was Walter William Moore and the Germans still acknowledge his contribution prior to WWII.

1936 European Champion Bernd Rosemeyer lost his life in one of the in~· edibly sleek Auto Union record breakers. The 26-year-old from Saxony scored his last GP win in the British GP of 1937.

A Busy War, and After . . .

War meant a complete conversion to military needs of course, but what that meant to the main Auto Union plants and NSU was rather different. Auto Union built, in their first year of war production, 33,646 engines for stationary use, 20,254 motorcycles and 5,111 assorted petrol-powered vehicles for military use. Horch and Wanderer took the bulk of the 55.6 million Marks made during 1940-41, Audi having the smallest percentage (3.2 million Marks). The workforce expanded dramatically, just as it did at the Munich and Berlin factories of BMW, reaching an astonishing 42,811 people in 1942, from a figure of just over 15,000 before the war!

Quantity, as always, was the aim of wartime production, but by 1944 the Allies were really pounding away at such production centres and company property in Spandau and Berlin was heavily bombed. The Wanderer works, where they were making Panzer engines under the Werk Siegmar title, was caught in what the company aptly described as a *Bombenhagel*, or "a hail of bombs" . . . The Horch Zwickau factories, and the neighbouring Audi (at Chemnitz: now

Karl Marx Stadt) were even worse hit. On March 5, 1945, shortly after the Germans had heard about the destruction of Dresden, the Audi and Horch works suffered two heavy night raids. By the middle of April they were under artillery fire from the Russians and by May 6 it was all over so far as that sector was concerned.

NSU at Neckarsulm put on production muscle rapidly in the war years, including 224 heavy machine tools and increased automation. A number of additional specialised tools made it possible for them to produce vital components for aeroplanes, U-boats and other machines at war but also demanded that increased floor space be acquired through 1942-43.

One of the most ingenious products NSU's fertile corporate brain (over 50 patents registered during the war years alone) created was a motorcycle sidecar where the "car" section was a multi-wheel mini tank! Neckarsulm's all-time low came on March 1, 1945, when some 36 bombers got through to complete their

All wheel drive is an old Audi NSU pre-occupation! Here's their version of the All Terrain motorcycle/personnel carrier, powered by a wartime 36bhp Opel engine. Below: an idea of what the bombs did to NSU's works. Ironically they became a repair centre for the US Army in immediate post-war years.

deadly missions. The works were damaged severely, but would be in a far better state to return to post-war production as the town fell to Americans, rather than the Soviets, whose occupation annexed all four Eastern German Auto Union factories. Incidentally this was not a unique fate in post-war Germany, for BMW's pre-war car production was centred in Eastern Germany and it took the Munich men rather longer to return to car production than most of their present West German rivals.

Auto Union Comes West

For their rebirth in West Germany, Auto Union selected the traditional car-makers' preference of a riverside location: Ingolstadt straddles the Danube in Upper Bavaria, whilst NSU continued on the Neckar river, located about halfway between Stuttgart and Heidelberg.

NSU went back into the motorcycle business post-war with a speed that was aided by a period as a repair centre for the US Army. New factory halls

NSU were 1954 World Champions in the 250 class with this Renn-Max ridden by Werner Haas. Note the use of trailing link front suspension and modern fairing style (even if the rivetter had a field day!) on the very high-revving four-stroke.

and general purpose buildings were erected and by 1949 some 3000 employees were shaking off the shattering past and making a new two-stroke single of 100cc: the NSU Fox, which had a fine reputation for excellent handling. At an astonishing pace, that will be familiar to those who studied the German post-war "economic miracle", NSU forged forward. In 1955, just under a decade after motorcycle production had properly resumed, NSU of Neckarsulm could claim to be "the biggest two-wheeler producers in the world" their output amounting to 350,000 units a year!

Sport played a part in the remarkable NSU revival, for they were running slippery 500cc record breakers to 290km/h (180mph!), this supercharged twin resting on two wheels. The 1953/54 seasons were the great ones for their motorcycle solo racing results, NSU achieving a 125 and 250 World Championship with the Fox and Max *Renn*, or "race", versions. In both seasons they scooped both 125 and 250 titles, the superb parallel twin Rennfox scooping all three premier positions in the 250 title hunt of 1954. From a quarter-litre engine, NSU wrung 39bhp at 11,500rpm — but it was capable of reaching 15,000 revs . . .!

In 1956 NSU were a memory on the racing scene, having withdrawn as suddenly at the close of 1954 as they had entered in 1953. To compensate they accumulated 62 solo motorcycle speed records, including the absolute figure

This near-115mph world record breaker on three wheels from NSU was driven/ridden by Herman Bohm. The other NSU World record winner, but this time on two wheels, was ridden by Wilhelm Herz and reached fractionally over 180mph in 1951.

of 339km/h (211mph) set by a supercharged twin of 500cc that yielded a tremendous 110bhp, or the same as a production Golf 1600cc provided in the seventies.

For NSU (initials originally drawn from NeckarSUlm!) 1957 was an important year, marking their return to car manufacture for the first time since their abdication to Fiat of 1929. Although the 600cc Prinz with its then fashionable rear engine and transmission was notable, it could well be that history finds the February 1957 NSU news of more importance: it was in that Winter month that the rotary engine debuted on the test bed. They had been working on the Wankel principle rotary motor since 1954, but it would be 1958 before the Felix Wankel tri-tip rotor was shown to the public, the 30bhp NSU Sportprinz retaining an engine location aft of the back axle, but introducing a very welcome dash of Nuccio Bertone flair in the styling of small German cars. We leave NSU in 1958 and return to Auto Union to see how they made out in the post-war scramble to resume profitable car manufacture . . .

The 1967 NSU Spider with Wankel rotary power was good enough to win the German hillclimb title for Siegfried Spiess.

Auto Union: A Tougher Task

Following the loss of its four primary manufacturing plants in East Germany one could have forgiven the four circles of Auto Union for quitting the stage, exit left. However, as already related they chose Ingolstadt as their site for a new start. Their chance of a second life came from the DKW military vehicles, for there were still some 60,000 examples to be serviced, inside and outside Germany. Initially Ingolstadt was just a spares depot, but under the leadership of Dr Hanns Schuler affiliated depots grew in Frankfurt, Munich, Hannover and Nürnberg. The complete operation became Auto Union GmbH (the German equivalent of a limited company) in 1947.

Currency reforms in the Summer of 1948 allowed pre-war Auto Union chiefs Dr Richard Bruhn and Dr Carl Hahn to raise capital for an embryo car manufacturer once more, so that a second formation of Auto Union GmbH was necessary in 1949. It immediately set to work making DKW motorcycles to the pre-WWII RT125 design; by the end of the year it was calculated that 1200 employees had made around 500 of these motorcycles and 504 of the surprisingly sleek *Schnell-laster* delivery vans, which had 22bhp two stroke engines.

As at NSU, the speed of Auto Union's recovery took away one's breath compared with the smugness to be found in some of the victorious allies when faced with post-war reconstruction. In 1950 Auto Union had 4500 employees

quattro

pumping out 24,000 bikes and 6800 *Schnell-lasters*; DKW were allowed to utilise their two-stroke techniques with a 23bhp twin for the *Meisterklasse* of 1950-52. By 1953 they had the first of many car-borne two-stroke triples, complete with the characteristic blue smoke and seductively smooth power delivery of 34bhp from 900cc; a very fair power figure indeed by contemporary standards.

During 1954 the workforce had more than doubled compared with four years earlier. Now 10,000 were aiding and abetting output of machines such as the DKW Hobby, the first German scooter with continuously variable transmission. By now AU had new production facilities in Dusseldorf and 83-year-old founder August Horch had died (3.2.1951).

Through the fifties, at least the early to middle years, there seemed little to stop Auto Union. They had some success with DKW in racing, including the 1953 Manx Tourist Trophy. The DKW triple, sold under the theme that a two stroke triple equalled a four stroke six for smooth power delivery, had sold 330,000 cars by 1959. Exports were going well too, Auto Union selling in 55 countries during 1953.

Quattro's Earliest Ancestor: Mercedes Step In

By 1956 the two stroke triple had been persuaded that 40bhp was better than 36, and DKW had the *Sonderklasse* so equipped. However the primary home for this engine over the years was inside the upright DKW Munga, a four-wheel-drive military machine that bore the Auto Union quadruple circles with pride in the 250 examples made in 1956, its first year. One such Munga was sponsored by Esso to complete a 150,000 mile round the world trip, "across country for friendship, goodwill, better understanding".

Direct Quattro ancestors in providing 4-WD behind the quad-circle badge were these three-cylinder two-stroke (using DKW-derived power plants) Mungas. A model later succeeded by the Iltis, which set Audi engineering thinking of other ways to apply the benefits of 4-Wd.

In 1957 over 11,000 Auto Union employees made over 123,000 assorted vehicles and Daimler-Benz AG decided this was too tempting a target to miss, particularly as the market for motorcycles in Germany was slowing down and causing many healthy companies with large two-wheeler interests to wonder how they would cope with a four-wheeler future.

On January 1, 1958, Daimler-Benz gained control by acquiring 88% of available Auto Union stock. One of their first decisions was to abandon motorcycle production: since the war the Auto Union Group had made over half a million two wheelers (519,000) and so it was truly the end of two eras when the new masters took over.

Under Daimler Benz, DKW continued to perform notably well with the two stroke cars, the last such machine introduced in 1964, while the DKW Junior series attracted both motor sport and commercial accolades. However, although the DKWs were a formidable force in European saloon car racing until the sixties, their rallying peaks were before Daimler-Benz ownership. In 1956 the "ring-a-ding" two stroke triples rattled their way to outright victories on three events that are now prestigious rounds of the World Rally Championship: the Safari in East Africa, Finland's 1000 Lakes, and the rough charmer Greece knows as the Acropolis.

Through the late fifties and early sixties NSU remained preoccupied with their rear-engined production cars and an increasing number of licensees for their Wankel motor. By 1963 NSU could report sales of 100,000 Prinz cars and nine licensees developing Wankels from 5 to 500bhp. In May 1963 the Spider rotary-engined Prinz sports car was in production. By 1966 it had proved powerful enough to annexe the German national rally championship in the GT class; a year later it won the hillclimbing title too, again in the GT class.

DKW F12 and later DKW junior could terrorise opposition in the small saloon car racing classes of the early sixties with their two-stroke triple power – a basic design also used by SAAB in their rally winners for Erik Carlsson and company.

Auto Union: Changing

During 1960, the Ingolstadt car production facility really "came on stream" manufacturing 61,938 DKW Juniors while Dusseldorf made 58,000 Auto Union-branded cars. Add in miscellaneous Munga output and Auto Union set a production record in 1960 that lasted until 1969. However this was a high point for the two stroke machinery and the early sixties turned into a grim period for Auto Union, production facilities at Dusseldorf being needed by Daimler-Benz and manufacturing isolated to the Ingolstadt plant.

In 1964 Auto Union entered a completely new era that links directly to the Audis of the eighties. Under Mercedes/Daimler-Benz ownership they had developed a range of four-cylinder four stroke motors that were ready for production in a new front-drive range of conservatively-styled four-door saloons first shown in September 1965. Yet before that sensational Frankfurt debut – where the clean lines, good accommodation and 72bhp motor of 1700cc were widely appreciated – Auto Union changed hands again!

quattro

The first of the four-stroke Audis that led onto the eighties technology was this 1965 Audi. It blended the Daimler Benz four-cylinder engine with modified bodywork from the DKW 102. The 72bhp result, which ended decades of two-stroke saloon cars from Ingolstadt, debuted at the Frankfurt show in September 1965.

The motive seemed to be that age-old motor industry compulsion to grow through acquisition. In this case Volkswagen were looking for additional capacity as well as a route through the sixties and seventies that held more variety than dependence on the even-then ageing Beetle.

Although the two stroke lived on a few years, notably in the Munga 4-WD that chattered on until 1968, the age of the four stroke and doubled capital resources swept Auto Union to a new emphasis on the Audi name under the leadership of VW boss Rudolf Leiding, who became chairman of the board of management at the new conglomerate. Even in 1965 the benefits for both parties were already evident as Ingolstadt assembled 52,200 of its own cars, plus 15,700 of the new Audis and 61,800 VW Beetles under a joint arrangement.

The year 1966 was notable for the astonishing progress Audi showed under new management. Output leapt from 15,700 to 63,500 of the latest four stroke front-drive car generation. Derivatives of the new breed abounded, all based on the front drive principles that have proved so happy to blend in with 4-WD today. First we had the Audi Variant, an estate version of the 72bhp saloon, and that was rapidly followed by an Audi 60 with 1.5-litre version of the four-cylinder engine and 55bhp. More exciting was the announcement of a 90bhp Super 90 Audi, again retaining the basic family look of clean conservatism, excellent carrying capacity, safe if rather soggy understeer-biased handling, and a legendary balance between mpg and performance that has been an Audi hallmark since the sixties.

The 1966-67 recession in the German new car market delayed effective introduction of the Audi variants but, by 1968, the master plan seemed to be back on schedule with a model that has great significance both to the Quattro and the eighties. In November the Ingolstadt premises were used not to preview

The short skirt sixties, seen in Bavarian style! The lady wearing the pelmet is being held up by a 1966 example of Audi's four-stroke Ingolstadt wares, the range expanded to offer from 72 to 90bhp that year.

the anticipated new factory extension, or some such other industrial event, but to present a flagship for the Audi saloon line: the 100. Of course today's "World Aero Champion" 100 is a very different car, but it represents a logical progression from that sixties front drive 100.

At the end of 1968 the faithful Munga cross country motorised-mountain goat ceased production. Some 46,750 had been made, and it was reckoned that Auto Union with DKW had produced a prodigious 2.5 million two stroke motorcycles and assorted four wheelers in nearly 50 years' association with this engine type.

Overall 1968 confirmed VW-Audi's return to meteoric progress with a 67.2% production boost and a 59.3% increase in exports. Reflecting that new confidence was a shapely new Audi for the Autumn 1968 Frankfurt show. The 100 coupe is remembered as something of a classic in Britain; a 115bhp version of the 100 that allowed 185km/h (115mph) to be reached with quite reasonable fuel consumption from the twin Solex-carburated engine.

NSU: Rotating Into Line

In hindsight it is easy to see that NSU were over-committing themselves to the rotary engine if they wanted to survive as an independent. The little sports coupes and convertibles and the rear-engined saloon range were joined by the award-winning Ro80. This was a truly stunning technical achievement, combining silky 115bhp twin rotor power, front-drive, electric clutch (control in the gear-lever knob) and swooping four door bodywork that would not look out of place in the aerodynamically super-conscious eighties.

quattro

Unfortunately the Ro80 was bugged with the now-famed problems of the rotary, including heavy fuel consumption and rotor tip premature failures: the engine was so smooth that it was terribly easy to over-rev despite the inbuilt precautions arranged by NSU engineers, including the largest red warning band I have ever seen on a tachometer from 6500rpm onward. In the initial LHD form the Ro80 sold at £2,279 on the UK market and provided slightly over 110mph in the highest of its three torque converter-ruled ratios.

The cost of creating the revolutionary RO80 was partially offset by sales of the rotary licence to outfits like Toyo Kogyo (Mazda), but by 1969 NSU needed new injections of capital from Auto Union, and therefore it was only a matter of time before NSU arrived inside the VW-Auto Union Audi corral, bearing with them the ill-fated 1.6-litre middle class saloon that would eventually emerge as VW's unloved K70.

Audi NSU Auto Union AG was officially integrated within the VW Group on March 10, 1969, and the formalised contract utilising the new name has held force since August 21, 1969. At last we had a group recognisable today!

The front door at Audi NSU in the seventies.

Quattro life abounds within the main car plant these days, the size of which can be judged from the aerial shot . . . and the works are expanding all the time.

Through the seventies and into the eighties it is tempting to see the 1969 car group as having progressed step by logical step but, aside from the Auto Union circles and the rotary engine work still going on at NSU, that logical progression really belongs to the VW-directed Audi side. Despite the major fuel crisis following the Arab-Israeli war and the severe world economic crisis that was only slowly beginning to ease when this book was written in the early eighties, Audi had continued forward whilst even parent VW suffered heartaches such as replacing the Beetle with something people would buy. Then, when the Golf answered all those problems, there have been more recent losses incurred as a result of two factories in America to worry VW.

Events during the seventies and eighties that are of great significance to the Quattro story were the birth of the Audi 80 mid-range saloon (Car of the

The 1969/70 range with individual brands still prominent. In the centre is the cleanly executed Audi coupe, whilst the surrounding products from Audi, Auto Union and NSU include 30bhp Prinz, with that range's usual rear engine layout, and the front drive NSU Ro80 (foreground, left). The Ro80 with a wind-cheating body and rotary powerplant, yielding 115bhp.

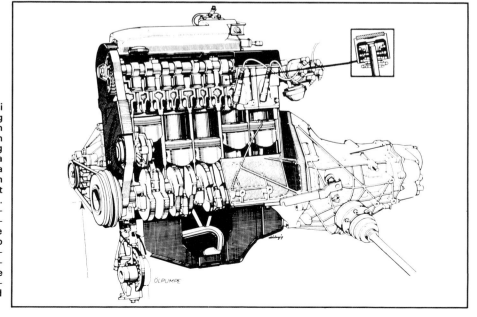

Summer of 1976 saw Audi set traditional engineering thought on its ear with the full scale production of their petrol-burning five-cylinder engine, a design which is now a feature of many Audis in the mid-eighties and at the heart of the Quattros. The strength of the bottom end was most generous and even the Quattro Sport's 300bhp engine used many components below the cylinder head line that were of 100/five-cylinder production origin and strength.

quattro

Year 1972); the five cylinder / 136bhp inline SOHC engine developed for the 1976 reskinned 100 saloon; the replacement for Munga in cross-country 4-WD ability, the Audi-developed, Ingolstadt-built, VW-branded Iltis, which appeared from November 1978. Finally there was the turbocharged Audi 200 executive saloon, then the most powerful front-drive saloon in the world, with 170bhp, announced for September 1979.

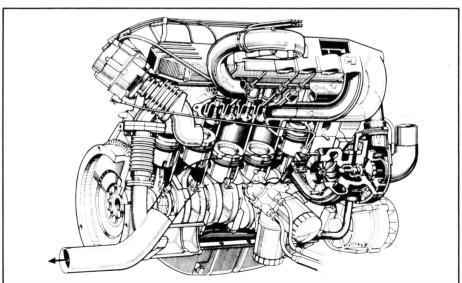

The Audi 200 engine in display form and cutaway shows a simple KKK turbocharger installation in the foreground along with the wastegate and dished pistons. Much of the Quattro's improved power output could be traced to the use of an intercooler.

The turbocharged front-drive Audi 200 development of the 100 provided useful pre-production turbocharging information, as well as a number of common components in the running gear, including the smart Ronal alloy wheels.

Audi coupe actually appeared *after* the Quattro, but in fact provided the basic outline of the 'earlier' car, minus the extended wheelarches. The floorpan was that of the 80 and it was strictly front-drive prior to 1984.

Kissing cousins: the 80 and the 100 both provided hardware for the Quattro programme, particularly the 80 on the body front. All Quattros prior to the 1984 SWB Sport were built on modified 80 floorpans, which had to be specially modified to incorporate a wider front to rear transmission tunnel, a rear axle and all the mounting points for rear drive components.

The pre-1983 model Audi 100 had a 136bhp version of the five-cylinder engine as its top fuel-injected option, and the front drive that was part of all Audis before the advent of Quattro.

quattro

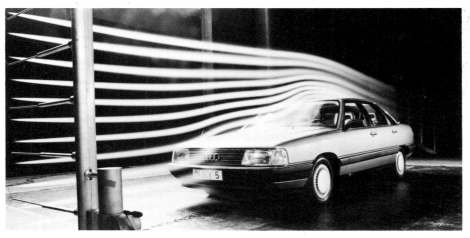

Wind tunnel development and an eventual 0.30Cd shook up the opposition when the Audi 100 appeared in 1983. Again front drive and five-cylinders lay beneath the skin — but the promise that every Audi model would have a 4-WD option in the wake of the Quattro's pioneering progress meant that the 100 would not always be just another front-drive saloon. Even if Renault had claimed a 0.28Cd for their 25 by 1984, the 100 will always be remembered for its pioneering production use of flush-fitted side glass . . .

The 1979 board who approved the Quattro go-ahead. (Left to right) R. Gerich; G. Kurrle; Dr Wolfgang Habbel; H. Kialka; Dr M Posth and Ferdinand Piech. Chairman Habbel and engineering chief Piech not only supported the Quattro internally, but were frequent rally spectators in the eighties.

Just over 30,000 workers — split broadly into 10,000 at Neckarsulm and the bulk at Ingolstadt — churned out 344,100 Audis in 1979 (less in 1980-82 because of the recession). Incidentally Neckarsulm production has mostly been used for American Audi derivatives and Porsche's 924/924 Turbo series. You may also care to note that the VW-Audi Group is collectively known under the V.A.G. initials, which are primarily used in Britain to denote their combined dealerships.

It was in February 1977 that Ferdinand Piech, an important Porsche shareholder and Audi management board member responsible for research and development, began to receive informal requests from his chassis engineering department regarding the use of 4-WD for a production Audi saloon. It would take the dryly humorous Piech — who headed Porsche's creation of the 12-cylinder legend that became *the* sports racer of the early seventies, the 917 — just one night to decide that, *if* 4-WD was to be part of their production plans, it would be better suited to a performance car than the proposed all-wheel-drive 100.

The Quattro was on its way . . .

Chapter 2

The Quattro concept: catalyst & reality

There had been plenty of four-wheel-drive vehicles before — military, agricultural, recreational, even Grand Prix racers — but none of them provided more than a hint of what Quattro would become . . .

Inside the massive four storey office block that houses the Audi Research and Development section, several thousand staff beavering away behind the metallic

The Audi R & D buildings before the carpark was full!

quattro

facing of the outer walls, a wiry engineer explained the concept that created the Quattro, and a new breed of Audis to provide at least the option of 4-WD throughout the range by 1985. His metal-framed glasses threatened by the ascending model Tornado swing-wing jet fighter that flies proudly above his generous desk space, Audi chief chassis engineer Jorg Bensinger recalled how

Jorg Bensinger: the Quattro's 'father'.

the 4-WD concept for a mass production car came to be taken seriously at Ingolstadt.

"Many years ago, I had the job of making speeches to journalists to explain the advantages of front and rear drive. I made up a chart [now translated into English and hopefully decorating these pages — J.W.] to help the writers, and me, see what were the advantages and disadvantages of each system.

"As we should all know today, very powerful cars, even those that are not for competition, are very difficult to drive at their limit. Of course it is not a problem to handle the difference in power on and power off for an Audi 80 1.3-litre, but when it comes to more than 200 horsepower in a rear-engined car,

Jorg Bensinger's translation of the thinking that led Audi to adopt 4-WD for road cars, rather than previous military or off-road use. Across you read the five rival drive layouts, to the side the chief characteristics, and the reaction of each layout, is listed. Put in British terms, the common examples of front-drive behaviour are most modern small and medium class saloons, the Mini popularising front-drive in the UK from 1959 onward. What is listed as "Conventional layout": front engine/rear drive, is becoming a minority system, but plenty of saloons from Mercedes and BMW follow this pattern, whilst both Toyota and Ford amongst the world's largest manufacturers, also use this layout for some products, this conventional system was always preferred in rallying until the supercars arrived, typified by the Quattro. Rear or mid-engine? Locations nearly always to be found in exotic cars, but Skoda and Porsche share opposite ends of the market-place with rear engines on the Estelle and 911 models respectively. That Porsche acknowledge the 911's deficiencies is emphasised by their 1983-84 development of an electronically controlled 4-WD system for the twin Turbo 911 rally model in Group B

	Front wheel drive	Conventional layout = front engine / rear drive	Rear or mid engine	4wd Front engine	Rear engine
Directional stability	Good	Good–satisfactory, often severely impaired on bad surfaces with power on	Poor	Good +	Satisfactory
Oversteer/understeer behaviour in corners with poor adhesion:	Can be set up for oversteer or understeer				
power off power on	understeer more understeer	understeer oversteer	oversteer oversteer	understeer understeer	oversteer understeer
"Lift off" reaction in fast bends	Can be influenced by setting up accordingly				
	Usually turns inwards slightly	Usually turns inwards quite noticeably	Usually turns inwards abruptly, difficult to control	Good	Good because tyre forces reduced by half
Traction	Satisfactory, not so good when loaden	Fair, better when loaden	Good	Very good + Ideal weight distribution	Very good
Stopping distance	Satisfactory	Satisfactory +	Good	Good Very good with inter-axle differential locked, same slip front and rear	Good +
Aquaplaning	Relatively harmless, directionally stable, early warning given by wheel spin	Critical, no warning with power on	Very critical, no warning with power on	Somewhere between front wheel drive and rear wheel drive, very little warning, but narrower tyre widths possible	
Usable space	Large	Moderate +	Small, divided luggage space	Moderate	Small
weight and cost	Low	Relatively high	Very low (rear engine)	Higher than front-wheel-drive or front engine / rear drive	

of 1985. Mid-engine layouts usually go with the supercars from Ferrari, Lotus and the like, but Renault also adopted this layout for the R5 Turbo and Lancia had it in the Rally 037 that won the 1983 World Championship. In the last column is the rare rear engine 4-WD layout (like that adopted by Porsche Group B) compared with Audi's front engine 4-WD. The Audi scheme of things was adopted by many other manufacturers of the mid-eighties. In these final two columns Audi obviously saw little difference in capability between rear engine 4-WD and front engine Quattro in manners. The important consideration was the lower cost of converting their front drive road cars to 4-WD, rather than re-engineering the rear end of their existing road range, or manufacturing a special, for the rear engine location.

or this kind of power in the front wheels only, then there are troubles for the driver — and this is the same when there is a front engine and rear drive with a lot of power, especially if there is bad weather . . .

"I studied three important things: 1) traction on all surfaces; 2) the high wear of tyres on high performance cars, no matter if they have front or rear drive — it's just terrible! Finally, 3) I look to the behaviour of these cars when you have to lift off the power in a big hurry in a corner", concluded the amiable engineer, whose hobbies include utilising his private pilot's licence, and whose past includes periods at Porsche, BMW and Mercedes.

Bensinger's conclusions can be seen in tabular form, but basically the pros and cons of front and rear-wheel-drive soon sent his mind to the obvious alternative of four driven wheels. "When I see the interesting possibilities of this system I ask myself; why not four wheels driven?" Bensinger grins at the simplicity of it all in retrospect and then frowned as he remembered The Snag. "This was very interesting, putting all these things on paper, but we had no possibilities to build such a car when I was thinking about such things. There were no parts in existence for me to make such a car . . ."

quattro

"I Was Convinced"

Bensinger waited literally years before there was a suitable Audi opportunity. It is worth pointing out that the experience of other engineers with 4-WD tended to put Audi off its application to a road car. Even Hannu Mikkola, before his first test drive in a Quattro prototype, expected "something that handled like a Land-Rover, or one of those things."

As in so many things that are created here but go abroad for production, Britain was a pioneer in 4-WD applications beyond the obvious off road utility vehicle uses. Stirling Moss won the 1961 Oulton Park Gold Cup with a 4-WD Ferguson-equipped P99 single-seater. Jensen of West Bromwich made 318 Ferguson Formula (FF) Interceptor V8 coupes for public sale between 1966-71. Ford of Britain supplied around thirty of their V6 engined Zephyr/Zodiac "aircraft carrier" saloons to the police and other interested parties for evaluation. In 1969 the same company chose the proven combination of V6 engine and Ferguson transmission to chalk up a competition debut win for the Capri, eventually making around seventeen such machines both for competition (televised rallycross) and assessment as possible limited production machines for their Advanced Vehicle Operation.

This may sound as though Ford and Ferguson were in the same development league as Audi a decade and more before the Bavarians offered their vehicle for sale. Yet, if you compare the Audi system and that of Ferguson, the excess weight and complexity of the British system becomes apparent immediately. For Audi, obsessed with weight in the fuel consumption and low cost manufacturing cause, there could be no question of considering anything like the Ferguson system. The answer lay in permanent engagement of 4-WD and maximum use of existing Audi model components, or those that were in the development pipeline, to reduce the costs and make those theoretical advantages Bensinger had so carefully analysed as a production possibility . . .

Quattro all-wheel-drive forerunners, Munga (left) and Iltis (right).

Bensinger had found his answer in, "1976 with the Iltis on the road, and then during the following Winter when we went testing in Scandinavia with it. You know it only had the 1.6-litre/75bhp four-cylinder and was *very* tall, with a short wheelbase. I didn't expect much handling from a machine with the centre of gravity so high in the air. But I was really pleased with its performance on ice and snow: I was convinced this was the way to go in the future . . .

"Sure, we knew about the Iltis ability on snow and ice, but I wanted to try 4-WD on better surfaces to see if the things I had written on my comparison chart would work out on dry roads too. When I came back from that Winter

testing I said to Mr Piech that we should do this 4-WD for a higher performance car, like a 100.

"Mr Piech was not very excited about this when I told him how good the Iltis had been; it was too early for him . . . but it was only the next morning when he telephones me and we talk about this idea. My first opinion is that we should put the equipment on Audi 100, but Mr Piech says 'we must convince the public of the advantages of 4-WD, and that we can do it at Audi. You know the customers see something technical coming from Mercedes, or Porsche, and they say OK, it must be better!' "

Ferdinand Piech stuck to his viewpoint and instructed that a high performance car be constructed, "maybe with motorsport possibilities; but that was *not* the point" recalled Bensinger. Today Bensinger feels that the Audi R&D boss was absolutely right in recommending the way for four-wheel-drive to arrive *chez* Audi. "Without high performance in a road car, and through rallying, there would have been no way to show the public all the advantages of our system", he stated firmly.

Before detailing how development progressed, Bensinger reminded us of the secrecy Audi imposed on the preliminary stage of Quattro development. "Nobody saw production plans that we had, not even the suppliers. Even when we had not shown the car at Geneva people from Mercedes, BMW and Porsche were asking me if we would really make this car. Nobody could believe it. I think they thought we were crazy — and some of the things I did, like making the first A1 prototype before there was official approval could have got me fired . . . but I had talked with Piech and everything was all right!"

High-Speed Development

Aside from the inspiration of the Iltis, forthcoming Audis such as the 200 Turbo (basic five-cylinder turbo layout), 100 (many suspension and transmission parts), Audi 80 (basic floorpan and some running gear) and the Audi 80-based coupe, all had major components to contribute. Thus the enormous speed at which Quattro coupe would whoosh from an idea to Spring 1980 Show sensation in Switzerland. Ironically the front-drive Audi coupe actually did not materialise until *after* the Quattro's debut in Germany, although the two arrived in Britain together, during 1981. Thus we had the situation where the Quattro launched the very similar coupe style — a bit of a shame for the mass production side at Audi, for this conventional coupe was eagerly anticipated as the successor to the well liked 100 fastback. However it does not seem to have done sales any harm, proving that you do not always have to unveil the most powerful derivatives after their less endowed brethren.

In March 1977 practical development began, an elderly 80 saloon equipped with the Iltis 4-WD system. That fundamentally differed from the layout used in the Quattro road cars because it operated on the "rigid" system, which simply means there was no centre differential to smooth out any differences between front and rear wheel speeds. Bensinger commented, "this rigid drive is not a system we could use in a passenger car of course because of the judder when turning, or when one set of wheels is sliding and the other is not. We just didn't have a centre differential available, so we used this drive to give us an idea how the car would be." Incidentally, the centre differential was abandoned in the Quattro rally cars too.

In asides to the story of that first prototype, a vehicle that officially did not exist (!), Jorg Bensinger made a couple of key points about Audi's transmission philosophy. "You should know we had always the possibility of making a 4-WD

quattro

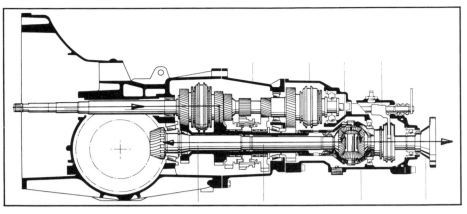

Schematic of the gear-box, showing the upper power transmission shaft from the engine, running above the front differential and transferring power to the outer gears of the lower transfer shaft, which is hollow. Power is taken to the cente differential and transmitted forward (within the lower shaft) to the front diff, and rearward to the propshaft. On rally cars a system without centre differential or hollow shaft simply interconnected front and rear directly, just as had been the case on the Quattro's military forbears.

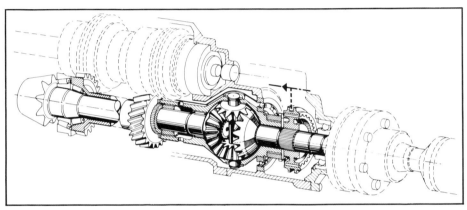

Another view of the hollow shaft transmission gearbox arrangement with the centre differential carefully displayed. Engine output arrives via the top shaft, and is split via input from the outer casing of the front section of the lower shaft, feeding it to the centre differential, before that middle differential's two pinion wheels deliver power rearwards and forwards. The latter goes through the solid inner to the lower forward gear shaft.

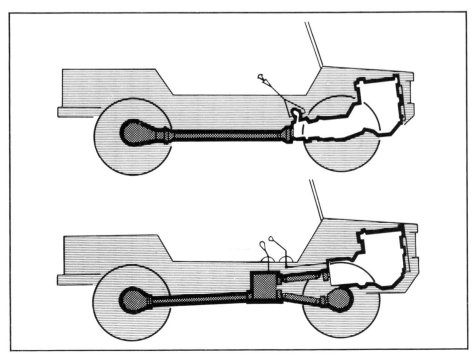

Top, the Audi solution for 4-WD with power transfer forward and aft, within one casing. Below, what they avoided and a feature of sixties British 4-WD systems: the separate transfer box to take in power and split it front to rear.

where the rear drive could be engaged, or taken out, like that for Subaru or Toyota, but we didn't like it. We had it, but we did not want to use it.'' Bensinger did not elaborate on their reasoning, but part of the reason must have been an extension of logic which said that the advantages of 4-WD outweighed any other system, so why should the driver want to disengage it? From the start Audi engineering was geared to providing a high performance system.

Providing just such a transmission whilst using as many existing Audi parts as possible, was the responsibility of former Mercedes racing engineer Hans Nedvidek. A burly and well dressed reservoir of transmission talent who worked on the Stuttgart competition cars, including the W196 of the Moss-Fangio era, during his 1950 to 1964 employment beneath the three-pointed star.

Dipl-Ing Nedvidek proudly guided me through the heart of the Quattro 4-WD system. Components adopted from Audi 100 and 200 production in the gearbox included the usual upper mainshaft, clutch and associated linkage, gear clusters that sit on the main shaft, bearings, synchromesh cones, gearbox housing and the original gearbox linkage — all traced their heritage back to 200 and 100 — although some strategic strengthening did take place, notably for the front differential.

To allow civilised four-wheel-drive a centre differential was incorporated aft and below the main engine gearbox shaft. From this differential power could be fed to the rear wheel layout and forward to the uprated front drive differential. How did the power get forward without a bulky external transfer box, such as featured in so many of the clumsy 4-WD installations that put Audi off such concepts in pre-Iltis days? Via an ingenious hollow shaft, whose 26.3cm (10.35in) long contained the shaft transmitting power forward from the centre diff, while wearing a conventional gear cluster externally: a two jobs at once approach that would warm any designer's heart and that ensured the simplicity and low weight that Audi sought.

It should be noted that the lack of a centre differential on rally Quattros from the earliest days was emphasised in 1983, when the Quattro A2 took on

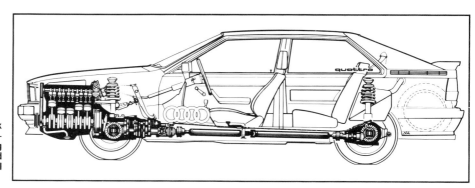

Quattro, front to back power unit and transmission layout, showing the three differentials and original cable differential locks.

External view of the hollow gearbox shaft. This vital component is only 263mm/10.35in long, but avoids the need for clumsy transfer boxes and associated heavyweight hardware.

quattro

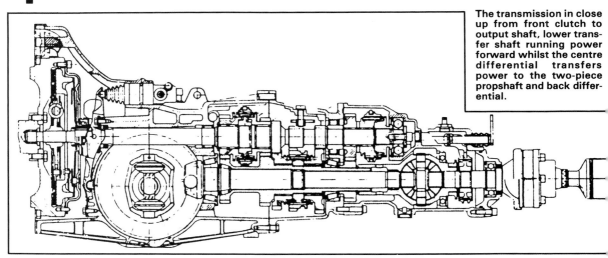

The transmission in close up from front clutch to output shaft, lower transfer shaft running power forward whilst the centre differential transfers power to the two-piece propshaft and back differential.

a shorter and lighter homologated gearbox casing that had no provision for a centre diff: previously a standard casing from the road car had been employed. In road and rally Quattros built up to the time of writing, the power is split 50 per cent to front and rear. Testing shows no advantage in handling feel or outright speed with any other power split.

The Quattro road car has always had the provision to lock middle and aft differentials, but the way in which this was done — and the engagement pattern — varied during production from the original twin Bowden cable operation that allowed each diff to be locked individually via transmission tunnel levers between the seats.

A sturdy but compact two-piece propshaft with a centre Kardan-joint took power back from the modified Audi 100/200 front transmission to the aluminium-cased back axle, which owed its existence to the Iltis programme of course, since front-drive Audis seem to do without back differentials very nicely! In fact it is the content of the rear differential that goes back to Iltis, as the casing was specifically developed for the Quattro. Some enlargement of internal components was necessary to cope with turbocharged 2.1-litre torque, rather than slogging military motors.

Development Speed

Using so many parts from forthcoming or existing Audis certainly speeded the engineering birth of Quattro. March 1977 saw the debut of the development 4-WD 80 Quattro-Iltis mongrel and March 1980, just three years later, the coupe Quattro had emerged to an almost literally hysterical press and public reception for the first Geneva Show of the eighties: a fitting trendsetter for the decade. Incidentally, the "hysterics" largely came from the German press who found *Auto Motor und Sport* had already printed a full, colour illustrated story. This, weeks before the international press briefing in a crowded Geneva conference room . . .

Meanwhile the serious development of the single modified A1-coded 80 hybrid, had shown enough promise in 1977 to attract full management support from outside, as well as within, Audi engineering. In September 1977 the project was given a development number and engineering expenditure was given official blessing: albeit *after* some five months of unofficial practical work had

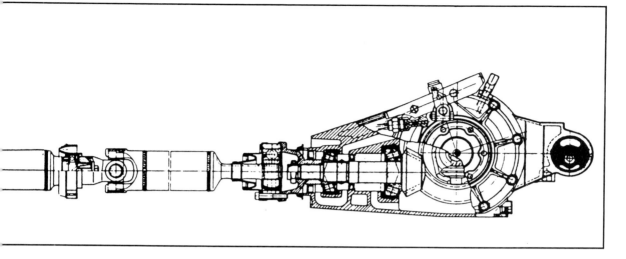

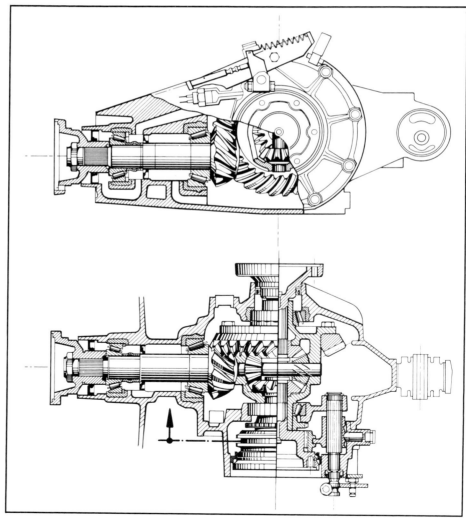

The back differential carries the lock-up mechanisms that were originally activated by lever and cable, or later by two stage switchgear with vacuum assistance.

quattro

commenced on that initial Audi 80-Iltis conversion. Rules are made to be broken, even in Germany!

In November 1977 the first A1, running a turbocharged five-cylinder motor of Audi 100 parentage and 200 development ancestry (without an intercooler at this stage) was assessed on the road and impressed so much that a formal project to build a production road model was put to Audi's senior management outside engineering, also in November 1977.

Once the project had been made official inside engineering, a small team was allocated to its progress. "Less than 12 of us were involved. Today our progress on production Quattro changes, like ABS brakes and these things, is slow because only four or five engineers can be spared from our other work to make Quattro changes", revealed Bensinger. All official engineering development projects are coded inside Audi with the prefix "EA". This simply stands for *Entwicklung Auftrag*, or "Development Exercise": in the case of Quattro the coding retrospectively applied was "EA 262".

Austrian Breakthrough

Inside Audi the arrival of 1978 coincided with a major demonstration of the embryonic Quattro's prowess as an extraordinary road car, badly needed to persuade senior management of the wisdom of going into regular production with a 4-WD high performance road car.

Austria's Turracher Höhe, Europe's steepest pass with gradients of 23% in places, was the January 1978 site for a full scale engineering presentation to management. The latter were represented by VW sales director Dr. Werner

Austria's Turracher Höhe, one of Europe's steepest public road gradients, played a strong part in Quattro development. A converted Audi 80 originally convinced top management that this was the way to go. Here is a 1980 pre-production Quattro going through its road tyre paces over the same terrain.

P. Schmidt and marketing chief Edgar von Schenck. After a full scale briefing from their engineers in the lounge of the Seewirt hotel, the original A1 prototype — the only car used this far in the project — ascended the icy incline with very little drama, utilising "ordinary summer tyres and no snow chains".

This January 1978 engineering showpiece transformed the Quattro development programme. In the ensuing two years of high-speed evaluation and progression of the Quattro, twelve prototypes were built in Engineering, "the first three with the Audi 80 saloon body and afterwards coupes were available", Bensinger recalled. A smile flitted across the engineer's features as he added, "you know at that meeting with Schmidt, he asked us 'who can sell even 400 such cars?' I was so pleased with the project that I said I would do it, if only he will let us go ahead!" At first the sales target was just the 400 needed for homologation in motor sport and to test public reaction. "Then it became 1500, then 3000 and 6000. Now about 5000 have been made" chuckled Bensinger happily, in Spring 1983.

In April 1978 it was time to pit a 160bhp Quattro prototype against the watch, a Porsche 928, and Hockenheim's race-track combination of tight infield curves and long pinewood-lined straights. The 240bhp Porsche, driven by engineering manager of Advanced Development Walter Treser (later the first competition manager in charge of the Quattro World Championship Rally team), as well as Jorg Bensinger, was little faster on lap times. That dry tarmac also provided a convincing Quattro endorsement. The Quattro's dry tarmac speed was seen as equally as important as the obvious wet and icy road, or off road, benefits. However it must be said that in motorsport terms the Quattro had yet to demonstrate that 4-WD *was* of *overall* stage time benefit on tarmac in the first three seasons of its life. A subject we return to in our later, sporting, chapters and one that obsesses many rally enthusiasts through endless alcohol-fuelled arguments!

By May 1978 VW's senior engineering director Dr Ernst Fiala had approved the plan to go into production with the Quattro concept. The practical result was the construction of a second prototype (A2) and by the beginning of 1979 the third and final 4-WD version of the 80 saloon-based Quattro forebears had been constructed. The A3 was primarily made to assess the road level of tune that would be offered in production coupes, providing 200bhp instead of Audi 200's non-intercooled 170bhp.

Unfortunately the second prototype met a somewhat dramatic end. Testing a 286bhp competition version of the inline five, with an eye to 4-WD action over the heated sands of the Sahara Desert in the summer of 1979, a fuel line exploded and the inevitable engine bay fire put a spectacular brake on that test programme! Incidentally the second and third prototypes were within a facelifted Audi 80 shell as publicly produced in August 1978, with a longer wheelbase.

As Autumn 1979 approached Audi had some vital negotiating to complete, for sports success demanded admission to the World Rally Championship which then ruled out 4-WD on qualifying events. Also there was the matter of getting a world class talent to drive the improved Audi at a time when Mercedes, Ford, Fiat-Lancia and others had more obvious attractions. How they tackled those thorns in the 4-WD crown is the subject of another chapter, but now we look at the way key Quattro components were developed.

Mechanical Melange

Aside from the transmission's ingenuity and clever use of 100/200 parts, the key to Audi's philosophy in the Quattro coupe was the use of a more sophisticated

quattro

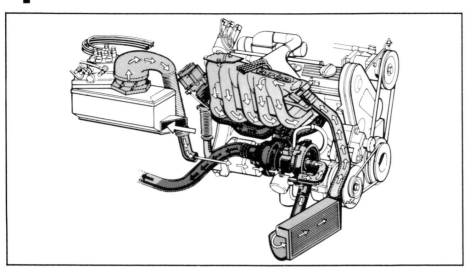

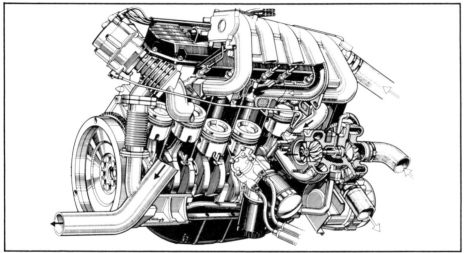

Turbocharging equipment, and the flow of air and fuel mixture from intake to exhaust, are clearly shown by this diagram of the KKK-equipped Quattro engine and its foreground intercooler. Next we have a superb factory cutaway drawing of the Quattro five, displaying the combustion space in the piston crowns, and the interconnected compressor and exhaust vanes of the KKK-26 turbocharger, again with air and mixture flow directions indicated. Note that the general installation of turbocharger and exhaust wastegate was as for Audi 200 on the slant five-cylinder engine. Our final picture shows how the complete installation looked within a 1981 production LHD Quattro. Not the easiest of engines to look after and therefore commensurate garage bills for service. Yet the power unit itself and the turbocharger installation has proved rather more reliable than used to be the norm for a turbocharged unit in the early eighties. Power output of 93.5bhp per litre, 200bhp total, was delivered with traffic docility; however, boosted performance "came on song" above 3500rpm.

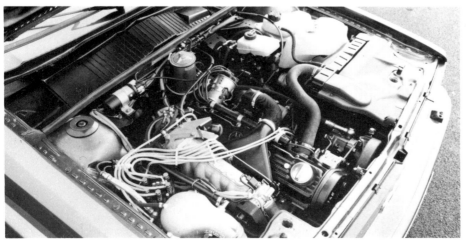

inline five-cylinder turbo than they were prepared to provide in the front drive large 200 saloon. The engine's inherent 6-bearing bottom end strength was not in doubt, after early trials with the best part of 300bhp, but to deliver that power smoothly — and with outstanding mid-range torque — was a challenge. Even senior personnel will occasionally admit that the combination of turbo-charging and a World Championship rally series that varies from searing sand to coagulated mud, or minus 30°C sheet ice, would be more easily met by a large 3 to 4-litre lightweight V8, in terms of providing instant torque. Yet Audi are in business to prove that fuel efficient engines of half that size can provide enormous power and championship-winning, or superb road, performance. For the turbocharged five is an inherent part of Audi's sales message to the public.

Key engine features such as the 86.4mm bore and 79.5mm stroke for 2144cc within an iron five-cylinder block, topped by an SOHC aluminium cylinder head, were basic also to the 136bhp fuel-injected motor of the Audi 100 as well as the KKK (Kuhnle, Kopp & Kausch) -26 turbocharged Audi 200. It is worth remembering that Audi's five-cylinder unit was unique in production car engineering when introduced in 1976. Even in the eighties no other mass producer has followed the Audi quintuplet-cylinder reasoning of four-cylinder economy with (almost) the smoothness of six-cylinder power delivery, at least so far as petrol-burning engines are concerned. There are five-cylinder diesels, of course, notably from Mercedes.

Using the 7:1cr and 0.82 bar-boosted Audi 200 unit as a starting point in Quattro engine development, the biggest contribution to the 30bhp gain of Quattro over 200T — using fractionally more boost (0.85 bar), but the same 7:1cr — came from the installation of a large 13-row aluminium air intercooler. This was positioned forward of the engine and front offside wheel, tucked away neatly in an engine bay corner.

The engine layout with the turbocharger and its foreground intercooler looking rather vulnerable in the front left-hand corner.

quattro

The intercooler's function was to lower the temperature of ambient air fed to the engine's induction system by between 50 and 60°C: the intercooler's finned air radiator being plumbed into the path of incoming air from the KKK turbo to the Bosch K-Jetronic mechanical fuel-injection. The cooled intake air provides a better base on which to build a more efficient fuel-air mixture, its denser mass giving the engine the equivalent of an increase in atmospheric oxygen content. That means a deeper-breathing engine of extra power – just as human lungs respond to extra oxygen content (within limits!) and allow extra athletic performance.

To extract the full potential of intercooling, Audi engineering specified sophisticated Bosch electronic ignition. This was controlled by a microprocessor programmed to react to 250 combinations of engine load; the key to the system's sensitivity being an induction manifold sensor to register temperature variations. These are relayed to the processor, which makes any ignition adjustments instantly to blend performance and economy in situations from toiling up an alpine pass on a summer day to cruising the *autobahns* in the depths of Winter. Without an all-electronic management system, detonation on over-run with a turbocharged engine can be overcome by supplying extra rich air/fuel mixture.

In production Quattro the "chip" brain of the processor instructs that ignition be advanced 50° BTDC (Before Top Dead Centre) which provides a more economical alternative during engine over-run situations, such as coasting downhill. Today, of course, many fuel-injected cheaper cars from Ford and VW feature the Bosch fuel cut-off system, but only BMW had applied that to a turbocharged car by 1980.

Detail engine developments for the Quattro road car included the expensive provision of an entirely stainless steel exhaust system, from top tubular manifolding to grouped twin tailpipes beneath the rear bumper apron. Compared with the Audi 200T, exhaust bore diameter was increased, that inside the top manifolding growing from 60mm to 65mm for Quattro. Also modified over the 200T was the intake manifolding to ensure a reduced journey for air on its boosted way from turbocharger to the injection for faster turbo response.

Engine intercooler (left) and oil cooler (centre) shown on Geneva Show cutaway.

The results of Audi's Quattro engine work were very satisfactory when compared with the 200T, and justified the extra expense of intercooling allied to electronic ignition and thorough detail development. In power terms the Quattro five developed 130kW (177bhp) at a leisurely 4500rpm, which was 4kW (6.8bhp) more than peak 200T output of 125kW (170bhp) at 5200rpm. The Quattro's peak was, and remains, in the road car, 147kW (200bhp) at 5500rpm with little point in persisting above 6000rpm as power drops away rapidly.

In a comparison of torque the Quattro provides over 200Nm (145lb.ft) from 2100rpm to 5500rpm, again with swift fall off in peak performance beyond 5500rpm. Maximum Quattro torque of 285Nm (206lb.ft) is at 3500rpm. The 1979 200T offered 20Nm (14.5lb.ft) less torque at its peak of 3200rpm and over 200Nm (145lb.ft) between 2400 and 5800 revs, altogether an efficient endorsement of the all-round improvements incorporated in the Quattro version of Audi five-cylinder engineering.

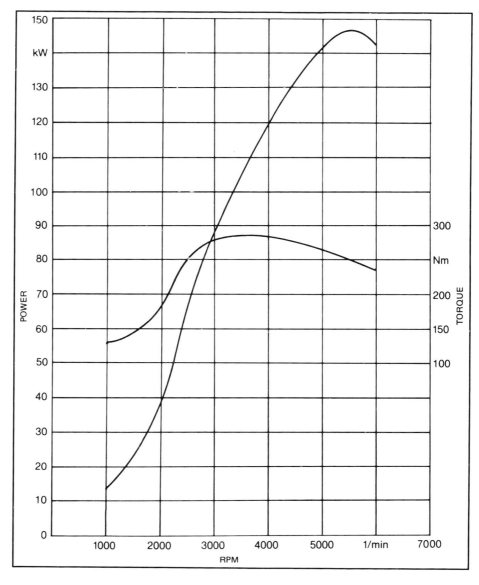

Power and torque curve for Quattro's five with noticeable torque "bump" between 3000 and 5000rpm. Just over 3000rpm there is the equivalent of 121bhp with another 79bhp added in the next 2500rpm.

quattro

Performance figures for the Quattro road and competition models are provided in the appendices, but it is worth pointing out that we are dealing with a coupe that, in its slowest production form, 200bhp, is capable of over 135mph and 0-60mph in 7.0 seconds, or tenths more, which places it firmly in the bracket of performers such as Porsche's 944 of 2.5-litres, BMW's 635CSi of 3.4-litres and the mid-engined Lotus Esprit, an unturbocharged 2.2-litre with 16 valves 4-cylinders and two-seater accommodation.

Running Gear

To provide a chassis worthy of permanent 4-WD, and the lusty engine, Audi's team plumped for an all independent strut/coil spring suspension layout and four-wheel disc brakes. Making wide use of existing production parts; however, it was the suspension system that attracted most of the adverse British comment for its on-the-limit manners. Detail changes were made during the production run, all incorporated as part of the Audi 80 Quattro suspension system too. Personally I encountered no original or current qualms about the car's handling — including 2000 miles around, and along some of, the sodden 1982 RAC Rally route — but drivers I respect have had worrying moments, or minor scuffles with the scenery at speed in the early cars. There is also no doubt that the 80 Quattro is 100% easier to point on ice, and much happier to oversteer at predictable angles.

Look at the front and rear suspension of the Quattro in its initial LHD form and you are baffled by the astonishing similarity between front and rear layouts. Your eyes did not deceive you, the back amounts to the identical MacPherson strut/triangulated lower wishbone front layout incorporated aft, but reversed through 180°! Naturally the front steering arms were replaced by solid transverse links in place of track rods, otherwise the handling could have provided a challenge worthy of even the most jaded journalist — rear wheel steering at 130mph!

However, "many a true word is spoken in jest" and it was in re-aligning the rear suspension that many subsequent Audi engineering hours were spent on the production and competition side, although the problems and solutions for road and rally use, were very different.

Although drawn from the same parts source, front and rear suspension systems offered different track widths (different width brake discs, a contributary reason) of 1421mm/55.9in front and 1458mm/57.4in rear.

Original Quattro Settings

	(Front)	(Rear)
Track	1421mm	1458mm
Camber	− 1°	− 1°
Toe-out	1°30	7°
Toe-in	0°	0°
Strut angles	13.8°	14.5°

The struts were taken from Audi 80 and 200 parts bins, the driveshafts also were existing Audi items, but swapped diagonally to provide the different lengths needed. Front and rear roll bars, the rear using the same layout as the front end, were also production parts.

Schematic drawing of the front and rear axles shows the basic suspension principles on which all Quattro development proceeded. Initially using parts drawn from elsewhere in Audi's range, and virtually identical front to back, as can be seen. The rally cars had to retain the strut and lower arm principles, but with replacement parts specially fabricated for the job becoming ever more common. The rear layout was altered on 1982 road cars and shared on introduction of Quattro 80. The 1983-84 Quattro Sport used the specially fabricated competition layout as a starting point. The long struts with their coil springs gave a particularly good road car ride without the need of gas damping. Note the front anti-roll bar is incorporated with the subframe, while the similarly shaped rear mounts from the body, aft of the subframes.

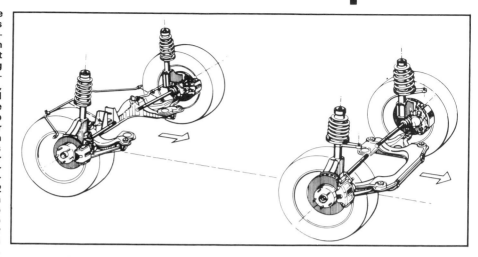

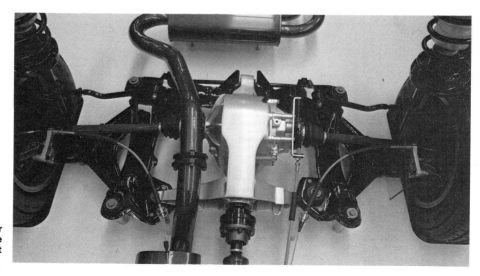

The front and rear suspension and drive layout, as displayed at Geneva in Spring 1980.

quattro

New for the Quattro was the development of standard power-assisted rack and pinion steering with the servo cylinder cast into the casing. As on Audi 200 the power-assistance for both steering and braking was derived from a central hydraulic pump, an engine driven ancillary rather than the usual manifold vacuum-actuated servos found in the majority of eighties production cars. The advantage is the consistency of assistance available at all times, and speed-related power steering: at higher rpm the steering feels as heavy and responsive as the best manual systems. For parking, or at low rpm, the assistance is considerably increased, providing lighter steering.

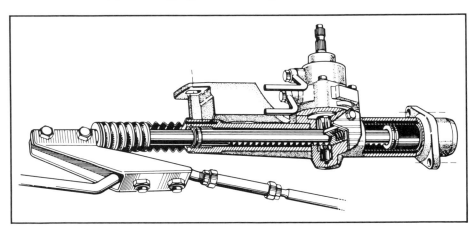

The power steering system for the Quattro has proved a vital part of the road and rally specification with its integral operating cylinder, rack and pinion, plus high pressure engine pump power supply. A power steering failure on a 1983 rally Quattro, left the driver's hands rubbed raw through gloves!

Although coil springs from Audi 80 (rear) and Audi 200T (front) were utilised, new gas dampers from suppliers such as Boge and VW were specified after development, especially for the Quattro coupe which has always featured an outstandingly good ride/handling compromise.

The twin circuit braking system with the servo assistance system described, and a pressure regulator to deter wheel-locking, also had 280mm/11.02in ventilated front discs and 245mm/9.65in solid rear discs. The new calipers featured an integral handbrake.

From the start two alternative alloy wheel choices were offered, the multiple spoke ex-Audi 200 Ronal, 6J × 15, and the five spoke Fuchs (who also supply Porsche for the 911 series) of 7J × 15. Recommended road tyres were always of 205/60VR marking: British cars originally arriving with Goodyear NCTs or cousin Fulda's low profile series in the main.

As ever in the UK, the use of a spacesaver 4J × 15 steel spare wheel with a T125/70 D15 "get-you-home" tyre of 50mph/1890 mile plus capability, was

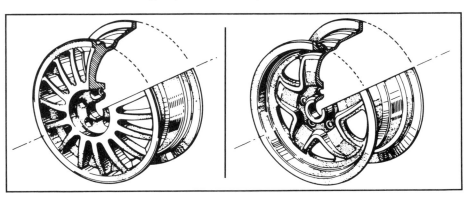

Two kinds of alloy wheel most commonly found on early Quattros. Left is the 6J × 15 Ronal road wheel and on the right is the Fuchs forged alloy five spoke (7J × 15) often seen as the narrow rally option and satisfactorily used for the Quattro's first three rally seasons for loose going.

controversial. Strictly speaking, such tyres were, and are, illegal to use. Porsche guard against prosecution by offering owners transport home in the event of a puncture, but this naturally only applies over the original warranty period: after that you're on your own! Audi really had no option but to use the spacesaver spare wheel concept, as the boot is a narrow pillar box orifice, biased in favour of a 92 litre/20.24 gallon petrol tank. In Britain owners of the early LHD Quattros were offered a full size spare when the legal doubt over spacesaving spares materialised. All RHD coupes came with full size spare wheels.

A Coupe Five-Seater

Not only were five-cylinders part of the specification, but this unique coupe also officially had five-seater capacity! Certainly the rear seat headroom offered by the then-unseen coupe fastback was exceptional by the old 2+2 coupe standards, but the rear accommodation was shaped as thought seating was on a quartet basis, rather than coping with an adult trio. However, seatbelts for five were standard equipment.

In a steel body based on the floorpan of the inspirational Audi 80 saloon (in which the pressings must be modified to take the propshaft's rearward path) Audi allowed a 2524mm/99.4in wheelbase, exactly as for the front drive coupe that would follow. Overall length was set at 4404mm/173.4in, width at 1723mm/67.8in and height at 1350mm/53.2in: the steel wheelarch extensions making the Quattro 41mm/1.61in wider than the subsequent coupe and fractionally lower, as well as 55mm/2.17in longer. The extra length came from the use of body-coloured bumpers in a plastic-finished choice of the four colours initially offered. Mocca cloth upholstery, with a vaguely chequered finish, was standard for the interior whatever the exterior shade. The choices were: metallics, Saturn, Helios Blue and Silver Diamond, plus non-metallic, Venus Red.

Skidpan testing with the 1980 pre-production Quattro reinforced the consistent understeer characteristic of the original Bensinger arguments, for and against, front-engine 4-WD.

The front spoiler was moulded into the front apron as an integral part of the squared-off coupe style: the bootlid, stretching down to the back bumper line, was also produced in plastic. A separate rear spoiler in black polyurethene accounts for 0.2 of the 0.43Cd aerodynamic drag factor, which was not widely quoted at the launch — a stark contrast to all the 1982 "hoo-ha" over the 100 saloon's world-beating 0.30Cd.

Standard equipment integrated into that two door steel and plastic pacemaker for features such as colour-keyed bumpers (Maestro in 1983, for example!), comprised items like the fluorescent rear strip across the tail, between tail lights (shades of Porsche) which included rear fog lamps. Quadruple halogen

quattro

headlamps with electric washers and H1 high beams, plus H4 low beams, sounded fine, but later models in RHD as well as LHD had important changes that transformed the lighting to illumination fit for such a swift night rider.

Even in LHD form, priced at less than £10,000 sterling equivalent in Germany, the basic specification included bronzed glass, laminated windscreen with top anti-dazzle strip neatly shaded into the tinted pane, and exterior mirrors, with power assistance and heating elements, seatbelts for the famous five and some very sporting front seats; the driver's adjustable for height. Leather trim was applied to the steering wheel's four spoke rim and the gear-lever's knob and gaiter.

Testing, testing. The pre-production Quattros fitted in a lot of mileage in mechanically 100% production trim as management ensured that quality, particularly of paintwork, met higher standards than originally intended.

Initial German options comprised cruise control, central locking system that included the boot lid, green tinted glass, sunroof (a lift-out glass panel; fitting a proper steel sunroof in Quattro or coupe really restricts headroom and the factory then did not approve . . .), rear window wiper and washer, those 7J wheels, heated front seats, vanity mirror, power windows and a variety of ICE (In Car Entertainment) cassette player/radio systems. Many of these items were part of the £14,500 original British specification, which was also based on LHD; RHD not being available until Spring 1982 in Britain.

Complete with 4 litres of engine oil, 9.3 litres of coolant and some fuel in the petrol tank above the back axle, the revolutionary new Audi Quattro hit the scales at 1300kg or 2865lb in British trim. Audi calculated that the weight penalty they incurred with 4-WD, compared to the alternative of front or rear drive configuration, was an extra 75kg/165lb over two driven front wheels and 35kg/77lb over a rear drive machine.

From the less than 20 Quattros manufactured before its Geneva Show debut, to Spring three years later when 4,851 Quattros had been made (rather more than *ten times* the original estimate!) plus over 5000 of the new 80 Quattro saloons, the permanent 4-WD proposition found owners not only across Europe, but also in America. Unlike most motorsport linked production cars, it sold strongly on its own merits rather than reflected competition glamour, or as a basis for further competition modifications.

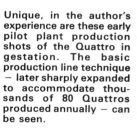

Unique, in the author's experience are these early pilot plant production shots of the Quattro in gestation. The basic production line technique — later sharply expanded to accommodate thousands of 80 Quattros produced annually — can be seen.

The Quattro road cars continued to progress and inspire a completely new breed of "High Tech" 4-WD Audis through the eighties, and we will return to that tale, after examining the enormous impact Audi and their 4-WD challenger were to make on World Championship rallying. The car that not only introduced a new 4-WD turbo concept which others had to follow — but also took a deliciously female crew to within an ace of winning the world title outright. After scoring the first female overall World Championship qualifying win ever recorded, (in 1981), Michele Mouton and Fabrizia Pons bounded to three more 1982 wins

quattro

Such diagrams were needed to make the public aware of the technology beneath the skin of Audi's March 1980 coupe. Here the complete layout can be seen, with its heavy bias toward most weight in the nose; the five-cylinder engine mounting forward of the front axle line in the Audi front drive tradition. Also on view are basic design principles like the strut suspension, vented front disc brakes (solid disc rear) and the lightweight 4-WD layout, with no need of cumbersome transfer boxes.

After all that, this was the result. The Quattro basks in Southern sunshine awaiting another photo-call to appear in the 1980 press pack.

and their title shot, all in a car largely developed by a man with Mercedes, *and* Ford contracts in his pocket!

Why that happened and how the Quattro concept rumbled through the results sheets of 1981/82 is our theme for the following chapters . . . A tale full of human drama as well as the high tech fight to turn such a complex car into a world-wide winner.

Chapter 3

Born to compete

The birth pangs beforehand were as nothing compared with the competition dramas enacted on the path to historic victories for rallying's first four-wheel-drive champion!

Ingolstadt prepared for World Championship rallying with outings like this 1979 assault on the Finnish 1000 Lakes. Once again the 80 paved the way for the Quattro, but this time strictly in 2-WD non-turbocharged form. The 1588cc four-cylinder engines were said to provide 160bhp at 7600rpm.

quattro

Although Audi press material naturally makes much of a glorious competition past of the constituent companies that we saw grow into Audi within our opening chapter, the competition world of the late seventies that greeted Quattro was totally removed from anything that the company and its employees had previously attempted. Of course motorsport had become more professional, jet-setting rally crews following the path of Grand Prix drivers in a constant whirl of pre-event practice, tyre and mechanical testing. Then there was an increasing need for media publicity interviews and demonstrations to justify constantly escalating costs.

However, the need for speed and endurance does not change, for "to finish first, you first have to finish" however much this cliché detracts from the essential truth of such an aim. It is obvious that many "experts" do not heed such basic advice, for there was never any doubt of the Quattro's speed over loose surfaces, which was established as an integral part of the engineering philosophy from the earliest pre-Quattro assessments of 4-WD. Yet when the car failed to finish events, an occurrence that was still far too regular in 1983, more power was still being advocated by some onlookers — and some who should have known better inside the Ingolstadt factory gates!

Yet Audi's preparations for a World Championship rally assault were meticulous and realistic. Even in 1973 Audi had initiated their Audi Trophy scheme, which offered 30,000Dm originally, but which had developed into a 150,000Dm prize fund by 1980. Together with the Trophy scheme to support those who used Audi's front drive products in competition came a new company

The Audi 80 also proved itself in European Championship racing, originally managed by key Quattro figure Jurgen Stockmar. At first it was thought that the Quattro would be used for circuit competition too, but World Championship rallying proved a full time occupation in the eighties.

pride in competition. The Audi 80 took particularly well to touring car racing and by 1977 former Solex carburettor competition engineer Jurgen Stockmar was enjoying his customer competition liaison role at Audi and getting increasing factory support. One of the drivers most commonly seen in these works-supported 80s was ex-Formula 3 racer Freddy Kottulinsky. Or Winifried Count Kottulinsky, Baron of Kottulin, as he was more formally known when not engaged in winning the European Formula 3, Formula Vee or Swedish national Championships that were accrued in an honourable racing career.

On the left is one of *the* key figures in Quattro progress over the years, Freddy Kottulinsky. Man temporarily in the centre of things is Scottish 1979 hope James Rae, whilst a pre-beard Harald Demuth is on the right with regular navigator Arwed Fischer behind. Completing the quintet is Kottulinsky's navigator Michael Schwaegerl. By 1984 Fischer was co-ordinating the factory Quattro team in the field.

Freddy Kottulinsky joined Audi in 1976 and assisted with development of the 80 as a rally car. In 1979 he finished seventh on the Portuguese World Championship qualifying round with an 80GLE, just a place behind fellow works Audi 80 driver Harald Demuth. These 160bhp Group 4 saloons were run in World Championship rallies of 1979, including the RAC where Demuth was 18th, and the two other team 80s managed 20th and 28th.

While Engineering were still developing the Quattro concept for road and rallying, Stockmar's low profile racing and rally competition management continued, but Jurgen's most important task was to ensure that the sporting powers within the *Federation Internationale de l'Automobile* (FIA) accepted a change in the rules governing World Championship rallying. A senior Audi executive told me, "perhaps, for competition anyway, this was the most important work that could be done for the Quattro. Before 1979 you could not earn World Championship points with a four-wheel-drive car, so it was vital that Jurgen worked hard on the FIA . . . It took him about six months of campaigning quietly, talking to other manufacturers and persuading everyone that it was a good thing for the sport that we should come with our four-wheel-drive car." Quite how Stockmar stage-managed his hard-headed opposition and persuaded FIA officials to the view that 4-WD would be very good for them, as well as inevitably giving Audi an enormous loose-surface traction advantage, is beyond this writer. However both Renault and Lancia-Fiat executives have separately commented that they were fully aware of the implications of 4-WD for rallying, but in both cases they felt they had a better answer with turbocharged and supercharged mid-engined machines of the "rally racer" school. Looking at Renault's Monte Carlo victory in 1981 and Lancia's string of 1983 World Championship wins, it would be easy to simply say they were right! In fact the technical trends that Audi established as key components in Quattro's layout have been enthusiastically imitated by other manufacturer's rival prototypes since Ingolstadt proved that turbocharging and 4-WD were such superior rally car elements that they could not be ignored. Examples? Peugeot's 205, which also has mid-engine location in the 4-WD turbo recipe. Those connected with the Ford Escort RS1700T — the front engine, rear drive flyer that was axed and sent to South Africa to repent — tell me that detailed plans existed for a 4-WD version. Austin Rover Group, Citröen, Mitsubishi Starion 4WD and many more, including New Zealander Rod Millen's Mazda RX7 4-WD conversion to challenge the USA monopoly of John Buffum and Quattro in SCCA events, all proved that the Audi team's 4-WD technical thinking was a truly worthwhile pioneering move in the art of covering rally terrain rapidly.

As was the case for road or race cars, Audi were far from the first to use 4-WD. The American scene had been enlivened by an enormous number of non-World Championship machines from Ford, AMC and Chevrolet that allied pick-up truck looks with 4-WD and anything up to 7-litres of V8 power to conquer any vestige of opposition in rougher off-road events. The lessons for rallying in African World Championship events were plain, Audi underlining that education when Kottulinsky won a class victory on the 1980 Paris-Dakar based Oasis 1000, a non-championship marathon covering 7452 miles, in the Audi-developed VW Iltis,

A New Competition Home

To house Audi's aspirations of World Championship success, a supermarket warehouse on the outskirts of Ingolstadt was acquired and converted into a two storey base for the embryo Quattro competition team. Audi management completed this move in 1979, ensuring that the new department was ''a closely integrated part of the Research and Development Division in order to maintain contact with the standard production cars''. Although you cannot see the enormous research and engineering office block referred to in our opening chapter, their presence inside the competitions department was stronger in 1983 than ever, with constant re-statement of the principle that competitions is part of R&D. The evidence that such a statement is not just PR floss lies in the construction of every car, particularly the engines and transmissions. The latter are all built within the main company's engineering sections and then transported the odd mile or so over to the squat clinic that the company label outside, in foot high letters, proclaims as ''Audi Sport''.

This way please, but don't forget our competition history . . . Sign outside Audi Sport's Ingolstadt dwelling.

Highlighted in the same corporate colour scheme of orange and two shades of mud brown is a proclamation to the effect that this is also HQ for NSU and Auto Union motorsport, even though V16s of over 500bhp and thirties fame are not high on the preparation lists within!

Basically the building is divided into ground floor workshop and stores, with the administration offices above. As you would expect the department is clean and well organised throughout. Only the drawing office on the lower floor and the admin offices, stuffed with the latest in electronic typewriter technology (from VAG-owned Triumph Adler; one of whose machines has been battered mortally to bring you these words) tell you that this is an office block that lives by communications and design. Oh, and by 1983, a spare room was stuffed with trophies earned by a staff of roughly thirty mechanics (twenty-seven in 1981), plus a quartet of foremen/chief mechanics, a draughtsman/designer on site and the small staff. When I paid my visits, in 1981 and 1983, there was a full time Public Relations office within, operated by book author and journalist Dieter Scharnagl with a secretary, and about half a dozen other white collar workers. These, including the competition managers (there have been three since Quattro's rally debut), making around forty to forty-five staff while the department is in World Championship action.

Lamp brackets too, have to be drawn up at Audi Sport.

Of course this is not the total depth of the Quattro competition commitment. Over in R&D there are mechanics and engineers with Quattro competition engine, differentials and gearbox responsibilities, a virtually fulltime testing programme and Matter & Obermoser's Matter-branched body construction to consider. All these efforts behind that small army of men and LT van service barges that have been the focal point for the rallying media since 1981.

Overall the competition premises are not grand in the fellow Bavarian manner of BMW, but they are extremely well protected against a casual visitor stumbling inside. The side entrance has the usual German strong metal frame and a squawk box-monitored lock, while some of the doors within — particularly to enter competitions main assembly area — would delight safe manufacturers of the ''Big-and-thick-is-Beautiful'' school. Outside there are usually interesting wide-wheeled Quattros and 200s slumbering in wait for their frequently forceful drivers, but inside the friendly atmosphere is a stark contrast to the impersonal building and assembled high technology.

Audi Sport LT van slumbers in Bavarian sunlight before the next great adventure, with rally car tail and heavyweight support truck also exhibiting the corporate livery.

Sports Personnel

Ultimately responsibility for Audi's ambitious rally programme has rested on the elegant shoulders of the dryly humorous Ferdinand Piech. As head of technical development since August 1, 1975, when he was appointed to the board, Piech really has been an inspirational driving force through the inevitable bad spells as well as the winning streaks. Ferdinand Piech has been with Audi since 1972, starting as a senior departmental engineering manager, but he is also a powerful and emotive figure in German motorsport history because of his Porsche links. The Piech family are 10 per cent stockholders in Porsche and Ferdinand is best known in racing circles for his design work on the awesome Porsche 917 flat-12-cylinder, sports racers of the seventies; he also contributed extensively to the flat-six-cylinder Porsche 911 classic.

Everyday contact between competitions and the main R&D "Mother Ship" will vary from queries on manufacturing special nuts and bolts to liaison on the constant development of an already sophisticated machine into an ever faster and more exotically lightened motor car. A device that has to compete in anything from a Corsican Summer road race to the primeval slime that slurps beneath the willing driven wheels of Quattros in such exotic climes as those of Africa and Southern America, or even Britain's Kielder Forest in November, which is about as prime-*evil* as they come!

Although Herr Piech stays in touch with the rally programme, much of the necessary, and recently increased, close contact between the sports and research

Ferdinand Piech.

sections is handled via Jorg Bensinger. In pure engine engineering matters, the contact point could be former Alpina-BMW engineer Dr Fritz Indra at Audi R&D, but also within the corridors of power at Audi R&D you will find chassis experts like ex-Ford and NSU employee Thomas Ammerschläger; although his primary responsibility is for the ride and handling of all road cars since his May 1981 arrival. Ammerschläger says "we always try to send one of our blokes along to help, or just to learn a little more, whenever they are setting up the rally Quattros". By coincidence Hans-Peter Gassen, the engineer appointed to look after all technical development work at Audi Sport, when Roland Gumpert moved on to an increasing management load in 1983, used to work for Ammerschläger at NSU.

Those charged with managing the Quattro's fortunes since its competition debut were Walter Treser (1980-81), Reinhard Rode (1981-82) and current incumbent Roland Gumpert. The latter bearded engineer held all the competition engineering and testing responsibility during 1981 and 1982 while Rode looked after administration. As ever two bosses didn't work out in the long run and Gumpert began to take an increasing managerial overlord role in 1982, with total responsibility evident during that year and formally confirmed for the 1983 season.

Walter Treser now runs his own successful tuning concern producing cabriolet and faster Quattros, amongst other products.

Reinhard Rode, still with Audi Sport but now with an accent on customer liaison.

That's Gumpert, always at the heart of the action, but this time a diamond pattern jumper emphasises a relaxed approach, before he had sole responsibility for a World Championship team. Then a look at Gumpert in 1982, and in characteristic working pose alongside Arne Hertz.

quattro

Both Treser and Gumpert shared strong engineering backgrounds. Treser was both an automobile and aeronautical engineer at Mercedes-Benz, but is best remembered for fourteen years at Pirelli in charge of tyre testing for the current generation of fat, low profile rubber. Walter Treser was also a very talented saloon car driver with European Championship wins to his credit in BMWs shared with men such as Hans Joachim Stuck Junior. Treser arrived at Audi in 1977, when he was 37, to an engineering job titled "Manager of Advance Development". According to Audi press matter Treser was, "responsible for the Audi Quattro project and played a considerable part in putting this unique new car on the road". By the time the press attended the Spring 1980 Geneva debut of Quattro coupe Treser had been working on the competition future of the model for about six months as a separate task: Jurgen Stockmar's diplomacy had by that time secured the legal right to run the car and acquainted perhaps the World's most wooed driver of the period, Hannu Mikkola, with the advantages of 4-WD. Yet there was never any suggestion in public that he would gain the top job on the sports side.

Reinhard Rode was far more of a competitor and company man. A former VW marketing executive, Rode supervised European Formula Vee, and then managed the Golf rally schedule, arriving at Audi in 1978 with eight years' VW experience and two-hundred & twenty rallies as a competitor. Fair haired and cheerful, the 35-year-old Rode was immensely popular with his staff during his managerial spell, but the demands of organising a team comparatively fresh to World Championship rallying, and the complex demands of the car, made it a very hard job indeed. Audi's management obviously decided they had enough complexities to face without the natural dilemma of two sports bosses, so Rode

The management not only had to make sure that the cars were built — and here you see some of the early machines under construction — but also to ensure that the mechanics were fit for in-field service. The contrast between workshop conditions and those found just testing is emphasised by the rear end picture of the mechanic wrestling with the rear suspension leg in mud and then in workshop cleanliness.

was gradually eased to one side in favour of engineer Gumpert: Rode was still with Audi Sport in 1983, primarily concerned with customer liaison. A big job as Quattros became increasingly the mount to have in Austria, Belgium, Italy, Holland, Britain as well as the USA and the car's native Germany. Quattros also often appear with great success in rallycross as well as rallies, placing a new set of hybrid technical requests upon Ingolstadt.

Roland Gumpert was 36 in August 1981 when he joined Audi Sport with a testing and engineering brief, but the East German emigrant joined Audi R&D Centre in 1969. There he worked with distinction on the 80 and small car the 50 (later VW Polo) prototypes as well as the Iltis. His first contacts with the company's 4-WD machine were extraordinarily successful as he team-managed the team's 1979 Paris-Dakar assault, in which they produced first, second and fourth places while his own back-up Iltis was ninth! Obviously a man to watch . . .

Away from the hustle of rally service areas Roland Gumpert can be one of the more charming men in motorsport. The deep blue eyes and constant laughter belie what must have been a pretty rugged conversion from a Silesian childhood to the life of emigrant, which led him to qualify in automotive electrical and mechanical engineering at Graz, Austria. He can be unfailingly polite, unless pressed for answers while the team and its drivers are beseeching him for instructions in a crisis! Gumpert's engineering ability to explain and explore from first principles, to the almost routine use of exotic materials and advanced techniques that are part of the Quattro, are exceptional.

The most successful driver and co-driver in World Championship rallying. As at the close of 1983 Arne Hertz (left) and Hannu Mikkola (right) were the men who had scored more World Championship victories than any rival, but they had not always rallied together. Ironically one of Hertz's former drivers was Audi team-mate Blomqvist, whilst Mikkola had been rallying with many co-drivers, most notably Gunnar Palm (like Hertz, a Swede) and present day Talbot competitions director Jean Todt. Another competitions boss to accompany Mikkola was Austin Rover's John Davenport and Roland Gumpert also sat alongside Hannu for the 1982 Ivory Coast Championship qualifyer.

Audi Approach Mikkola

Convinced that they had the technical answers to the problems posed in rallying, Audi's next logical step was to arrange a meeting between the revolutionary rally car and the most successful World Championship driver. At the time matching Bjorn Waldegard in a point-for-point Championship title chase, which the Swede eventually won by a point to become the World's first official World Champion rally driver, Finn Hannu Mikkola was 37-years-of-age and riding rally crests with ever more grace. In 1979 alone he won four world title qualifying

quattro

rounds and he had two of the most lucrative manufacturer's contracts possible: Mercedes, for the vast V8 coupes in which he had a Bandama win and a Safari second, plus Ford and their then ubiquitous Escort. Hannu won the Portuguese, New Zealand and British World Championship events, in the Ford, during 1979.

Mikkola's rally career had started in 1963 with a Volvo PV544 and had included outings in factory Lancias and Toyotas, Fiat Abarths and Peugeots besides the two spells at Ford of Britain, where his ways with an Escort netted a selection of silverware that began with the 1968 1000 Lakes and a £250 one-off fee! Subsequent Escort achievements encompassed a hat-trick on the 1000 Lakes from 1968-1970, another win in 1974, a Safari victory for 1972 and the 1978 RAC. But these were just the jewels amongst a solid record of Ford success in Championship events, there were many other wins including those in the British home international series and the 1970 World Cup of London-Mexico mileage.

Mikkola went rallying outside Ford between 1975-77, winning the 1000 Lakes for Toyota and Morocco for Peugeot's ungainly 504, but the best thing about that period was the start of a partnership that was to be equally important to Audi. An alliance between co-driving and driving talent that is equally surprising for the co-operation between Finland and Sweden as it is for representing the epitomy of professionalism: on the Quattro wings it just says "H. Mikkola A. Hertz". To any enthusiast and to Hannu himself Arne Hertz, partner to top Swedes such as Blomqvist and Andersson in the past "has one *hell* of a strong will too win. Always he is fighting to give me a chance, always for a better position . . . He is a fantastic man and that is why he is the most successful co-driver."

Mikkola recalled the approach from Audi when I interviewed him for *Motoring News* prior to his sensational RAC Rally win in the Quattro (a speedy flip in fog proved no more than a hiccup on the way to a five minute victory!) during November 1981. "It was a phone call from Jurgen Stockmar in 1979. He asked me to come and talk. I said I had already decided what I was doing in 1980. No point to come and talk! He carried on, asked me to come for a couple of days to Munich and Ingolstadt, plus I would have the chance to drive a 4-WD turbo car. Wouldn't that be interesting . . .?"

Stockmar's persuasion won the day. The Finn with a Ford contract and a Mercedes agreement for anything Ford were not doing, went to Germany. It was October 1979 . . .

Audi company documents state, "in the Altmuhltal between Ingolstadt and Nuremberg Mikkola made an abrupt turn off the main road onto a rough cross country track."

Mikkola recalled that the prototype was one of the 80 saloon type and "I take this car for half an hour, all around. Put it in the gravel forest roads: Stockmar gets out, he doesn't want to ride with me! So, all alone, I drive this car, and I could see the idea behind it. I could see it could be good . . . Really good.

"I was quite surprised. I knew it would have traction, because I had been with the Ford 4-WD Capris. But, when Timo was looking *really* good in this car, the front differential has failed, so it is only a two wheeldrive! The handling was my surprise. All the people tell me how it will be, just terrible, but I find it very different to a Land-Rover! I did not change my mind about Ford and Mercedes in 1980, but Audi said to me — what about 1981? We agreed that I would do testing for them in 1980 and maybe come to an agreement for 1981". Of course that is exactly what happened, so Mikkola has an integral part in the Quattro's competition development that dates back a year and several months *before* the car's debut.

In retrospect Mikkola outsmarted all his world class rivals. The Quattro, heartache though it had been on occasion, has consistently proved the benchmark to judge loose surface performances and there was the astonishing

coincidence that both Ford with their obsolete MkII Escort and Mercedes with their Fat Cat coupes were out of the sport by the close of November 1980! It was that month and year in which Mikkola signed his 1981 Audi competition contract . . . which was unusual in modern rallying in that it asked for his exclusive services and lasted more than 12 months.

Armed with a David Sutton-prepared Escort for comparison purposes and the challenge of mastering a completely different driving technique to the rear drive cars in which he had always excelled, Mr Mikkola and Audi set about developing Ingolstadt's ingenious *Wunderwagen*.

Ready to go in 1980, when Audi completed a testing season with no official World Championship entries.

Chapter 4

Weighty progress

Getting the Quattro show on the rally road was not difficult — keeping it there was another matter!

Splat! At home in a local gravel pit-cum-test ground that has hosted innumerable factory Quattros and where some early punishment sessions provided important preparation pointers

"At first the engine temperatures were wrong, much too high. The engine was not nice to drive, there was *nothing* under 4000rpm. You had to wait, and wait, for any power, then it would go like *hell* [said with a broad grin of delight] until 7500!" Mikkola's first impressions of the Quattro were forthright additions to the painstaking kilometres of the development engineering team around Treser, which included Kottulinsky. Most of the mileage prior to Mikkola's arrival had been biased toward preparing the road car for its Spring 1980 Show debut and exploring the basic strength of the five-cylinder engine in turbocharged form.

Having the talents of a "Flying Finn" at their disposal meant that Audi could spend weeks in 1980 simulating World Championship rally conditions. Mikkola remembered Greece (The Acropolis) and Finland (1000 Lakes) as events they virtually recreated in testing, but for the public the first demonstration of the Quattro's potential came between October 29 and November 2, 1980. The event was the 44th round of the sprawling European Championship for Rallies, the Portuguese Urbibel Algarve, and Audi had arranged for Mikkola/Hertz to act as the O-numbered Course Car.

Thus Audi were able to see the Quattro's potential on an event, without being officially entered, with the bonus that much of the loose terrain was exactly the sort of stage mileage that would confront them on the Portuguese World Championship qualifier.

First public appearance for the competition Quattro was on the 1980 Algarve in Portugal, when Mikkola and Hertz piloted the course car and proved the efficiency of the Quattro for competition. It was estimated that they would have won this European Championship round by more than 20 minutes!

While that week's rallying headlines were dominated by what was to prove the briefest of contractual relationships between Walter Rohrl, Ari Vatanen and Mercedes, the Quattro's performance was hardly less sensational. Mikkola was fastest on 24 of 30 stages, but it was significant that the stages Hannu was not fastest on amounted to tarmac sections gobbled up by Bernard Beguin's privately-prepared Porsche 911. However this Quattro Course Car's times would have won the event by the best part of *half an hour*, compared with eventual winner and 1980 European Champion Antonio Zanini's times!

The Algarve sortie merely confirmed, in public, that the combination of

quattro

Mikkola/Hertz and Quattro would be dynamite to rallying's establishment, although some rivals took comfort from the fact of Quattro's slower tarmac times and the quality of opposition. It is worth noting that the team were able to bypass the requirement to deposit the car overnight in *Parc Ferme*, spending nocturnal hours fettling the machine. One aspect they emphasised was to experiment with differing final drive ratios and limited slip differential action to alter the balance of the car.

Inside the 1980 development Quattro, a production four spoke steering wheel and a complex dash that already has the now-familiar layout of later cars with central tachometer and speedometer in the bottom left-hand corner. At the time Hannu reported the main power band as between 4000 and 7500rpm.

Development engine bay with the familiar long runs for the turbo air inlet (left) and intercooler to injection, over Audi embossed alloy rocker cover. At the time 300bhp was estimated (Autumn 1980) and 309.5lb. ft torque.

Peter Foubister of *Autosport* was present for Quattro's Portuguese practical debut and his shrewd summary of the Quattro's potential included the following comments, "turbocharged and quieter, four-wheel-drive and less spectacular, the car appears with none of the dramatic sideways style which rally fans throughout the world have come to love from Mikkola; it was as if the vehicle was contributing far more to the speed than has been the case in the past."

Later on Foubister summarised, "in many ways the comparison must be drawn between this new weapon, and the modern F1 circuit machines, where the biggest problem is that the machine is doing the winning, not the man. To date it has been true to say that a really talented driver could get results with a slightly inferior motor car. Now it seems the reverse will be the case. Whatever happens between Group A and B, Audi are sure this will be their rally car for the future."

At the time Mikkola felt the Quattro's traction and handling qualities were "incredible". He drew some comparisons with the beloved Escort thus, "it is

Off on its Algarve course and testing duties in 1980, the Quattro was an immediate centre of attention and notably quick over the dusty gravel stages it would later conquer as part of Portugal's World Championship round.

quattro

not like driving an Escort, where you control the car with the throttle. With this car you do not drive sideways. The only places where the car was slower than an Escort were very twisty sections, or into hairpins."

Looking at the tarmac performance of the Quattro in Portugal subsequently Mikkola felt, "the only area where the car was not competitive in Portugal was on tarmac and we have learned of many areas where we can improve the car. We were running on very narrow racing tyres, and they 'went off' quickly and it became very slippery to drive. In that area we have a lot to do, although on gravel it is maybe the quickest car there is."

Hannu's Running Mate

Although 1980 Championship performances of factory-supported but specialist-prepared Audi 80s in European races (Manufacturer's title) and the German Championship (eight class wins for Harald Demuth plus repeated top five overall placings) were creditable and led to some speculation that Demuth would be "Mikkola's [team] Mate" the factory's Quattro crew selection was a lot more complicated.

As not only a German company, but also one proud of its role in the south German state of Bavaria, there was one natural choice — a man who was also to show that he had more all-round talent than anyone else in world class rallying with two world titles at the time of writing, and a good chance for a third. All this in just the five seasons that an official World Championship for Drivers has existed!

The name on Audi's driver preference list was Walter Rohrl. Walter came from nearby Regensburg, had worked in the area prior to his rallying fame (as a PA to the Bishop of Regensburg) and was to be 1980 World Champion via Fiat's boxy 131 saloon . . . "Unfortunately", as one Audi insider explained, "Walter comes to see us for the negotiations before, just the day before, he goes to talk to Mercedes. That was a bad thing, and you cannot blame him for taking the better offer the next day!"

Meanwhile Audi were also negotiating to procure the best possible driver in France, a very important export market. Sports spokesman Dieter Scharnagl told me, "we had not planned to take a girl, just the best driver who was available at this time. Men like Jean Pierre Nicolas were not interested, he was retiring anyway, and Michele was simply the best we could have. This was very lucky for us, as it is obvious that she is much better than a man for PR purposes."

For the volatile Michele, who won her first international in Spain with an Almeras Porsche in 1977 and had proved as fast, if not faster, than the best men in World Championship contests like Corsica, where she was fifth for Fiat France in 1979 and '80, the Audi decision was a complete surprise. Giggling to Mike Greasley in *Motoring News* Michele recalled, "it was a big catastrophe for me! It was a very important time and very difficult to decide". For Michele there was a good chance of going further overseas with Fiat France, where she was known and respected for her abilities, as well as valued for her bubbly friendliness — and the move to World Championship rallying on a regular basis would demand the loss of her previous regular co-driver (Annie Arii). Instead her fiancé had recommended Italian Fabrizia Pons, whose waif-like appearance belies an early career spent in motocross and rally driving before she switched to navigating in 1979. Both Audi's 1981 lady choices were born in June: 23rd and 1951 for Mouton, 26th and four years later for Fabrizia — Mouton attaches some importance to this in the instant *rapport* the female crew immediately displayed.

If only all BP representatives looked like this . . . Michele Mouton and Audi made history together.

Italian by birth, former World Champion points winner as driver . . . Fabrizia Pons came into Mouton's life as a co-driver at Audi.

Announcement of Audi's pioneering 4-WD plans, with Hannu Mikkola/Arne Hertz and Michele Mouton/Fabrizia Pons as factory crews, was made in the second week of November 1980. Under the direction of Walter Treser it was confirmed that homologation into FIA Group 4 was confidently expected on January 1, 1981, (correct — J.W.) to make a serious assault on the World Rally Championship. The cars would be in Audi corporate colours, although BP's support of Mademoiselle Mouton sometimes led to their colour scheme being grafted over the basic Audi message. Trade support was headed by the French Kleber concern (later taken over in a business and competition sense by Michelin), with the names of Boge dampers, Castrol oil, KKK turbochargers and Recaro seats also neatly displayed on the first three Quattro rally cars exhibited to the press.

Walter Treser made it plain that Audi's ambition would extend to countries such as Belgium, Britain and Italy in supporting national teams. From the start there was strong interest from the rallycross fraternity in the Quattro concept, it's traction off the start line was enough to win most of these sprint events. Treser also committed them to a racing future that has yet to materialise with Quattro, "we would like to see the car in the European Touring Car series eventually", he commented at the Ingolstadt launch, adding for an end quote, "we are certain that the Quattro will be very competitive in the future on tarmac". Writing this in 1983, it is easy to say that Quattro coupe never did win a World Championship event based on tarmac (eg: Corsica, or even a dry Monte), but the 4-WD concept seemed likely to succeed over dry and smooth surfaces when incorporated in the 1984 season Quattro Sport. It is also worth adding that Michele's historic first World Championship victory for a lady (San Remo 1981) was taken despite a route that covered about 50 per cent asphalt and the Portuguese performances of 1981-83 (two wins and a five minute lead lost by mechanical trouble in 1981) were also over a route that contained a high percentage of black top.

quattro

Audi Sport workshop are well-equipped, but far from the suave showcase that BMW have, less than an hour's drive south. The basic bare shells, in the background, were the heart of factory rallycars until the rapid evolution moves of 1983.

Original Specification

Glance over a specification such as that of the Quattro road car, four-wheel-drive, locking differentials and 200bhp turbo engine. There is a strong temptation to think that it should not take a great deal of further technical work in order that it be prepared for the rigours of rallying. Wrong!

Just like every other competition car that has evolved from a production base, the Quattro has grown progressively further away from its roots as the seasons roll by. The principles of five-turbocharged-cylinders, a five-speed gearbox, four-wheel-drive, four-wheel ventilated disc brakes and all-independent strut suspension remain within that chunky body, but very little is left of that original car — even the external appearance altering rapidly as the bodywork accommodated ever wider tarmac tyres, a taller rear wing over the huge external oil cooler and the adoption (in two stages) of even lighter plastic bodywork with extra cooling slots, particularly notable around the front of the back wheel arches. As ever, the chief objective in the Quattro programme materialised as more power for less weight, allied to a burning desire for reliability and substantial handling refinements.

Unique items abounded as Audi's technical expertise was plumbed, perhaps the best known being the electro-hydraulic clutch activation from a gear-lever knob to aid the mandatory left foot braking technique, but on more routine matters sophistication also abounded. The power steering was vital and was retained, even with a standard four spoke wheel initially, from the road car. Aluminium was widely used from the start, both in the reproduction of standard external body panels and in the amazing "chassis-within-a-chassis" — Matter alloy cage that extended from behind the front bumpers to the rear, picking up suspension and body loads *en route*.

Basic modifications to prepare for Group 4 competition in 1981 went along the following lines. The bodywork was highly specialised and, as usually is the case today, was the work of Matter & Obermoser. They ensured not only that all the body welds were extraordinarily strong, but also fabricated everything from the roll cage to the myriad minor bracketry needed to attach sundry rally equipment to the still primarily steel bodyshell.

Ready for battle with a comprehensive roll cage and oil cooler plumbing clearly displayed beneath the bootlid.

Matter took a basic shell from the small ex-pilot plant that has produced seven to ten Quattros a day since September 1980 and returned a white-sprayed competition masterpiece. The alloy tubular frame inside the two-door body ran transversely across the front of the engine bay before leading back to the braced top mountings of the forward suspension struts. The alloy frame, essentially on cross-brased dune buggy lines, formed a roll cage within the cockpit before picking up the rear strut mounting points.

Also in aluminium were the front wings, bonnet and doors, while the bootlid was in plastic and always carried a larger spoiler than that of production Quattros. Matter also fabricated the 120 litre/26.4 gallon fuel tank and the original dry sump oil tank. The dashpanel was a quick release alloy sheet and carried six-dial instrumentation, dominated by a 10,000rpm tachometer. Other information

Inside the 1980 rally Quattro with the large road wheel still evident along with footbraces (note horn push buttons for co-driver's feet) and electronic Halda navigational equipment. Today's Quattros have an even more complex cockpit.

quattro

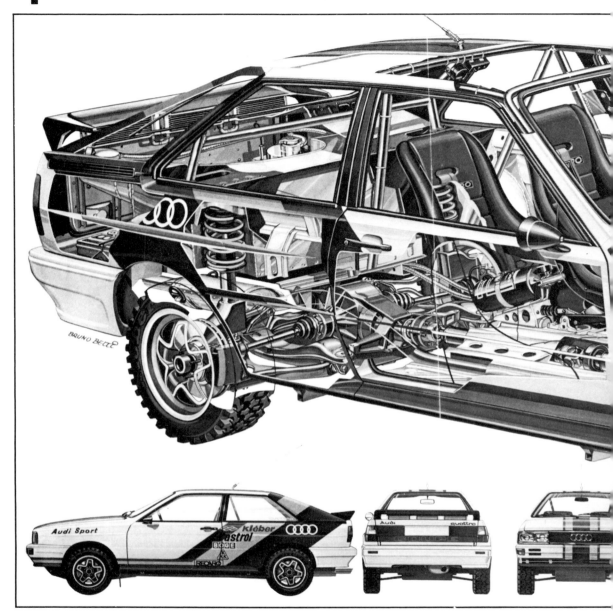

relayed by dial was oil temperature, boost pressure (no cockpit adjustment), water temperature, oil pressure and the mandatory speedometer was tucked over to the left. Unfamiliar then, but commonplace today, was the new breed of Halda electronic navigational trip distance recorder.

Cockpit details included fixed-back bucket seats for both occupants on some initial works Quattros, an enormous low oil pressure beacon light in orange, and massive foot braces for both passenger (who could foot-pedal the horns) and the driver. Overall the cockpit was slightly messier than today, but its information was probably easier to assimilate as development over the years has tended toward the usual rally car over-complexity.

Despite the widespread use of lightweight equipment, excess pounds

quattro

The principles of a turbo-charged five-cylinder with 4-WD permanently engaged, and strut suspension, remained in the rally car. This cutaway of the original competition car reveals how the production intercooler (usually at the front left-hand corner of the engine bay, looking front to rear) has been replaced by the large central intercooler with its large bore pipework feeding over a distance that is almost Alaskan in comparison with some turbocharged rivals today. This view also emphasises that the turbo casing size went up considerably for competition, and that the rear disc brakes were converted to ventilated units.

(compared to the previous generation of sub, or near-1000kg/2200lb, rally Escorts and the like) always preoccupied Audi. It is a cornerstone of VW and Audi road car engineering that performance and mpg bonuses are available through weight reduction, and you will normally find in any routine road test confrontation between a group of similar class cars that VW-Audi have produced the lightest contender. For the rally car, complete with five intercooled and turbocharged cylinders, and four-wheel-drive, there was bound to be a weight penalty. In its first year of rallying the factory reckoned 1220 to 1240kg (2728-2684lb) was the usual weight span, which compares with just over 1300kg (2600lb) quoted for the standard road car.

Dimensionally the Quattro would tend always to grow fatter, but the

quattro

standard length of around 172in and a height of less than 53in were features of the original rally car. Audi quoted a fractional increase in width of body (from 1725mm to 1733mm, or 0.3in!), but more substantial track increases were reported. At the headlamp end 1465mm instead of 1420mm, up 1.77in, and 1502mm instead of 1460mm at the rear, a boost of 1.65in. As far as I am aware these figures are for a Quattro equipped with the competition Fuchs 6J × 15in forged-alloy wheels and Kleber cross country rubber; obviously the 10J × 15 alloy wheel and appropriate racing-style Kleber slicks increased total track considerably.

The principle of permanent all-wheel-drive was retained but the details were subject to a great deal of test mileage, originally front and rear effectively coupled without any differential action, via a solid shaft. There was no limited slip for the front and a ZF 75 per cent limited slip torque setting for the rear wheels. In its original and early competition form there was a lot more obstructive understeer than by the close of the 1981 season.

As of January 1, 1981, three differential ratios were listed − 4.11, 4.55 and 4.87 − with a five-speed competition gearbox that had the following ratios (standard Quattro in brackets): first, 3.00 (3.6:1); second, 2.0 (2.125:1); third, 1.50 (1.36:1); fourth, 1.217 (0.967:1); fifth, 1.040 (0.778:1). A classic example of closer ratio rally gearing with the accent on acceleration, rather than top speed. Depending on the combination of ratios selected and attendant wheels and tyres the company reckoned top speeds from 108.7mph to 158mph and 0-62mph capability of a helmet-banging 4.9 to 5.2 seconds, both of which are slightly quicker than exotica such as Mr Porsche's 3.3-litre/300bhp 911 turbo! From rest to 100mph was covered in 12.8 to 13.5 seconds in company tests prior to the 1981 season. It impresses this writer that *Autocar's* test of the 2778lb, 1981 spec, Quattro campaigned by David Sutton Motorsport in Britain during 1982 produced 0-60mph in . . . 4.9 seconds! And 0-100mph? That took 13.7 seconds, so next time Audi tell me something is true, I will already be halfway toward belief.

Engine Modifications

Producing extra power from the dimensionally unaltered 2144cc five was not a problem − ''we could have given Mikkola 350 horsepower in the beginning'', shrugged one engineer, ''aah, but to make that power of the best kind for rally, yes, that was a problem!'' Even by the close of the first season, it could be seen that providing instant response − particularly over ''blind'' terrain as is found on the Lombard RAC − and the best possible pulling power, these were priorities over sheer horsepower.

Even the original engine bay of the rally car looked very different to that of the production car. Missing was the small intercooler in the left front corner (assuming you were looking front to rear) and the Bosch K-Jetronic injection. The intercooler had been shuffled over, to live behind the quad-ringed grille in front of the radiator. The larger cacity KKK turbocharger was thus relatively uncluttered in its corner to the right of the inclined five, but its compressor had the awesome task of shovelling air to the distant intercooler before it was returned for injection induction: a distance measured in feet rather than the usual inlet tract inches.

The injection itself was changed to a Pierburg-branded mechanical DVG layout, which metered fuel on the basis of rpm, throttle opening, boost pressure and engine temperature. As Audi's experience of World Championship terrain expanded the number of camshaft alternatives multiplied to alter power delivery, but the original profile was almost gentle by competition car standards, providing 300bhp between 5500 and 7000rpm. By contrast the normal car peaked at 5500

and 200bhp, drooping to just under 200bhp by 6000rpm. The reported rally car torque curve sounded wonderful in comparison to the standard car. It was said that 420Nm (304lb.ft) instead of a production 285Nm (206lb.ft) was available some 250rpm *below* maximum torque of the road car, *ie*: 3250rpm instead of 3500rpm. As we all know, getting test-bed results to produce road performance can always be a problem and Audi put in an enormous amount of work on the engine and its ancillaries, including using smaller turbocharger turbines and casings, to provide the instant pulling power that rally drivers demand when the unexpected occurs.

Aside from the enlarged intercooler in its new position and the new induction and ancillary systems, Audi chose to reduce compression ratio to 6.3:1 instead of 7:1 and to up boost from a roadgoing 0.85 bar (12psi) to 1.5 bar (21psi) as a basic starting point. They could always provide more boost, and did, even during the original test year and subsequent seasons, but it was never Audi philosophy "to give the driver the way of turning up boost. We put in the screw, but not the screwdriver", in the words of one competition engineer on the original car.

Chassis work to contain a claimed maximum of 320bhp at 6500rpm from the still SOHC and 10-valve motor was far from extensive compared with the sort of equipment Roland Gumpert was evaluating in 1982-83, but all the usual rally strengthening tricks were employed for the steel lower wishbones (extra cross bracing), tie rods, steering knuckles, engine mountings, gearbox mountings and the points for attaching and mounting the rear differential and front and rear subframes. Completing the protection measures were aluminium underbody trays front and rear.

The hydraulic dampers were unusual — amongst European rally cars in coming from Boge, but like those Fuchs forged wheels, Audi felt that what was good enough to earn them the mantle of being Porsche suppliers, was good enough to earn Audi's competition patronage. In fact there is good reason to think that Audi deliberately selected suppliers who would give a service less in demand by other competitors, particularly in the case of that original exclusive Kleber tyre contract. Incidentally Kleber also supplied the rubber envelope for the fuel tank, which had the usual foam filling.

At first the braking system was only mildly modified from standard, retaining brake pipes that apparently owed their parentage to the Audi 80, and using

quattro

For show, rather than go on those road Klebers an Ronal road wheels, th competition coupe pose ready for the 1981 seasor

standard 280mm/11 inch diameter brake discs at the front. The rears were vented discs also 11 inch, but that was a slight increase over the production 245mm/9.65in. No hydraulic servo was used, but the rear wheel handbrake was hydraulic and pressure bias adjustments were provided. Nice to see that AP, as well as Castrol, kept the British supplier flag flying right from the early days of the project.

Thus Audi spent over 12 months honing a design that would mean as much to World Championship rallying, in establishing a design principle, as Colin Chapman's Lotus ground effect car did in Grand Prix racing. Could Audi prove that 4-WD for a high performance car was the logical answer over the widely-differing Championship rounds. Or would the critics' cries of "too complex", and "it'll never work on tarmac", be proved painfully, and tremendously expensively, true?

After three seasons of Audi Quattro as a Championship contender we draw our conclusions through the following chapters. Be certain that the writer was pressurised by those old clichés about triumph through tragedy, the depths of despair, and things couldn't get worse . . . could they? Yes, all these hoary old chestnuts had to be manfully resisted. Such a tale requires only straight recollection to provide a motorised plot of more character intrigue and exotic background locations than you would find in *Lucrezia Borgia & Family meet James Bond*!

All the other competitor would see? Complet with the original sma rear wing and oil coolers the Quattro ready t revolutionise Worl Championship rallying . .

Chapter 5

1981: Bizarre !

Competing in selected World Championship rounds, primarily in Europe, Audi scored three victories including an historic first for a lady — but there was a dark side to the season too . . .

FIA homologation number 673, effective as from January 1, 1981, contained the Group 4 recognition Audi needed to compete internationally with the Quattro. That such recognition was granted at all was a mute testament to the diplomacy exercised by Jurgen Stockmar over six months patient politicking, and to the determination of Audi themselves, for there was also the not inconsiderable expense of launching and manufacturing the minimum 400 cars to enter Group 4 — knowing that the rules would change for the 1982 season.

Austrian Audi loyalist Franz Wittman, then 30-years-old, was paired with Kurt Nestinger in factory Quattro "IN-NV 90" to debut the Quattro officially. Between January 9 and 11 the Kleber-shod coupe romped over perfect icy conditions to demonstrate the inherent advantages of 4-WD against a mediocre opposition. The seventy-four other starters on the European Championship Austrian Janner Rally, sponsored by Audi backer Castrol, stood no chance. Wittman/Nestinger whooshed the latest in high technology rallying home to a 20m 50s win over the rear-engined Skoda 130RS of Norway's John Haugland after 380km/236 miles.

It had been ample warning of what World Championship rallying could expect if conditions on the January 24 to 30 Monte Carlo Rally proved to be anything other than consistently dry tarmac . . .

Naturally the opposition for Audi's first Championship challenge in the World

quattro

Series was considerably tougher, but it should be first explained that — in line with motor sport's apparently insatiable desire for obscurity through technicalities — there are two World Championships: one for Drivers and one for Manufacturers. A Championship round for Drivers may not count for the Manufacturer's title! In Audi's initial year they scored one win on a Drivers-only qualifyer and two on events that counted toward both series, which is the more common (and prestigious) occurence.

Monte Carlo counted toward both Championship series, but like Le Mans and Indianapolis in motor racing, it really does not seem to matter what status is attached to Monte Carlo, for the event is bigger than the series and provides an irresistible draw for any car maker with sporting ambitions. The regular controversies just seem to add to the attractions of a Mediterranean location on the basis of "any publicity . . ."

Although Walter Rohrl, 1980 World Champion for Fiat, had become available when Mercedes withdrew from rallying so shortly after signing Regensburg's favourite rallying son, Audi stuck to their moral and contractual obligations. Resisting any last minute pressure to run a third car for Walter they fielded the long-awaited double duo of Mikkola/Hertz and Mouton/Pons against a first class Monte entry. Renault, as the home team, were there to defend technical and patriotic honours with the mid-engined turbo R5 — the first of the purpose-built and technically-inspired rally cars for the eighties after generations of almost exclusively front-engine, rear-drive winners. The exception to the rule? Lancia-Fiat's Stratos-Ferrari hybrid: a mid-engined winner in the seventies, that only became unfashionable in its backers' eyes when they wanted to push the sales of 131 saloons.

Fiat themselves had two 131s, a Ritmo and low profile support for the ex-works Stratos of Bernard Darniche. Opel brought two of the Ascona 400 machines, Talbot brought two of their cars, and there were a pair of obsolete, though still effective, Escorts from Publimmo (Bjorn Waldegard) and Rothmans (Ari Vatanen), plus a single Datsun.

In the weeks prior to the event Audi colours had become familiar to the hardy residents of the tortuous hillside roads of Southern France for, as with 90 per cent of World Championship events, reconnaissance to make pace notes is permitted on the world's best known rally. On the event the specially rigged and rather slow VW LT vans (with standard 2-litre petrol engines; the base on which Porsche 924 power unit was developed) staggered over the tiny twisting roads and hummed along motorways with literally tons of spares for rallying's new superstar car. It was estimated that anything up to 30 service vehicles were out serving the needs of the two team cars, but some of these were the roadgoing Quattros ("Chase Cars") used to monitor progress and assess conditions constantly, aside from the ice note crews — the latter including the ubiquitous Kottulinsky for the Audi cause.

"The Monte" is unique amongst world class events in retaining the varied starting points and concentration runs prior to the competition proper. Normally modern rally cars just breeze into Monaco after several days of boredom, though there has been a recent trend toward providing at least a taster of competition action *en route*. For Audi the omens of a dramatic year ahead, began immediately . . .

Michele Mouton had started work for Audi in the Vosges region on December 5, 1980, tyre testing, and commented wryly "the Audi team do not know the meaning of the dead season" as she worked through all but the Christmas days on not only the competition cars, but also giving TV interviews and all the other activities that inexorably pressurised the attractive Mademoiselle after Audi's announcement of her employment. Unfortunately the Monte provided only anti-climax: her coupe stopped rumbling its way South after a

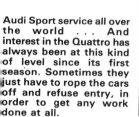

Audi Sport service all over the world ... And interest in the Quattro has always been at this kind of level since its first season. Sometimes they just have to rope the cars off and refuse entry, in order to get any work done at all.

petrol halt on the way down from her Paris start to the concentration run!

Officially the reason given was dirt and water in the petrol. Despite changing the accessible components in the injection system, no permanent cure could be found and the Quattro was towed over 70 miles in an attempt to keep it in the event! Unsurprisingly that was duly noted. Local officials at the Aix-les-Bains would have been forced to exclude the Quattro, so the team gave up prior to that point: an unjust reward for all concerned. Aix also witnessed a significant hiccup from the alternator on Mikkola's car, although it was the long-term import of the injection problem — repairing it swiftly and ensuring reliable operation — that was to be significant for Audi during 1981; eventually forcing the engineers to plumb the system again with a number of important duplications for speedy service and reliability.

Mikkola's Monte was certainly spectacular. The first stage was suitably snowy in surface and 14.12km/8.76 miles long. Mustering all his recently acquired left-foot-braking technique, Mikkola mashed the mid-engined Renaults into the snow banks, 50 seconds faster than Bruno Saby and 54 seconds faster than eventual winner Jean Ragnotti. The second test comprised 43.54km/27.03 miles and Mikkola was 1m 57s faster than Saby, 2m 1s quicker than Ragnotti! All the time the Quattro was in good heart the others might as well have been competing in a separate treasure hunt. When they arrived in Monaco after six slippery stages, Hannu Mikkola enjoyed nearly six *minutes* advantage over his flustered rivals. The alternator belt-throwing problem (attributable to the pulley) began to intrude at frequent and unwelcome moments. After eleven stages it was calculated that Mikkola was 7m 35s behind a new leader, Jean Luc Therier's Porsche 911SC, but the bothersome belts were only a contributory factor.

quattro

Looking remarkably standard by mid-eighties comparison, the 1981 Monte Carlo rally car for Mikkola/Hertz performed sensationally, but suffered a lot of accident and mechanical damage. Mikkola led the first ten stages and set more fastest times than the eventual winner.

What happened? Mikkola explained later that he was at that critical midway point between left and right-foot-braking, because he had to change gear and then preferred to use right foot braking and left foot for the clutch: "my foot slipped off the brake pedal", said Hannu with disarming frankness. The Quattro punted a low bridge parapet, the abrupt halt damaging the driver's side front wheel so badly that Hannu was advised, via the radio, to simply remove it and carry on to the end of the stage and subsequent service assistance. Even Mikkola couldn't master the disabled coupe, which ground along on the brake disc to the inevitable conclusion that it once again hit the scenery. Hannu didn't give up, and made it to the service area, where they replaced the major components — suspension strut, drive shaft — leaving frills like broken engine mounts and other tasks to be cleared up later. Although the car was eventually restored to competitive condition, the tousled "IN-NP 50" Ingolstadt number plate one of the few legacies to betray there had been an "about 140km/h bang", in Hannu's words, there was "too much of the dry stages and too much time spent with the alternator belts", for the Audi to do more than reaffirm its competitiveness with a fastest time on the Cul du Corobin (16km/9.94m). Even with a substandard car a long slippery stage like Croix de Bauzon (27km/16.77m) produced a time only one second slower than Ragnotti's pace-setting Renault R5.

Although the Quattro did not retire until it had an even larger accident on the 26th of 32 special stages that made up the 1981 Monte, there were other mechanical problems that gave its rivals heart. The Audi mechanics and their managers were inexperienced in tackling rallying's unexpected deviations from plan, of which there were two prime examples: a missing steering arm bolt, left lying on the gearbox after the rack change, which lost them 40 minutes on SS17 and the final accident which was attributable to brake failure at nearly 100mph, possibly a legacy from the earlier dramas. Luckily Mikkola was on a quick uphill section when the centre pedal sank to the floor because a linkage rod was displaced: Mikkola told Rupert Saunders of *Autosport*, "I was going so fast I almost caught the car in front as I was having the accident!" A rock face brought the Quattro's Monte to a harsh conclusion. For journalists used to reading great portents in "the writing on the wall", there was plenty to write about — and much speculation about *when* the Quattro would win a World Championship round, rather than *if*.

Mikkola led all 25 stages of the second World Championship event Audi contested, the Quattro's liking for a freezing atmosphere and icy surfaces resulting in an apparently effortless 1m 53s win over compatriot Vatanen's old Escort. Mikkola was quickest on 15 stages versus 5 for Vatanen!

A Perfect Quattro Event

Sweden were the hosts to the next World Championship round, an event counting only toward the Drivers' series, although it had long been admired for its professional organisation and challenging format over snow and ice covered terrain. Whirring through this white landscape came the new age in rallying — the predominantly white Audi (IN-NV 90, the car used by Wittman in Austria), its occupants looking suitably space age in their white Simpson helmets.

The result was a carefully paced win from the front for the solo works entry (Sweden felt to be too specialised for a driver of Mouton's Mediterranean background). Mikkola setting fastest times on the opening four stages, slacking off to let the opposition from Blomqvist's Saab, Vatanen's Escort and Airikkala's similar Rothmans-David Sutton Motorsport Ford show its worth. Altogether Hannu and Arne were fastest on 15 of 25 stages and won by 1m 53s. Arne Hertz made sure that they always stayed in touch with the opposition, even whilst taking things comparatively easy, so they ran the remaining ten stages always amongst the fastest five. For Mikkola it was a case of taking no chances and ensuring the health of his complicated coupe, but "easy" for Hannu does not mean dawdling, for that has its dangers, as he has discovered in the hardest of lessons over the years.

Mikkola summed-up Sweden as, "I knew after Monte we could win. The cold air in Sweden was good for the turbo and I didn't have to push the car much. Ari (Vatanen) got a bit close in the middle stages, but I had a feeling he was going over the limit to do this." Fellow Finns were second (Vatanen) and third (Airikkala), contributing to an historic 1-2-3 as this was the first occasion on which the Swedish had been won by anyone other than a Swede. Furthermore it was the first World Championship victory for a 4-WD car.

For Walter Treser and the Ingolstadt team, plus the management who had stuck their necks out in gaining even higher level support for the Quattro programme it was a very pleasing vindication of the scientific approach to rallying. However, if anyone thought that Audi would now just steamroller their way through the World Series, the season held a lot more unpleasant surprises . . .

quattro

Onlookers complained that the Quattro virtually stopped on sharper corners, but here Hannu Mikkola shows how a nice long slide can cheer things up on the way to the Quattro's maiden World Championship victory, February 1981's Swedish.

The Bad News

A good result certainly sent Audi back to the drawing boards in good heart. As a matter of policy it had been decided to give the Easter African Safari a miss. Expense and the need for specialised preparation, along with an early need for practice cars disrupting the rest of Quattro's debut season preparations, were primary reasons — so they had from February until April to finalise preparation and recce notes for the April 30 to May 2 Tour de Corse. Another specialised event, one that amounts to a timed tarmac race over very narrow roads, with more twists per kilometre than any other championship round.

While Audi were working hard on the Corsican cars, clipping a little weight and installing larger diameter cross-drilled vented discs of Porsche Group 5 ancestry, as well as boosting the five-cylinder engines to an official 350bhp via a camshaft of racing rather than rallying bias, there was another loose surface and tarmac championship commitment to meet. The March 4 to 7 Portuguese contribution to both World Championship series.

Audi sent the usual factory pairings to Portugal, Mouton getting a brand new car because the factory had developed a 40kg (88lb) lighter body in association with Matter. The "diet" was based on thinner metal gauges and increased use of plastics, including distinctive "eyebrow" spats for Portugal. Another reason was because two factory Quattros had been severely damaged in road accidents! Mouton's "lightweight" was measured at 1188kg (2619.5lb) with nearly half a tank of fuel and was finished in black, red and silver rather than the corporate Audi colours; it also bore Mikkola/Wittman's "IN-NV 90" registration plate! Both Mikkola and Mouton were given more powerful engines, a decision ratified on the eve of the event, a maximum 1.5 bar boost replaced by 1.8 at low rpm. At higher rpm a boost limiting valve modification allowed only the previous 1.5 bar. A second camshaft profile was also introduced at this point and the official output was 340bhp.

Mouton got off to a comparatively leisurely assault on the event: he was not happy with the brake pedal feel, and was later troubled by characteristic injection maladies. Meanwhile it was Mikkola versus Vatanen from the outset;

New grille with pronounced beak and single headlamps with wheel-arch eyebrow extensions were amongst the 1981 improvements, along with the huge rear wing and larger oil coolers.

quattro

the Quattro pulling away from a class field — including an aviating Markku Alen in a temporarily three-wheeler Fiat 131. On tarmac as well as dirt Mikkola's Quattro set a demanding pace. After 16 of 46 stages in the first night leg, Hannu held a 1m 48s lead over Vatanen. The second leg saw Mikkola and his masterful mount increase the gap to nearly three minutes over his former Escort team-mate.

Then, with almost half the scheduled stages completed, the Quattro suddenly ceased running in mid-test. It was so sudden that Mikkola suspected an electrical fault and changed everything to hand. On attempting to restart again, the five locked up, a valve having demolished a piston. Increased turbo boost? The revised wastegate? The revised cam profile? All were possible contributory factors, but Hannu took this and subsequent setbacks philosophically — ''I don't get angry anymore. No point to do this, it does not make things any better.''

In contrast Mouton started to pick up some pace. By the close of play she was fourth, setting seven fastest times. Obviously the lady had now made up for her deficit in Quattro competition mileage and was learning at a rate that one would expect from such a fiercely determined competitor. How else could one judge a performance that saw her set two more faster times than Vatanen, that supreme ''hard trier'' amongst the Finnish elite?

Corsica swiftly demonstrated that this Portuguese premonition of Mouton's capabilities was absolutely accurate. This time it was Mouton's turn to wear an ex-Mikkola number plate (IN-NR 87) in conjunction with her BP-inspired colour scheme with central black stripe; both cars slightly uprated in power as earlier described and wearing larger spats and deeper front air dams than before.

Mikkola had not enjoyed any luck on any Corsican Championship round at the time of writing, and 1981 was no exception. It just doesn't seem to be his sort of event, and it's one of the few that the Scandinavian contingent have generally found harder to conquer than any other Championship round: from 1972 to 1982 it was won only by French or Italian drivers. It took the Italian based

Quattro's tarmac dress for 1981, wide wheels supporting Kleber's earnest efforts to find the answer to the kind of smooth-going understeer exhibited here. Car is the victorious Sanremo mount for Michele Mouton/Fabrizia Pons.

Markku Alen driving a Lancia to crack the jinx for Finland in 1983 with a surprise outright win on an event that depends for success on racing precision and monotonous months of note-taking preparation. A superb spectacle, but a wearing grind for the crews.

So it was that Mouton outshone Mikkola in Corsica 1981, setting one second fastest time and featuring in the top six for six of the eight stages she covered. That was two more than a miserable Mikkola . . .

In both cases engine failures were responsible for the retirements, Mikkola's hastened by excess turbo boost because of a failure in the sophisticated wastegate to cut excess pressure; at least one piston collapsing under the strain. Mouton's machine had extra tensioning pulleys for the fan belt and when one of these wobbled off into the toothed cam-driving belt there was ensuing mechanical carnage. Dr Piech was on hand and *Motoring News* correspondent Gerry Phillips scooped up the significant reaction of Audi's development chief, saying that Piech was "horrified and proclaimed that development methods should not be allowed to become so unsophisticated. Indeed he felt that the Quattro should benefit from the standards employed in the exacting aviation field rather than the less rigid ones of the automotive industry." It would not be long before engineering and management heads rolled . . .

The Really Bad News

The year's nadir came in Greece on the picturesque Acropolis. The team notched up some historic firsts, running a three car team that was disqualified only after dominating the event and providing the first ever World Championship round to be led by a woman.

The Audi-entered three car team featured new detuned machines for Mouton and Mikkola, while Franz Wittman appeared in an older example. It was to be Walter Treser's worst and last outing as team manager although the 300bhp power trim for the fives seemed to provide the extra reliability Ingolstadt had been seeking.

At first the dusty heat and relentless schedule over imposing Greek trails seemed to suit Audi to the tips of all driven wheels. Mouton beat everyone on the opening stage outside Athens and Mikkola then took over to such effect that he led the rapid Vatanen Escort by over six *minutes* after the first 797km/495 mile leg to Kalambaka, Mouton four minutes and more behind Mikkola and over 2m 15s ahead of Vatanen. With 68 survivors from 138 starters and Wittman running strongly too, Audi could have afforded themselves some complacency if it had not been for their previous record, and a gathering row with the technical inspectors on the event about the Quattro's detail specification. Just six stages into the second leg Mouton's Quattro bashed its rear suspension askew, the result of a progressively deteriorating ball joint. Mouton dragged the car to the next service area on three-wheel-drive.

Knowing that a rear ball joint was the cause of the problem, Treser crawled under the rear of Mikkola's Quattro prior to the arrival of Mademoiselle. They were still refuelling the Quattro . . . Whump! The rear end of the Mikkola coupe was enveloped in flame, Treser rolling out from underneath with his hands and face partially burnt. The fuel burning on the ground could have inflicted even worse damage had it not been for an heroic Arne Hertz. He drove the car forward, away from the terrifying ball of flame that had literally engulfed the Quattro's hindquarters. Incidentally the Audi's engine was running throughout the incident, as is normal practice, for reasons of turbo mechanical sympathy, and ease of starting.

quattro

Treser was treated for burns by the team doctor while Mikkola took the car over to Talbot's Coventry service boys for a check over, before carrying on in the lead of this torrid Greek Championship qualifyer. Treser carried on managing the team through the dramatic remainder of their event, the doctor continuing a treatment of pain killers and dressings for the right arm and the left of the gallant German's head.

Still the Audi dramas continued, Mikkola's car suffering a rear differential failure that transformed it into a limping front-drive horror: albeit one that was still in a reduced lead prior to the start of the final leg, 2m 51s ahead of compatriot Vatanen as Mouton had lost time with that suspension bother. The Audis were set for the final assault with Mikkola leading, Mouton fifth and Wittman tenth, but destiny decreed they would not return to Athens in glory . . .

Besides her earlier use of three-wheel-drive, Mouton also covered the best part of 24 miles with front-drive after a rear driveshaft broke. Following the Treser fire incident service was somewhat shambolic for Audi, but with all the Quattros in apparently rude health despite the dramas the team looked forward to a good night's sleep at the Lagonissi overnight halt.

While the team relaxed along with rivals from Fiat-Abarth, Datsun and Rothmans/Sutton Escort team behind second place man Vatanen, the scrutineers were busy in *Parc Ferme*, the closed overnight car park for competitors. They inspected the three Audis and found them illegal on grounds of carrying batteries in front of the co-driver's seat, for which the Ingolstadt organisation was fined over £200. There was dispute over whether the batteries were simply being carried overnight in readiness for the morning start, or if (as in the case of Mikkola's car as an example) they were wired into place for regular use, so Audi were not excluded for this offence.

However all three cars were disqualified by an esoteric and rather belated decision on the legality of running without the inner pair of their quadruple headlamp layout. Not so obvious when all the auxiliary Carellos were in place, Audi in fact used the inner headlamp space for a flap that, under air pressure fed ducted air to the engine bay. Naturally Audi tried everything they knew to continue under notice of appeal, but the organisers were adamant and the battered team packed their bags for home, Walter Treser returning for further burns treatment in Germany.

The benefit of hindsight does little to illuminate this sordid Acropolis affair. Audi were not reinstated in any form, and Ari Vatanen reluctantly accepted the "honour" of winning an event under circumstances far from the straight fight he and Mikkola understand as the only way to win. It was implied at the time that a suggestion had been made to the Greek organisers by one of Audi's jealous rivals that the cars be inspected in respect of batteries and lights with particular care. One can understand the reasons for such a suspicion as such thorough mid-rally checks are rare — and one would have thought the headlamp item a natural for a scrutineering row *before* the event started: shades of Monte Carlo and the Minis, except they were at least able to scoop up the moral glory, whereas Audi were denied the right to continue in mid-event. Unprecedented in the author's limited experience of technical offences on World Championship events. If it was a rival, nobody has come up with proof enough to print and withstand the laws of libel . . .

All Change

''Walter Treser (41) has relinquished his position as manager of Audi Sport and will again resume responsibilities in the Research and Development Centre of

Audi. Mr Reinhard Rode (37), long-standing team manager, takes over as the manager of Audi Sport.'' That was the English version of the German press statement issued in late June. Hospital or no hospital, the disqualification of three team cars, with the impuning of Audi honour, had to be paid for by one man: even if he had played such a large part in the practical development of Quattro. Walter Treser was OUT!

Today Treser still works with Audi products, but he has his own specialist preparation business, making machines like 130mph Audi 80 Quattros and the like. Innumerable conversations with company insiders left me in no doubt that Treser was deeply respected for his mechanical abilities and straight talking, but mistakes were being made that humiliated Audi in public and Treser's scapegoat role was inevitable, particularly given the daily interest in the project by a man like Ferdinand Piech, used only to succeeding, and unimpressed by some development details.

The Ingolstadt assembly shop at Audi Sport, before the 1981 RAC Rally, emphasised a new era had truly begun in world class rallying.

Rode became the high profile manager in June, but by the time I paid my first visit in Autumn 1981 there was no mistaking where the real power lay. Roland Gumpert, promising R&D engineer with an Iltis 4-WD pedigree that showed he was keen enough to get really involved in competition (ie: driving the back-up Iltis in that successful Paris-Dakar sortie referred to earlier), was definitely on the way up. After the Acropolis fiasco he was drafted in to look after all technical matters and by the time I visited he was ranked as an equal to Rode. It would only be a matter of time before "Captain Nice" Rode, promoted in the opinion of insiders a little beyond his management capabilities, was entirely replaced by "Mr Engineering Efficiency" Gumpert. For 1981 we can assume that Rode looked after team admin while Gumpert tackled the car with a fundamental brief to ensure its reliability.

Lines to engineering inside the main company centre were dramatically shortened, Jorg Bensinger taking much of the day-to-day input from Audi Sport while Ferdinand Piech continued to take ultimate responsibility — and a personal interest signified by attendance at everything from test sessions to selected events. Gumpert summed up the technical brief succinctly as, "in all things we must first make sure it does not break. Because if we have a breakage, usually it must take longer to repair than in other cars."

Unfortunately mere management changes were not enough to avert the wrath of the Gods, and Audi's astonishing ability to become involved in rallying

quattro

controversy recurred in August. First there was an important development programme to implement . . .

Audi opted out of the South American events from the start, leaving Talbot and Rothmans/Sutton with their Escort for Vatanen to pick up World Championship points in what was becoming a very close contest with Talbot's Guy Frequelin. Whilst the Finn and the Frenchman wrestled with the Argentine and Brazilian rounds, scoring a win apiece, Audi applied their PR slogan of "Progress through Technology" to the potential of Quattro in rallying guise.

First apparent sign of the new approach was a brief outing for Michele Mouton on the non-Championship Mille Piste: a rough event which provides manufacturers with the chance to air forthcoming rally models. Michele's BP-backed machine appeared with a new grille that covered up the gap left by the absent inner headlamps, as well as allowing mechanics better frontal access by protruding proud of the bonnet. The outing was not a success, Mouton eliminated by low oil pressure at an early stage, but the grille featured on all subsequent works Quattros, solving the legality problem in FISA's opinion.

Tragedy Masks Potential

For the August 28 to 30 sprint that is often called the "Finnish GP" or more formally the "Rally of 1000 Lakes", Audi Sport were back up to three cars, Wittman's supported by the Austrian operation, but also fully works serviced and supported. The new front grille was neatly integrated into the bonnets of the works cars, lifting up *a la* Mercedes to provide excellent front end access, which was, unfortunately, needed as engine problems were the talk of practice and cost Mikkola a likely win in the event.

After just four stages Mikkola had drawn out a slim lead over an intense war between Alen's Fiat and Vatanen's Ford, but Wittman was the one in the spotlight. His Quattro slithered into the crowd after a flying finish board had become obscured by spectators and Raul Falin, President of the Finnish Automobile Association, was so severely injured that he later died.

Naturally such an incident aroused strong feelings and the organisers issued an order that Wittman be barred from further participation, alleging dangerous driving. In fact it had taken some time for the extent of the incident to become apparent — those on the spot found that Wittman was unaware of anything more than a slight scrape over a flying finish, which is not that rare an occurrence to an experienced rally competitor. When it was realised that the injuries to Mr Falin had proved fatal, Audi withdrew Wittman's car immediately. A later police enquiry completely cleared Wittman from any charges in connection with Mr Falin's death, but the Austrian and co-driver Kurt Nestinger had already been through a harrowing inquisition in public, plus hours of police inquiries at the time, so the whole incident was more traumatic for the organisers and Audi's crew, than one would have expected.

Meanwhile in the 1000 Lakes itself, Mikkola bid fair toward keeping alive the tradition of Finnish home victories until the Quattro's motor lapsed onto four-cylinders. Still Hannu managed to keep the conventional Fiat and Ford four-cylinder opposition at bay, but in the end 26 minutes (over 4 minutes in penalties) were required to change the camshaft, for it had worn its lobes to such an extent that the motor was misfiring.

Mikkola set about retrieving lost ground with the kind of desperate determination and skill that is the hallmark of all top "Flying Finns" and was battling with Henri Toivonen's Talbot for third overall when the Lotus-engined Talbot quit, leaving Mikkola a fine third, less than 2 minutes behind Alen, who

had been beaten by Vatanen's Ford with a margin of 59 seconds after a superb second-for-second stage battle of the kind Finns provide when trying to win their home event. Incidentally the only non-Finn to win 1000 Lakes was Stig Blomqvist in 1971, the Swedish SAAB driver who was to mean an awful lot to Audi in the eighties.

Audi also had a second finisher, not in the top ten. Michele Mouton and Fabrizia Pons put on one of *the* most gutsy first-timer performances ever seen in Finland to finish 13th in this specialised event. While Mikkola was in the top five, fastest on 29 of 46 special stages, Mouton was thoroughly enjoying herself in the unfamiliar world of ultimate commitment over forest roads.

Mouton settled into the rhythm of Finland's stages after the halfway halt, moving from 16th overall to a final 13th, despite perpetual problems with the fuel-injection, a broken halfshaft and a landing heavy enough to bend the steering linkage out of true! On the very last stage she was just a second behind Blomqvist (then in a Talbot) tieing for seventh quickest, and grinning broadly at the challenge of something completely different.

For Hannu Mikkola there were over three times as many fastest times as his nearest rival could muster on the 1981 Sanremo, but no victory . . .

Driving Back to Happiness . . .

Just two World Championship roads remained in Audi's 1981 schedule, for the African Ivory Coast qualifier had also been ruled out from the start. Unlike much of the preceding season, Sanremo in Italy — a mixture of tarmac and dirt going — and the predominantly forest track RAC, would bring Audi a realisation of the potential that had first been apparent on February's Swedish.

Audi brought three Quattros to bear on the problem of breaking the Sanremo opposition. Mikkola had a new chassis, the 20th constructed by Audi Sport, while Mouton was back in Audi colours after using BP decor for the Summer season and Audi had made a bold choice of a native Italian driver for the third works car, 23-year-old Michael Cinotto. All three cars showed cooling modifications, partly based on extensive testing in the Sahara using sections that are routine for R&D trials of future road cars. Most obvious was the large

quattro

rear oil cooler and associated high wing. In the boot was a new Swiss-manufactured oil tank of 18 litres/3.96 gallons instead of the previous 10-12 litre/2.2-2.63 gallon design.

Fuel delivery problems once again attacked the Audis on the event and Hannu Mikkola was in trouble from the first stage, falling right to the tail of the meagre field, 56th of 66 starters. There seems little doubt that this cost Mikkola the rally, for after a lot of engine ancillary replacements had been completed a final desperate injector change brought the Quattro to permanent vigour. Of 61 stages Mikkola was then fastest on 30, some 22 more than the winner could manage!

Picturesque Pisa provides a rest halt for the victorious works Quattro on the Sanremo World Championship round. A fitting historical background for a car and driver that were also making history . . .

"Winneress" actually, for Michele Mouton overcame spells of brake trouble, three and two-wheel-drive (not an inherent fault, by and large, for an errant brake caliper left her with a broken driveshaft on one occasion) and Ari Vatanen to win by 65 seconds from Toivonen's Talbot. Vatanen clumped a rock face in a pre-arranged "do or die" attempt to slash the 35 second gap to Michele during the final night. History had been made and Mouton had so much confidence from this point onward that anyone dismissing her achievements on the basis of "the best car" was on inferior 2-WD ground. For the lady's times were never far off that of the men in similar equipment — and more frequently became faster, leading to more wins in 1982/83 that proved this was no freak result. *Magnifique!*

Cinotto? Sensational to look at with a natural sideways style that produced some fabulous times, the Italian crew of Cinotto/Emilio Radaelli returned with the second leg lead to Pisa; holding it for 15 stages. Then Cinotto eventually lunged off into the hard bits, possibly prompted by the recovery of Mouton, who swept up the field and past the youngster a couple of stages before that accident!

here are plenty of other pictures – some of which you have just seen – of Michele Mouton on her way to the first ever World Championship rally victory by a lady, but this AT-produced classic by Maurice Selden just sums up that 1981 Sanremo, with its "on-top-of-the-clouds" winning feeling. Some of the bar stool loungers even forgot that they'd reckoned Audi picked Michele as "just a gimmick old boy . . ."

With Ivory Coast outside their schedule Audi's 1981 World Championship finale came on the November 22 to 25 Lombard RAC Rally, 65 stages (40 of them in dark dampness of varying ferocity) that had to be driven largely on instinct and any previous knowledge, for reconnaissance notes were, and remain, specifically forbidden. For the top Finns that presents few problems: Vatanen, Mikkola and Airikkala are all familiar drivers and winners of the British home internationals. Although it is only fair to point out that expatriate Finn Markku Alen has not been a regular, but still performs magnificently over UK soil.

For Audi the question of familiarity with the terrain was as important as in Finland, because Michele Mouton was once more tackling something outside her experience. As before, but bucked up by her October Championship win in Italy, the dusky Mademoiselle swiftly displayed her mettle to such an extent that Audi's after-testing notes recommended that she be given the larger casing KKK turbo, as used by Mikkola, for the event, instead of the smaller unit. This is deeply significant because it implies commitment on behalf of the driver: a commitment to keep the big turbo blowing and therefore working the engine high up the rpm scale, while a smaller unit could be specified for situations where instant low down power was required, basically because an error had been made on entry speed.

Gumpert & Co inside Audi had been refining the injection system to provide instant plug-in accessibility of all major components, back-up high pressure pumps and constant separation of air at every stage in the injection plumbing. By-and-large their efforts improved things considerably, but Audi's could still be made mundanely uncompetitive beyond 1982 by malfunctions in this department: the difference was an answer that could be swiftly found! Filters and pumps were simply mounted on panels which required only the removal of a nut and fuel snap connector.

quattro

As part of the "to finish first, you first have to finish" philosophy the suspension had been considerably toughened, particularly in the fabricated lower arms that link wheel hubs to body front and rear, so that the drivers could brush rocks without instant retirement or the kind of breakage that Mouton suffered on Acropolis to the rear suspension.

Tyre testing with Kleber up against their rivals prior to the 1981 RAC Rally at Nant yr Hwch. The factory stuck to Kleber primarily until the close of the 1982 season although Blomqvist provided a notable Michelin test bed when he began to appear regularly in 1982. From 1983 onward Michelin was the Ingolstadt contract, but David Sutton Cars in Britain ran the cars under their care (including Blomqvist's 1983 RAC Rally winner) on Pirelli.

As ever the combination of Mikkola and the slightly de-rated Quattro (320bhp officially with an 8000rpm limit and maximum torque "around 3500rpm") provided the story. From the Chester start the first day meandered through the well-attended public park and stately home initial menu, Mikkola an effortless 40 seconds up on Tony Pond's Vauxhall Chevette HSR after less than 17 miles competitive motoring!

Leaving the public gaze for the forests of the Lake District and the doggedly determined super enthusiasts who watched quartz halogen briefly turn the rainy, often foggy, night into brief spasms of electric daylight, Mikkola foundered on the seventh, Grizedale, stage.

Waiting in the next service area we saw the screen-less Quattro pound into view with the lightest of roof dents and slightly frayed bodywork the only evidence of their flight from a 90° left to inversion. As ever Mikkola was brutally honest and reported, "I was just going too fast. We could see nothing at all really, and there was not time to do anything. I think I am lucky with the 4-WD. As soon as we can get spectators to put the car the right way up, then we can drive back up the bank. I do not think we could have done this in an ordinary car — and it really did not lose us too much time."

Pond led for three stages. When they went into the bleak windy wetness of Kielder forest, the biggest artificial forest in Europe, Mikkola swept back to the head of the field. Using perhaps 1.6 bar as the maximum turbo boost the Quattros lapped up the wind, rain and mud — plus any trace of opposition. By the eleventh stage Mikkola led, and he stayed totally in command until the

This was the condition in which Michele Mouton's Quattro began the 1981 RAC Rally. She held third for most of the event and then slipped off permanently on the snow during the last leg run for home from North Wales. Note Carello auxiliary lamps, wide wheels for tarmac and the post-Sanremo large rear wing.

finish, where he was 11 *minutes* 5 seconds ahead of new World Champion driver Vatanen, despite constantly keeping himself in check to ensure that no more excursions spoiled an entirely convincing demonstration of mastery from car and crew.

Mademoiselle and Signorina had their moments too. They arrived with flu and snuffled their way through Audi's pre-event press functions with surprising grace and pale faces. They got into the swing fairly easily, 13th after the Sunday public stages and then sploshing through all the forest mud to reach third overall in Carlisle. Kielder detuned them a bit, an horrific diet of no prior knowledge and squalling rain about as alien to this Mediterranean duo as the Sahara is to a Mancunian!

It did not take long for Mouton to re-establish herself back in the leading trio, but she inherited Audi's mechanical maladies for this event. On the 41st stage the gearbox went for two speed operation, first and fourth. Changing the unit was an hour-long job and had to be delayed until something like that service time could be found and some of the 27 Audi service vehicles effectively deployed at a small Welsh dealership near Llanbyther. The BP-backed Quattro bombed back to action along lanes that were temporarily dry, making a magnificent sight as the turbo over-run flames illuminated Welsh hedgerows for the entertainment of those who had watched those grim minutes of concentration as the Audi mechanics under Gumpert's supervision heaved aside technical niceties on the partially prepared Quattro to convincingly break the hour mark for the box swop: for a conventional front engine rear drive rally car the times for such a change can be under 10 minutes! By 1984 gearbox changes in 18 minutes had been recorded by Audi Sport workers in the field.

Back on the Welsh trail Mouton was briefly fifth, then fourth as Jimmy McRae's Opel suddenly lost drive after a halfshaft failure: now if Jimmy had been in a Quattro that elusive top RAC placing could have been realised, which is the way to look at the Quattro's technical specification. Permanent 4-WD gives much more than complexity takes away, and both the company and its drivers had proved its plus points most convincingly over the RAC stages.

quattro

Pretty! Mikkola and Hertz pound toward their first Quattro win on the RAC Rally. Mikkola led all but four stages, and won by 11m 5s.

"Thing about Quattros is that they're terribly boring to watch . . ." Hannu Mikkola demonstrates why rally drivers need as many driven wheels as they can get. All this despite the fact that he had already been over on the roof once (note masking tape around screen) on the 1981 RAC Rally, an event he ruled and which began a train of Quattro victories that showed signs of repeating the Ford Escort domination of the seventies, in which H. Mikkola also played a part . . .

However, there was no fairy-tale ending for Mouton. Into the Northern Welsh daylight and the event's only noticeable frosty snows, Michele plunged off the straight and narrow. The Quattro lay stricken on its side like a beached whale that could not be budged. After 57 of 65 special stages, six fastest times (27 times in the top six) Mouton and Pons were out, sadly missed. Not only were they supremely competitive in a way Britons had not seen since Pat Moss, but they also had a lovely sense of humour. Ask how the 'flu was and a small white Snoopy doll with a red tongue would be drawn from the door pocket or the dash (the latter if it was a road section) and its red tongue displayed alongside that of the crew.

Admiring Mouton's speed through the long straights of Dalby I was a little bit taken aback when she said she was scared. "How could anyone who set those times have time to be scared?" I foolishly asked. She made to pull me into the passenger seat. "You sit there at 180km/h (111mph) and see how close those trees are with the car, ah, she is everywhere! You try it . . ." Like most of the Brits, I was enchanted, and that is rare for the bunch of cynical survivors who report the RAC by pounding soggily and sometimes wearily around the 1700 to 2000 mile route.

Thus the RAC provided Audi with almost the exact high note on which to finish their first season of rallying. Michele would go into the history books along with the car and Mikkola just seemed to get faster and faster as the technicians solved the problems and sought even higher performance from the Quattro permanent 4-WD concept. That first season had yielded fifth in the Makes series (won by Talbot, Coventry) and third (Mikkola) plus eighth (Mouton) in the Driver's Championship.

Tackling more events with a better-developed Quattro for 1982, how could they fail to dominate? Read on!

Chapter 6

1982: The Lady is a winner [3]

For Mikkola a Championship season to forget, but Audi keep on learning and Michele Mouton demolishes the males on three Championship rounds. Ingolstadt finish the tough season as Champion Manufacturers with a lot more Quattro speed to come . . .

Although Audi had refined the Quattro recipe for 1982's season most conscientiously, they had neglected to ask the gentleman Hannu Mikkola refers to as, "the Big Man up there", to provide Quattro-favourable weather in Monte Carlo. In conditions guaranteed to delight the local tourist board and promote envy in any northern European heart during January, Monte Carlo was at its sunny picture postcard best. Barely a slippery slope in sight. So the usual pairings of Mikkola/Hertz and Mouton/Pons — augmented by Cinotto and Radaelli in a third Ingolstadt warrior, sponsored by the R6 cigarette company — could expect none of the technical traction advantage that is a Quattro driver's right over ice and snow.

The Quattro appeared in Monte as a thoroughly developed loose surface machine, but the team were painfully aware that even Klebers softest slicks and the lowest practical ride height on the widest rims that could legally be installed under the glassfibre wheelarch "eyebrows" were far from a complete answer. Mikkola's machine still weighed fractionally over 1200kg and the size, emphasising how handy a short wheelbase would be over mountain twists, tended to emphasise the Quattro's negative qualities. While the SWB Quattro had been under development since the previous season, Ferdinand Piech really hoped that it would never be necessary — and with the notable exception of the Tour de

1982: the season Quattro arrived as a Champion's choice. Here's Harald Demuth's Schmidt Motorsport-serviced Quattro, winner of the German Championship. Note the "extensions-upon-extensions" wheel-arches so clearly shown in this superb Kraling picture, a photographer who provides many of Audi's outstanding publicity pictures.

Front drive technique? Stig Blomqvist became a Quattro force to reckon with in 1982. Note front Kevlar sumpguard on the victorious Sanremo works Quattro.

Corse, which *demanded* such a Quattro for any chance of success — Audi were able to carry on competitively with the original Quattro coupe until 1984.

Back at the Monte in 1982, Mikkola's machine sported a more vigorous camshaft that extended the rpm range by 400 compared to the previous season's RAC specification. Hannu reported to *Autosport* readers, "it is much, much, better. The torque is there and it is good from 3700 and it goes right up to 7800rpm, which is the most I used on the Monte."

quattro

It must have been tempting to use more, for Mikkola "had just started the third stage, and it was no more than 100 metres before quite a hard right-hand corner, and when I went to the corner there was no grip at the rear at all". The result was a rapid spin and equally instant deflation of the tyre on a damaged rear Ronal. Mikkola lost a lot of time, compounded by an unsurprising subsequent rear driveshaft failure. On the 1982 Monte, Audi could not afford any time losses.

For, following Sod's Law, Mouton had discovered some ice — and it was just where the team dreaded it, on a section that it had not been possible for her ice note team (composed mostly of friends: Mikkola used professionals Lampinen, Saaristo and Britain's John Taylor) to enter. Mademoiselle from Grasse had covered but 10 stages before she hit home terrain, hard! The Quattro whipped straight off into a stone wall with force enough to knock Fabrizia Pons out and eliminate the fourth-place female crew immediately. Only two stages before Cinotto had also charged the scenery and headed for "an early bath" following a front wheel puncture, so Audi Sport had just one, delayed, charger to support . . .

Backed by R6 cigarettes, the wealthy young Italian Michael Cinotto put in some very promising Quattro performances that too often ended in retirement. Here, on Monte Carlo, Cinotto and Radaelli retired after just six stages when a front wheel puncture produced a trip into the unyielding scenery. Opel won the event, with Mikkola's Quattro second, and Mouton, a retirement (again) on the Championship event closest to her birthplace.

Mikkola certainly dug deep into a store of Monte knowledge that goes back to 1967. He manhandled the cumbersome coupe into ten fastest stage times, only three less than the man who dominated that 1982 event, factory Opel Ascona 400 driver, Walter Rohrl. Hannu also managed eight second-quickest selectives to nine from Walter and was third fastest on three occasions compared to "Big Wally's" tally of five third-fastest times. From eighth place after the initial tyre and driveshaft dramas, Mikkola wrestled his way into third and was then promoted to second when Opel factory driver Jochi Kleint left the twists of the Turini and let the Quattro snuffle along the wheeltracks of the amazing Ascona. Except for a wrong tyre choice that saw Mikkola gaining on Rohrl, the Opel continued to set the tarmac speed standard. On the traditional 100-strong last leg Rohrl was 31 seconds faster than Mikkola during the first two stages and 25 miles of competition. Mikkola then settled for second place and valued championship points, the Quattro finishing 3m 43s behind the Opel and nearly 10 minutes ahead of those legendary Monte mounts, the Porsche 911s, which were very competently driven private examples on this Monte Carlo Rally — by Jean Luc Therier and Guy Frequelin. Also privately entered on a Monte that was notable for the size — nearly 300 — rather than the quality of its entry, were the fifth and sixth-placed Renault 5 Turbos of Saby and Snobeck, which pursued the Porsches home and reminded us that Renault had won the event only a year previously.

Of all the events in the World Championship calendar Sweden's snow and ice obviously offers Audi every encouragement to hope for leading results, but if one looks at the record it's actually Britain's RAC that has also been unfailingly kind to the Quattro with three wins in three years recorded when this was written.

Sweden 1982 proved the case. Although a Quattro did win, establishing a precedent that has also been maintained, it was the *wrong* Quattro from the viewpoint of a World Championship chance for Mikkola and Audi! What happened?

Quattros began to arrive as a rallycross force in 1982 as well. Here is Austria's Franz Wurz at play in his factory-supported machine: later in the season he would earn a ride in Argentina with a works 80 Quattro.

Audi Sport entered two factory cars for their regular drivers, using Swedish Timi tyres just for this event and 22mm (0.87in) studs. A third ex-factory car joined the line-up of Quattros, the refettled 1981 RAC machine, for Stig Blomqvist in Sanyo-sponsored Swedish blue and yellow. It would be former Saab front drive factory driver Blomqvist's first appearance on the World Championship scene with a Quattro (although the Swedish continued to count only toward the driver's title), but he had already begun to contest the Swedish national series with this borrowed Audi. Indeed, he'd even had time to find out how easy it was to crash the car on an earlier Swedish event!

Held deep in the coniferous forests of Sweden's Varmland, the event had less ice on the ground than usual, but there was still plenty of snow piled up on each side of the stages, ready for Swedish regulars to assess its braking potential after the traditional bank-bouncing technique had been deployed. However, for the Finn who became the first non-Swede to win this three day specialist classic in 1981, banks became a sore subject in 1982 . . .

From Mikkola's point of view the event started predictably enough with a fastest time over the short opening stage. For Blomqvist, tipped to win by many who knew his prowess with front-drive's left-foot braking technique — a driving style that makes a lot of sense over slippery surfaces in a Quattro because it turns its natural heavy understeer to oversteer at the jab of the centre pedal — the initial stage held drama of the pop, pop, bang, grunt and silence variety.

quattro

Stig Blomqvist scored his sixth Swedish rally victory and showed he could turn faster stage times than Mikkola after an electrically-troubled start to the 1982 Swedish. Mikkola went off into a snow bank whilst leading and was tapped further into touch by Mouton's sister Quattro! Michele finally finished fifth, to begin her 1982 World Championship points collection whilst Mikkola's eventual 16th reflected a season that would be full of misfortunes.

The Quattro's five-cylinders had been quietened by "a failure inside the car's black box and the fuel-injection stopped", according to Reinhard Rode. Blomqvist's persistent probing into the under-bonnet vitals yielded the answer to the problem with reasonable rapidity, switching in the spare engine management box, but he was now 113th, or second from last, and had lost 2m 47s to Mikkola.

Blomqvist is not the chatty kind of driver who delights the media with instant quotes (although he will usually answer an engineering or tactics question with concise illumination that reminds you his world class rally career covers two decades), but ask Stig to perform the rally equivalent of a three minute mile – preferably in the dark, over sheet ice, and he'll just get on with "Mission Impossible". That 1982 Swedish proved the point, for on the second stage Blomqvist was 13 seconds faster than Mikkola in 8.8 miles. The third stage provided 14.2 miles for Blomqvist to prove his mastery over home terrain and 4-WD by returning a time a sensational 53 seconds swifter than Mikkola. By the finish of the event Blomqvist had set the fastest stage times on 16 of 25 sections: after just three stages, he was back in the top twenty!

Meanwhile Mouton and Pons were having an active event too, for the second stage saw the turbocharger plumbing spring a leak, depriving the ladies of any boost for their five. On the very next stage there was a puncture, so at this point it looked as though Audi's fortunes rested entirely on a Mikkola win. Particularly as Stig's eagerness to whittle every second out of every snow bank had cost the Swede a one minute jump start penalty, dropping him from 13th to 14th and meaning that he was 1m 43s in arrears of Hannu when they reached Karlstad. However with two days hard rallying to go Blomqvist was fourth already and obviously set for further improvement.

Just six stages totalling 62 miles were left between Mikkola and victory when they restarted for the final leg, early on Sunday afternoon. Mikkola began confidently with his narrow-wheeled Quattro teetering to fastest time on the first stage, but four tests from home disaster struck, and struck once more to be sure! Over 29 miles long and by far the longest individual stage on the event, Haljibyn seduced Mikkola into an uncharacteristic error. The leading Audi Sport entry with its unbelieving crew as helpless passengers understeered straight on into a snow bank. Just to make sure it could not be extracted Mme Mouton tapped it back into place as the hapless Mikkola and Hertz fought to free it from that freezing grip!

As ever Mikkola admitted it was his fault, although there were consistent reports that he had been unhappy with the amount of understeer shown by the Quattro under stress. Hannu obviously felt that he had not been fully concentrating, sharing with Vatanen the conviction that it is usually safest to travel the normal Finnish flat-out gait as, "you are less likely to make mistakes this way. Always the concentration is 100%".

Mouton also had to dig herself out of a nearby snow bank while Blomqvist went on to certain victory, over 2.5 minutes ahead of the two-wheel-drive opposition. When you consider that rivals included Ari Vatanen's Escort, Walter Rohrl's Ascona 400 and Per Eklund's privately-entered Saab 99 Turbo, and how much time Blomqvist had lost earlier in the event (3m 47s in time penalties and electrical repairs alone), the 4-WD's effectiveness is heavily underlined.

Mouton and Pons dug themselves to fifth spot, but Mikkola was outside the points after nearly half an hour in that bank, finishing 25th of 68 survivors. Now Hannu had some hard motoring to complete in forthcoming Championship rounds if he was to gain that coveted driver's title — which had always just eluded him in the years since its formal inception in 1979. At this stage of the season it looked as though Walter Rohrl might be set to become the first driver to take two Championship titles, leading Blomqvist, while Mikkola and Vatanen tied for third.

Quattro rampant in Portugal. Michele Mouton scatters stones in this fine study of the Quattro driver's understeer-killing technique. Fabrizia Pons peeks over the scuttle, from a vantage point well aft of Michele!

quattro

Mouton Emerges

Portugal provided the third round of the Drivers' series and the second in that for Manufacturers, a 1428 mile route over four days providing 397 first class rallying stages. Of this mileage the majority was loose surface, but the Competitors started with an all-tarmac 41 miles that saw Opel's Henri Toivonen on top.

Audi presented three Quattros — none of them with the alloy block homologated in December 1981, which was still undergoing final development — to be driven by Mikkola/Hertz, Mouton/Pons and that Quattro loyalist from Austria, Franz Wittman: it was his first factory Championship appearance since the 1000 Lakes tragedy.

After scratching out a small advantage over the opening seven stages, poor Toivonen suffered a puncture and Mikkola was through to lead. With the prospects of long dirt stages ahead it would have been a foolhardy punter who took odds on anything but a convincing Quattro victory for Hannu . . . but the fool could have been half right! Mikkola crashed in fog (shades of 1981 RAC), misinterpreting the severity of a fast left-hander so that the crew got lost on their pace notes. The effect was immediate and dramatic. "I didn't really have a chance, as I was driving maybe 50kph too fast and just getting ready to brake. You couldn't see more than 10 metres and suddenly this bend was *there*", recalled Mikkola.

Michele Mouton's first win of the 1982 Championship season came in Portugal. That country had never been very kind to Mikkola prior to 1983 — remember him joining Vatanen in a double Escort roll for the Sutton/Rothmans equipe. So it was in 1982, when Hannu went off whilst leading a Championship event for the second successive performance

The leading Quattro was eliminated after 11 stages, but for Audi Sport there was compensation from the emergence of Mouton as the new leader. It was no carefully-paced inheritance either. The vivacious Frenchwoman in the striped black BP overalls would finish the event having scored in the top four stage times on *all* 40 stages, 18 fastest times amongst them. She had shown that stamina and spectator-dodging ability, two vital attributes in a driver on the Portuguese, could be allied to a brand of female speed that owed equal success to Audi technology and her own muscle-straining ability to compete.

Mouton's 13 *minute* lead over Eklund's second-place Toyota, was

accompanied by a fine third overall for Wittman and Peter Diekmann in the oldest Quattro chassis present. Aside from Mikkola's accident it had been an invigorating Ingolstadt result, Audi sweeping to the top of the manufacturers' points and Mouton four points behind Rohrl (sidelined after an accident in Portugal) in the Drivers' contest.

The next rallies in the World Championship calendar were bound to leave Audi at something of a disadvantage. Although the team budget is a multi-million one — according to non-factory sources, there always have been considerable financial restraints on the events attended by Audi. The Easter Safari, based in Nairobi, was out of bounds for Audi in 1981 and 82. It was only with reluctance that Audi contested the 1982 South American World Championship round (Brazil), having omitted that long and expensive foray in their debut year, while only the 1982 fight for the Championship and an extra budget dosage, courtesy of Marlboro, took them to the Ivory Coast later in the season.

So Safari was out, but Rob Collinge/Mike Fraser showed what 4-WD could do in Africa by holding a top five place on Safari in their private Range Rover. It didn't make it to the end, but there were three Subaru 4-WDs in the lower half of the final top ten that year!

Portugal was no gentle cruise to an inherited lead and a 13 minute winning margin. *Mme* Mouton set more fastest times than her world class male opposition could manage with the kind of gritty driving shown here, on one of Portugal's most photographed corners.

Pre-Event Destruction

Audi were in Corsica with what was becoming the normal three car line-up: Mouton, Mikkola and Wittman driving. Evil luck struck even before the event, for Mikkola's car was severely damaged by a team mechanic and was one of two lightweight Quattros chosen to debut the aluminium block five. They hurriedly gutted Mouton's practice Quattro and rebuilt it with all the goodies they could salvage from Mikkola's mangled machine, but it was to prove a fruitless effort as the gearbox would provide only neutrals after less than a mile of the first stage! The aluminium cylinder block contributed 22kg/48.4lb of the average 100kg/220lb weight saving reported by Ferdinand Piech in an interview he granted me in November 1982. The block was initially tried in 200 customer

quattro

Audi 100s without telling their German-based owners. Reliability was good and many more 100s were so-equipped, along with the 1984 Quattro Sport. However engine builders outside Audi, and inside, discovered cracks in the block after some World Championship events — notably Blomqvist's 1983 RAC-winning engine.

Wittman's historic Quattro, the one used by Mouton to win Sanremo 1981, was eliminated after 10 stages with engine failure attributed to the head gasket; the Austrian had not set a top six time on this specialist Corsican challenge of a thousand twists and turns. Even Mouton, rugged survivor after innumerable scrapes including a one-sided wrestling match with Corsican countryside that resulted in a leaking back axle, broken seat mountings and demanded new steering components. An interior fog, due to the lack of heating arrangements on the lightweight tarmac specification machine, was the cause. After all these woes even Mouton could manage no better than seventh with just three top six times. I say "even Mouton", not only because of her Quattro role as the leading 1982 Championship challenger, but also because her Fiat France record included better overall results than could be achieved in the Quattro — and Corsican rallying is just the sort of terrain over which Mouton originally made her name.

Winning habit! Although her car suffered mechanical maladies in the earlier stages, Michele Mouton went on to crush the Acropolis Championship opposition by just as wide a margin as in Portugal with this kind of driving. In fact it was Opel driver Toivonen who was left with defending male and 2-WD honours, and even the flying Henri could manage less than half the number of fastest times posted by the lady . . .

May and Corsica had not been kind to Audi or Mouton, but the May 31 to June 4 Acropolis Rally (round five in the Manufacturers' series and sixth for the Drivers') held the chance of doing something to close the gap between Audi and Opel and Rohrl and Mouton. A quartet of Quattros contested the event against factory opposition from Lancia's supercharged mid-engined 037 (then still struggling to overcome the mechanical fragility that had dogged its pioneering

Leader on 48 of 55 stages, Mouton's Grecian Acropolis win put her into second place in the driver's series to begin a year-long duel with Walter Rohrl. Audi also went into second position behind Opel for the manufacturer's title.

quattro

wheeltracks) and the Rothmans Opels of Rohrl — Mouton's arch-rival for the Drivers' title, even at this stage — Toivonen and Scotland's Jimmy McRae.

Audi's drivers for the 584 frequently rough and usually loose surface stage miles in the 2,174 mile route were Mouton, Mikkola, Cinotto and Wittman. All but Cinotto's coupe had the alloy block engine and enlarged intercoolers. It was noticeable that Audi Sport were now bringing in 1981 World Champion Escort preparation team, David Sutton Cars at Acton, to help out with servicing. This was a natural tie as Sutton had sold the Rothmans-backed Escorts at the close of 1981 and was engaged to contest the British championship on Audi's behalf with Mikkola managing the majority of the driving (see chapter 9).

Audi seemed to be in trouble almost straight away, Mikkola's opening fastest time followed by the destruction of the front right wheel's lower suspension link and the departure of the wheel, strut, et al! Mikkola struggled the nose-diving Quattro off the stage with Arne Hertz perched in the rear of the cockpit, behind Hannu, to balance the weight distribution! Cushy life, is that of a top international co-driver . . .

Mikkola's persistence was not repaid, falling out of time after repairs had been made. Wittman put in a useful performance with 23 top five times, including four of the quickest, but also damaged the front end. The afflicted steering parts were renewed but he was OTL after 33 of 57 stages, by which time Cinotto's brief but spectacular outing — three top three times in nine stages — was over: defunct electrics, demanding a diet of batteries in the stage parts that service crews couldn't reach.

Mouton Moves Ahead

Mouton? Following a bout of initial fettling for the turbocharger to cater for a lack, and then a surplus, of boost and some attention to the steering ("either the car is crazy, or I am crazy!"), the lady moved ahead of the Lancia and Opel squads. For all but seven stages she held the lead, 13m 37s ahead of Rohrl after five days competition. Now she had 20 points to make up on Rohrl and Audi had scored 58 to Opel's 74 — and there was the longest journey of all to take . . .

New Zealand, a country of such olde worlde English charms that Australians swear the air crew tell you "turn back your watches 25 years", was the late June setting for the sixth Championship of Makes qualifier, and the seventh round in the series for drivers at World Championship level.

Audi took two Quattros to NZ, Mouton's the 30th complete car constructed at Ingolstadt for competition, both equipped with alloy block engines and slightly more compact casings for their KKK-K27 turbochargers in the interests of better forest road throttle response. The Finns aptly describe the NZ stages as being rather like a super RAC with longer and smoother stages that everyone seems to enjoy mastering. The point is well illustrated by the provision of individual stages of 50 miles and more on the 1982 event. Mikkola country?

Certainly, but flying to the other side of the globe was not enough to set the fair-haired Finn's personal 1982 gremlins to rest! After setting four fastest times in the first six tests, pulling out a little lead over Mouton, Rohrl and 1979 World Champion Bjorn Waldegard's Toyota, Mikkola found his Quattro reduced to a misfiring 30mph cart. An electrical sensor was pronounced guilty in the injection's electronics, but Mikkola was down to seventh by the time they had the Quattro running properly.

Waldegard held a scant lead over Mouton with Rohrl looking after World Champion points business, and third place. Mouton's attack on the lead was delayed by the loss of a rear brake assembly, torn off on a rock, but it was the

15th stage of 38 that hurt really badly. Mouton sending the dispiriting message over the airwaves that she had stopped with "no oil pressure". In fact a pressurised line from the boot-mounted dry sump tank had detached itself and the mechanics were later able to connect everything up and drive away without engine damage. Michele had been conscientious in saving an engine, but her candidly admitted lack of mechanical knowledge had cost her dearly, as it would again in 1982.

The long haul to New Zealand resulted in retirements for both works Quattros, but both had also led the event. Here Mikkola parades before the impressive Kiwi crowd in the Quattro that lasted longest and set the majority of fastest stage times.

Mikkola charged mightily at Waldegard's lead, aided by some clever tyre choices to within 15 seconds of the Swede. Then, with nearly 190 miles of the 644 stage miles left to complete the Quattro faltered. Its electrics died completely, losing the Finnish-Swedish crew 10 minutes and any chance of victory. This was followed by retirement when a steering arm pulled apart to finish the Quattro tri-wheeler finally.

Rohrl put in another canny outing in NZ to place third behind the shock Toyota 1-2 finish order, giving himself 84 points to Mouton's 54. On the Championship of Makes side the tally was equally unfavourable with Opel amassing 88 to Audi's 58. Now the two German rival manufacturers and the French lady's contest against the lanky Bavarian Opel driver would have to travel to South America.

The Marlboro *Rallye do Brasil* replaced the cancelled Argentinian Codasur event as the seventh qualifying round in the Championship of Makes, besides its original status as the eighth counter in the hunt for points amongst Championship drivers. The Argentinian event was forced out of the series owing to the political aftermath of the Falklands conflict.

quattro

The entry was headed by the factory Quattros for Mouton (the car she used in NZ) and another ex-Mouton coupe, this time the Acropolis winner, which Mikkola used. Only Rohrl attended for Rothmans Opel and Datsun were represented by multiple Safari winner Shekar Mehta.

Once again Audi used an Anglo-German team of mechanics and management, Roland Gumpert overseeing the technicalities whilst David Sutton and British co-driver cum 1982 RAC Rally *routemeister* Phil Short concentrated on the event service and administration. Both Quattros had similarly mixed pre-event preparation, Mouton's coming directly from New Zealand after a local rebuild and Mikkola's via Ingolstadt. Both had beefier steering arms of fresh design to circumvent the previous failures and the possibilities of contact with the suspension under heavy load.

Really this Brazilian adventure should not have counted toward the World Championship, last minute sacking amongst the organising team and the high number of alcohol-burning vehicles in the miniscule 58 car entry leaving chaos and ineligibility as most observers' memories of five days rallying.

Battered but victorious Michele Mouton finally beat errant road cars and sturdy Brazilian scenery plus World Championship rival Walter Rohrl, to win Brazil's Marlboro-sponsored event. Mouton and Pons won by over 35 minutes and set 13 more fastest stage times than even Walter Rohrl could produce.

Mikkola's miserable season dragged on, his opening section battle with Rohrl abruptly curtailed when the Quattro slid over a bank, caught out by a change from dry adhesion to wet mud. Mikkola and Arne Hertz could draw no practical help from Mouton, who showed Good Samaritan spirit by stopping despite her desperate need of Championship points. It was two hours before they could have the car dragged out, albeit still in the official running. However the battle was between Rohrl and Mouton, the lady spurred on by mechanical misfortune — a spell on three-wheel-drive — and the knowledge that Herr Rohrl freely expressed the opinion that her driving was a far less significant factor than the Audi's technical specification. At the end of the first leg and 129 miles of special

stages Rohrl had 1m 53s over the lady, who was 33 *minutes* ahead of the Mehta Datsun. There had been endless wrangles about maximum lateness as the organisers fought to keep some cars in the event — five would be classified as finishers — but Mikkola/Hertz were excluded. They were rather relieved to be winging their way to 1000 Lakes practice, as they knew the 1982 challenge from Stig Blomqvist posed a serious threat.

Mouton battled on, meeting trucks on "closed" roads, as did so many competitors, and biffing a VW into touch on a road section. Yet at the close of the second leg, she was only 1m 12s behind Rohrl. The third leg should have had eight tests but three were cancelled (the organisers heading for an international allcomers record on stage cancellations owing to incipient chaos). Now Mouton was 23s behind the Rothmans Opel . . .

The final leg had nine stages scheduled, one was cancelled, so Mouton and Rohrl fought over 158 stage miles of mainly loose surface going — surfaces often changing abruptly with heart-stopping consequences for the drivers. Mouton stamped firmly on Rohrl's magnificent attempts to get on terms, the lady setting eight fastest times, including a 1m 51s quicker time on the 38.5 mile longest stage of Coletas. Here she was aided by Walter losing a plug lead temporarily and demanding it be re-located. The German's substantial "off" came toward the close of this marathon, which resulted in him finishing the stage with the front wheel of the Opel tucked underneath its normally pristine paintwork!

The subsequent repairs to Rohrl's Opel cost over 30 minutes in penalties, but he still finished second and retained his Championship lead with 99 points to Michele's 72. In the Makes fight Opel had 97 points to Audi on 68 with Datsun a distant third. With Rohrl definitely missing the specialist 1000 Lakes, Mouton and Audi had a chance to slash that deficit further during August.

Audi Wins — Mouton Loses

Utilising the talents of the only current Championship driver to have beaten the Finns on the 1000 Lakes, Stig Blomqvist, and ensuring that he ran on Michelin throughout, providing a demonstrable advantage over Audi's contracted Kleber covers (that should have been used throughout by Mouton and Mikkola), showed how serious Audi had become about the Manufacturers' title. They prepared two brand new cars, Mikkola's the 34th chassis out of Ingolstadt, and also had on hand the old chassis 16 as a filming car and Roland Gumpert's glorious red Group B prototype with the plastic wheelarch extensions and a generally business-like look that was to become familiar in 1983. There seems little doubt that Audi Sport resorted to Michelin rubber for Mouton and Mikkola despite the Kleber stickers adorning Audi's factory cars. Incidentally Blomqvist's car was reputed to be Mouton's Portuguese car, although it wore a different registration plate.

The opposition? Opel relied on the talented Henri Toivonen and a local Swede in the fight against Audi whilst Lancia debuted the lighter and more powerful evolution Group B derivative of their 037 mid-engine wonder. Ostensibly this was one of the most powerful cars on the event, with over 310bhp, but as Ferdinand Piech said to this writer in a late 1982 interview of Audi's "330bhp, between 7200 and 7700rpm. I must tell you these are strong Bavarian beer-carrying horses, not the smaller ones of Italy!"

On this occasion we had little chance to evaluate the challenge that Lancia would present, for the supercharged engine with water-cooled compressor overheated from the start.

Although the 1000 Lakes has the shortest route in the World Championship

quattro

calendar, it offers a lot of action. In 1982 it measured 892 miles with a creditable 463 stage miles also providing the best stage to road mileage ratio of the year. Most of the top Finns approach the event as a memory test, relegating the prepared pace notes to the role of reminders, rather than dictating the pace over every blind hazard. The going is typical Scandinavian forest with the famous brows putting a premium on placing the car accurately with maximum commitment before you can see the horrendous truth!

Neither Mouton nor Mikkola were free of small engine bothers in the early stages, Mikkola's machine misfiring when one of the fuel pumps struck and Mouton's unevenly boosted by the efforts of that well known trio who hide under the KKK trade name branding. Blomqvist might have opened up an advantage at this, but a puncture cost him the best part of a half minute, a simply enormous deficit by 1000 Lakes white-hot competition standards. At the end of the first section's 60 odd timed miles, Mikkola had 14 seconds over Toivonen's Opel, with Blomqvist another 14 seconds in arrears. Mouton, with all of six days' practice behind her (they reckoned Toivonen had practised just one test over 20 times!) was a cautious eighth.

Blomqvist now displayed what he could do in a Quattro, skipping through the lengthiest stage (15.7 miles) some 22 seconds swifter than Mikkola managed and taking a 4 second lead at the close of 18 stages. It was on that longest section that Mouton went missing, aviating her Quattro with such verve that she smashed a front differential and consequently over-steered her way into a ditch-bound roll with the aid of rear-drive only. It had been a tremendous effort in which she had run in the top five, but the dispassionate historian would say she might have tried to rectify the situation for the car was undamaged for practical purposes, after the roll, and there was the chance of crucial championship points . . .

At the front, battle royal between Blomqvist and Mikkola had resulted in them pulling over five minutes ahead of new third man Airikkala; Toivonen having lunched the front of the Opel. This enormous margin was maintained despite a further puncture for Blomqvist, who certainly looked to have the legs of Mikkola on the Finn's home event. At the end Blomqvist had set 21 fastest times to the 12 of Mikkola, but with no threat from rival marque opposition, the Quattros were adjusted to low boost and asked to maintain order, Mikkola narrowly in front of Blomqvist to the finish. That is exactly what happened, but as would become increasingly the case in 1983, the press all spoke unhappily of such deals to maintain status quo.

Thus Mikkola won his first 1982 Championship round by 28 seconds and

t last! Mikkola had to ait until August before coring a 1982 World hampionship win. Appropriately it was on the nnish 1000 Lakes, and ought his tally up to an nmatched six victories this event. Aside from e familiar jumping flight eded to score the uattro's first win on the innish GP'' we also ow Hannu and Arne lebrating; Mikkola has n Juhr learning how to pe with fame on dad's .

quattro

Audi scored a notable 1-2 against the finest opposition the World Championship circus could then provide. The Ingolstadt team left with no improvement in the Drivers' series for Michele, although Mikkola and Blomqvist were tied in fourth position, whilst in the Makes' series Audi had closed to within 11 points of Opel.

October's protracted points accumulator toward both World Championship titles was the subtle Sanremo event. "Subtle" because it contained such a balanced split between tarmac and loose going that the results were in doubt right to the last of 56 stages within its six days of roaming from Italian Riviera to picturesque Pisa.

Six-Strong Quattro Squad

Audi mounted a massive effort to keep their title hopes alive. Effectively three teams, the factory, David Sutton Motorsport and Germany's Schmidt Motorsport (who ran Harald Demuth's German Championship-winning 1982 Quattro) were present to run six Quattros: all with the aluminium block engines. Additional filters were added to the already complex Quattro petrol filtration facilities within the boot, and larger diameter and thicker brake discs were available for mountainous tarmac use. Tyres were a tortuous subject, the factory trio for Mouton, Mikkola and Blomqvist wearing Kleber stickers with Pirelli rubber beneath. The machines for Cinotto/Radaelli, Demuth/Fischer and Wittman/Diekmann tended toward Kleber for Wittman and Pirelli for the Italian and German-maintained Quattros. All three factory Quattros were drawn from those appearing on the 1000 Lakes; Blomqvist continuing with his factory mount rather than the Quattro, of 1981 vintage, he had to wrap up the Swedish series before the Summer was over.

Lancia's quartet of 037s got off to a desperate start with two factory-supported machines damaged on the first stage and a Ferrari fastest overall. Over such typically tight Mediterranean tarmac the Quattros could only bide their time looking for gravel road glories to come, but Wittman was out on the second test, smashing the Quattro's front against solid scenery with enough conviction to push the front wheel back toward the passenger compartment.

Mouton was in trouble on the third stage with an unnoticed rear wheel puncture — she had felt a transmission problem was the more likely cause of the Quattro's lurching progress. This left her 17th overall, and later meant Audi were unable to execute the planned handover of the event from Blomqvist to Mouton for maximum points in the Drivers' Championship.

Over 125 miles of gravel, in Tuscany, was the next task on the agenda before the overnight halt at Siena, by which time the Quattros had moved into commanding positions. Initially Blomqvist had to depose Alen's hurrying Lancia, for Mikkola was deep in the throes of a transmission saga that had been sparked off by a puncture on the opening stage of the second leg: Hannu fell to tenth after a driveshaft failure, gearbox change and differential replacement. All for a puncture!

At Siena after a total of 24 stages the order was Blomqvist, nearly two minutes ahead of Alen's Lancia, the promising Cinotto third, Demuth fourth, Mouton sixth and Mikkola eighth. Cinotto's place had been achieved with help from a bridge parapet that destroyed a wheel rather than let the errant Audi loose on the countryside beyond.

Looping South before running up to Pisa for another overnight halt away from base, the next 18 stages held the only heavy rain of the rally. Only Alen's Lancia seemed to stand in the path of Audi's squadron and that lapsed onto three-cylinders after 37 stages, leaving the Quattros in first to fifth place! However,

quattro

Stig Blomqvist (right) and Bjorn Cederberg won Sanremo at their first attempt, scoring the quattro's second successive win on the Italian championship round.

quattro

as ever at Audi, life was not that simple. Mikkola had survived a bonnet, unsecured on its front retaining pins, that flew open in mid-stage and Demuth had soon lost that fifth place, hacking down telephone lines after attacking a wall on the conclusion of that loose surface leg, but the German Champion continued. Now Toivonen was fifth, Demuth sixth.

Mikkola's long charge up-field — he was to set 18 fastest times and nine second quickest, exactly as for Blomqvist — had secured second place, 2m 37s behind Blomqvist after 49 stages. That was the position prior to a last night composed of seven special stages on twisting tarmac that suited Opel's Michelin shod saloon car "racers" rather than Audi's 4-WD coupes. To prove the point Opel's Toivonen and Rohrl drove their hearts out, their cars stripped of all but the bare necessities in an effort to snatch victory. Only Opel drivers set fastest times that night, but even then it was not enough to deprive Blomqvist of a fabulous first San Remo appearance and victory, secured by 2m 16s over Mikkola. Hannu had just 11 seconds over Rohrl while Mouton was only 35 seconds behind her World Championship adversary in fourth overall. *Quelle Domage*! Toivonen took fifth after a late charge error, Cinotto finished an excellent sixth, but poor Demuth was sidelined five stages from the finish with a sickly engine.

Having just two rounds of the Championship for Drivers left, and one to decide the Makers' series, the points position was: Rohrl 101 versus 82 for Mouton and Audi leading Opel for the first time in months by 104 to 102. Now the sexist struggle between *Mmes* Mouton/Pons and *Herren* Rohrl/Geistdorfer transferred to the swirling red dust of the African Ivory Coast, round 11 in the World Rally Championship for Drivers and a non-starter for Makers.

The Blomqvist/Cederberg Quattro on its way to defeating not only Lancia on home ground, but also World Championship rivals, Opel. Audi left Italy in the lead of the manufacturer's title chase, Mouton remained second overall in the driver's series and Blomqvist moved into third place.

Religious Noting

The pessimistic Rohrl certainly had no real desire to compete for Opel in Africa, a Lancia contract pocketed for 1983 made sure that only the thought of a second Championship was reason enough to attend. The Regensburg rallyist left it to co-driver Geistdorfer to do the recce, while Mouton and Pons slaved away at their notes with near-religious fervour. Neither Audi or *Mme* Mouton had rallied in Africa before, although a private Quattro had appeared in the previous year's event without success.

Three hours before the start of the late November African qualifyer, Michele Mouton was told her father had died. She started the event simply saying, ''my father showed me the way into rallysports. Knowing my position, he would say yes to the question of carrying on''. Driving the Quattro Mikkola used in NZ, Mouton had some very special service support. Jorg Bensinger was along with the regular mechanics and Gumpert was sharing Mouton's ex-NZ Quattro with Mikkola, the pair formally entered but there purely to support the girls — as were Blomqvist and Hertz in another ''spotter'' Quattro, renewing a partnership that had ruled the roost in their seventies Saab era.

An enormous route length of 3102 miles, and humid heat that boosted cockpit temperatures to apathy-inducing levels in the Quattros, provided a tough background to this classic confrontation. One that could always be unexpectedly resolved by one of the all-too frequent oncoming trucks.

Although Mouton was never really happy with her Quattro, and Mikkola

quattro

was stranded for over 4.5 hours with a differential failure — which also meant that Gumpert was not available to practise his dual engineer/flying administrator rule effectively — the position at the close of the second leg and more than 1550 miles of exhausting rallying was a good one for Audi. Michele had nearly an hour in hand over Rohrl!

African rallying is a very different affair though, as one can judge from reports of the Opel breaking a rear damper and getting stuck in a river, losing its fanbelt in the process. Even with over an hour's advantage Mouton was not safe, for it took 58 minutes to change a gearbox and she had already needed both a front differential and a radiator replacement. Also typical of the African rallying problem was the fact that three crews had to dispose of a fallen tree before they could continue, eventually solving the problem by becoming lumberjacks and sawing the obstacle apart.

With a final leg of 410 miles to complete from a 4am start Mouton was feeling the pressure. Rohrl's casual approach, and the Opel team's African Safari experience had resulted in Walter keeping an ever closer watching brief in a constantly fettled car whilst Mouton, deprived of the usual close contact with Mikkola and Gumpert, was unsure of the car mechanically. That led to extra demands and confusion for the mechanics. At the 4am restart things began badly when the fuel-injection played up, demanding 25 minutes work and costing her that grimly maintained lead.

Perhaps the most courageous drive of Michele Mouton's career came on Africa's Ivory Coast. Recently bereaved she fought Rohrl and the environment to lead and crash on several occasions; finally she was defeated and the Quattro retired. With that retirement went the lady's chances of taking the 1982 title . . .

Game as ever, the ladies hurtled back into the fray, which was being conducted largely in misty fog with the added charm of dust-laden atmosphere in case anything useful was left visible. A downhill T-junction claimed Rohrl, who was unable to restart his car until the chase Opel came on the scene. At the same junction, Mouton flipped the Quattro. The gallant girls enlisted enough help to get the coupe back on its wheels again. Yet, without the aid of their pace notes, and with the help of the fog and a pressing need to make up time, another accident soon intervened. The combined efforts of the multi-national

Audi service crew got the wounded Quattro moving again, but when the right front suspension collapsed every effort from Gumpert, Blomqvist, Mikkola and two German mechanics was not enough to set the battered car and crew to rights. Besides, Rohrl was long gone on his way to the victory that decided the male destiny of the 1982 World Championship of Drivers.

Airborne service administrator Phil Short recalled Fabrizia Pons signing off from the wrecked Quattro with emotional finality, "it is over. We are finished". Michele was denied the chance of becoming the first Woman World Champion in the history of motorsport, but for Audi there was still that Manufacturer's title to pursue in the last, British, qualifying round.

Fitting Finale

Michele Mouton thus came to Britain for her second RAC Rally as runner-up in the Championship; Rohrl being simply uncatchable on 109 points to the 82 of *Mademoiselle*. In a year in which she had scored three outright victories to the pair at each end of the season scored by her rival, such a result may have appeared poor reward. However, recall the jeers when Audi announced that Mouton would be the second works driver for the Quattro? The complaints that she only got the drive on grounds of appearance and the accident of birth of being female? How many of those pundits would have imagined that *La* Mouton would not only prove she could be on the pace, but also score a win, never mind *three* victories? Or that her record would leave Hannu Mikkola way behind in the Championship race? The Mouton we saw in 1981 was beginning to gain World Championship confidence, following that historic San Remo victory. The Mouton who bubbled back to Britain in 1982 was an intoxicating mixture of proven driver and southern French belle.

The plaudits were shared amongst Audi's ladies in Britain, for Fabrizia Pons received the acclaim of her fellow co-drivers in the form of the Golden Halda Award. This compact trophy was presented to Fabrizia by Gunnar Palm at an Audi dinner held in the 1982 HQ city of York, and completed the male establishment's recognition for both occupants of this Quattro's cockpit. In previous years the Halda award had been taken by men like Arne Hertz (the most successful co-driver on the basis of World Championship wins) and Dave Richards, 1981 co-driver to World Champion Ari Vatanen.

To preserve their fragile lead over Opel in the Championship of Makes, Audi once more appeared to dig out every known Quattro combination to defend their honour. Audi Sport fielded their usual pair, Mouton/Pons and Mikkola/Hertz; Hannu in a brand new car with Michelins and the associated special Fuchs wheels needed to complete the event on the French covers. This despite the retention of Kleber advertising upon the Quattro's flanks! Mouton did use Kleber for the event in the car she had used on San Remo.

The factory had two very useful tweaks, both cars sharing electrically-heated front screens to combat the misting interior that was a feature of hard-driven Quattros in English downpours. The second "tweak of the week" was confined to Mikkola and was unofficially fitted: an electric switch was taped to the gear-lever. This operated the clutch without the driver needing to press a pedal, thus cleaning up the foot-tapping routine that every top Quattro driver had to go through whilst exploiting the famed left-foot braking technique. Such a modification is really only beneficial on the loose where the application of brakes and power simultaneously is used to kill understeer and promote a manageable tail slide. For the RAC it proved particularly useful as the driver often needs to change line halfway through a corner, the event covering a route that competitors

quattro

cannot reconnoitre in advance. The British event is the only one in the World Championship to ban advance noting of the special tests, demanding that the driver reacts to each situation as it develops, rather than pace note it and drive (particularly over dry tarmac) more in the tidy, committed manner favoured by racing drivers. Incidentally the electro-hydraulic clutch worked via an additonal high pressure reservoir in the engine bay that pushed the clutch pedal to the floor with an almighty thump, whenever electrically commanded by the gearlever switch. It added weight (over 20lb) but was a general Quattro fitment the following season. The system, based on an accumulator, was particularly appreciated on loose going to tidy up necessary left foot braking and clutch operation moments.

Aside from the two factory Audis, David Sutton Motorsport were asked to provide service support for four cars with varying degrees of Ingolstadt backing. Closest to the works was the Pirelli-shod ex-San Remo winner for German Champion Harald Demuth, who had an RAC finish to his credit in the Audi 80, and was paired on this occasion with solicitor cum ex-Talbot team co-ordinator John Daniels. American Champion John Buffum took another English solicitor along — Neil Wilson — in the BF Goodrich Tyre Co's Quattro (which had been fighting a year-long duel with Rod Millen's Mazda in the USA, during which the Mazda developed 4-WD too!) while Lasse Lampi/Pentti Kuukkala had a Sutton re-shelled Quattro remnant that owed something to Mouton's Monte wreck. Finally Ford-contracted Malcolm Wilson, another of Britain's perennial international hopefuls, was paired up with *Motoring News* scribe and experienced co-driver Mike Greasley in "LYV 4X". This Quattro featured a Terry Hoyle iron block five (Mouton, Mikkola and Demuth had the alloy units) and had won the Welsh in Waldegard's hands, and two more British home international rounds when driven by Mikkola.

Mikkola mashed any opposition on the York-based RAC Rally to take his fourth win on the event and Quattro's second. Mouton was second and there were four Quattros in the top ten that year.

quattro

The RAC's 1800 mile route with some 450 stage miles, heavily biased toward unknown forestry roads to decide the five day competition, could have been designed for the Quattro. Especially one in the hands of an experienced 40-year-old Finn who had already matched the winning record of three victories, never mind a brace of second places in recent years. In 1982 Mikkola simply demonstrated what an awesome combination he and the Quattro are over British trails, where frequent uphill bends leave the 2-WD opposition paddling for loose surface grip. Then a Quattro simply whooshes upward at the same sort of startling velocity that it displays away from a loose surface standing start.

Mikkola led the first six stages over the well attended public park format with four out of five fastest times, but there was a surprise when they entered the smooth and rapid tracks that wind through the Forest of Dean. Markku Alen, like Mikkola a startling forest performer in Ford Escorts in the seventies, took his detuned 290bhp Lancia 037 by its Kevlar neck and charged it through to lead Mikkola from stages 7 to 16. Mikkola counter-attacked as they entered the mid-Wales forests, and was back on top after a run that included beating allcomers over the famous TV Rallysprint stage of Esgair Dafydd.

Thereafter it was a question of watching Mikkola control the event via Hertz in such a masterful manner that even such a sordid season as Mikkola's 1982 began to fade from memory. After 36 of 69 scheduled stages Hannu had just under 4 minutes over the brilliant Toivonen (leading the Opel effort: naughty Walter had been sent home after refusing a Rothmans promotional appearance!) while Alen was third. Demuth was next best Quattro, just ahead of *Mademoiselle*, whilst Buffum was also in the top ten.

British terrain suited Quattros to the tips of their four driven "toes" in 1982, for only one of the sextet retired — and that was with suspension damage after falling in a Kielder ditch in a burst of competitive politeness (Lasse Lampi).

One of the annual RAC highlights of the early eighties was American John Buffum's visits to the UK. Usually accompanied by the brave Neil Wilson they gave the Quattro stick and it never did die. Here they dive-bomb their way to twelfth on the 1982 RAC, in a car that eventually previewed a narrow Quattro, as well as a SWB version!

quattro

Demuth ran as high as second but lost six minutes in Cumbria when he parked on a rock.

Mikkola came back to York a 3m 37s winner over Mouton, whose performance through the unyielding rain-lashed wastes of Europe's largest forest, Kielder, justifiably helped her hold off a late tarmac charge from Toivonen's Opel. Alen was fourth, then the Lancia's best ever Championship placing, Demuth fifth and Malcolm Wilson made it four Quattros in the top ten at tenth.

John Buffum? His Quattro was battered on both sides to the point where it looked as though the factory might be investigating a narrow Quattro as well as a short wheelbase prototype! After a brave performance in which he set three fastest times to the 27 of Mikkola, 16 of Mouton, 7 of Demuth and 4 of Wilson, the cool American became the first US citizen to drive to the finish of an RAC, arriving 12th.

After 10 rounds of the World Championship of Makes, and 12 in the series for Drivers, Audi finished the year as Champions with 116 points to the 104 of Opel and 57 of Datsun. The factory Quattro drivers finished second and third to Rohrl, Michele with 97 points and Mikkola with 70. Fourth-placed Blomqvist had the Quattro to thank for most of his 58, but his RAC eighth place was achieved in the last outing of the 1981 Championship winner, the Talbot Sunbeam Lotus.

With permanent 4-WD the Quattro was a natural for European rallycross events. Here Franz Wurz in the Quattro and Norway's Martin Schanche (Zakspeed-powered Escort Mk2) dispute the old and new technology benefits. By 1983 Schanche had constructed a 4-WD Mk3 Escort at Gartrac to take on the Quattros for the 1984 season . . .

1982 Retrospect

Looking back at 1982 Audi had certainly made much of the progress they could realistically have hoped for with such a complex rally car needing highly skilled technical support over some of the world's most varied and inhospitable terrain. They had the Makes' title and had narrowly and honourably missed the title for Drivers with a female driver choice that had originally been derided far and wide.

Reliability rather than competitiveness remained a primary concern. There were more instances of driveshaft and gearbox/differential trouble than there should have been and the fuel-injection system, perhaps because of its intricate failsafe precautions and advanced electronic management of engine needs, had failed on at least six critical occasions to provide accurately proportioned fuel/air mixture when required. Hannu Mikkola was a particular victim during the season, but it's also quite possible that the African early morning failure on Mouton's machine caused her to subsequently hurry through fog at such a pace that the accidents were inevitable.

Loose surface Quattro competitiveness had become a legend, one reinforced by the RAC Rally at the close of 1982. Ferdinand Piech told us in November 1982 that he hoped "we don't need a new car. For sure, while we make minutes and half minutes on the special tests there is no reason to make something else". Yet this remark could really only be applied to events on which dirt road mileage was in the majority, for we saw in Corsica that the car, even driven by a Mediterranean specialist like Mouton, was simply not covering tarmac fast enough, a problem abetted by its size which sometimes demanded backing up around hairpin junctions! Some British transmission experts felt that the lack of a centre differential could have been *the* significant factor in the Quattro's cumbersome tarmac hairpin performance, rather than the size of the car. These sources reckon that the strong slow speed understeer could be cured, and an easier time for the transmission and tyres would result by using a centre differential.

For such tight corners − and to stop the type of situation we saw on the 1982 Sanremo where the Opels could bite great chunks of time away from Audi over the tarmac sections − Audi needed the shorter wheelbase Quattro, which had been under intermittent development since 1981.

Yet the small engine team, developing a four-valve-per-cylinder derivative of the five for the "short" Quattro, were far from ready. Group B for 1983 would give Audi the chance to make some significant weight and power improvements to the existing car.

Thus 1983 would see the original Quattro concept dive into a third season of titanic World Championship struggle − this time with Lancia as their most effective opponents − while the Engineering R&D team prepared the SWB Quattro for public show exposure later that season.

However, there was a little something to spread the Quattro concept to a much wider audience in 1982. We journalists had the terrible ordeal of jetting to St Moritz to find out more at first hand . . .

Another nice one from LAT. The atmosphere of World Championship rallying and the fanatical interest with which the series is followed are properly captured in this shot of Michele Mouton's Portuguese winner. During the year she and Fabrizia Pons secured three World Championship wins to finish second to Rohrl in the title hunt; taking her total winning tally to four outright Championship victories.

Chapter 7

Spreading the legend

Work to improve the Quattros offered to the public culminated in better suspension control in a cheaper, non-turbocharged extension of the four-wheel-drive theme: the 80 Quattro. Meanwhile sales of Quattro coupe spread as far as the USA in 1982 . . .

"We had only 10 to 20 Quattro coupes ready before Geneva 1980", recalled Jorg Bensinger in conversation three years later, "and we knew this must be only a low production car for us. There was just part of the floor space set aside for us at Baur in Stuttgart to make up the bodies for Quattro — where they must make up the transmission tunnels from the Audi 80 floorpan, among many other things". Yet, even before the first cars were delivered to the public, there was a fundamental change in Audi's managerial attitude to the new offspring in its sales role . . .

Following the spectacular show success at Geneva, where the cutaways made as much impact as the complete car as onlookers craned into every technical aspect, Audi's top management took the decision that quality control, particularly of paint standards, should not be just the same as their existing front drive range, but superior. Now this was quite a demand and much of the time between Quattro's Swiss show debut and the first deliveries to the public during the Autumn of 1980 was occupied with this task. Remember that the Quattro uses a mixture of materials in its external panel work and management wanted assurance that the finish of these panels would offer at least the same durability and quality as the simplest steel saloon. Judging by the finishes, metallic and otherwise, of the earlier cars we see today, Audi's production people came up

Sensational Spring **1980** debut for the Quattro coupe came at the Swiss Geneva motor show. Note that this pre-production car is on the Fuchs five-spoke forged alloy wheels, later much more familiar in rallying use for forest roads.

On its correct Ronal multi-spoke alloy wheels, the Quattro prepares to carry this Audi gent off to the Casino to make enough money to support the laughing ladies.

with the exterior answers, although the original check-pattern interiors are beginning to look frayed in the 40,000 mile plus examples we have seen.

Bensinger pointed out that "at maximum", they had 20 engineers and mechanics involved with the Quattro project. "We build only a small number of cars, and we must use production parts as much as possible. OK, if you want a completely new car, or a lot of production changes, then there must be more people and money than we had."

When production for the public began in Autumn 1980, at the smaller pilot build hall within the main factory gates, there was little more for the Audi press

quattro

Busy life: this pre-production Quattro appeared in many of the press release pictures as well as acting as a demonstrator for journalists at Geneva. Here Rex Greenslade researches for *Motor* whilst Clive Richardson took the picture for *MOTOR SPORT.* It is no exaggeration to say that many of the journalists were stunned by the car's super snow performance on road tyres.

department to trumpet about their already-fabled newcomer, although they did manage to wring a couple of lines about the possibilities of optionally installing Mocha-toned leather for the seat, door and headliner trim. Much more welcome would have been the ABS, *Anti-Blockier System*. The Robert Bosch of Stuttgart electronically-managed anti-lock brake layout that would have made the Quattro as effective in stopping on slippery surfaces as it undoubtedly is under acceleration. In September 1980 the large-scale production Audi 200 Turbo gained ABS as an option, a feature we were still waiting for in British Quattros three years later. In Germany ABS went into Quattro and 80Q production after the 1983 summer holiday.

At the rate of up to nine Quattros a day it did not take Audi's skilled pilot plant workers long to make the balance of the 400 cars needed for the sporting authorities to recognise the Quattro in Group 4. As of January 1, 1981, revolutionary cars from Ingolstadt could compete, and by this time Audi were beginning to get some feedback on the sometimes unduly coarse road manners of the original cars.

As ever it took some time to get their production answers to these problems on stream: much of 1981 was taken up with the 4-WD priority of spreading the message back from whence they had first proved its effectiveness: the Audi 80. Also those awkward British wanted Quattro too, but they could be kept quiet with an initial batch of highly specified LHD machines available in March 1981. There are more details in our chapter on the Quattro in Britain, but basically British cars came with power windows, electrically-heated front seats and central locking, plus a few other minor features that were not standard items in Germany. The British were not allowed the optional 7J × 15 alloy wheels and initially the price tag went up several thousand pounds in the trip across the channel!

IN-NJ 66 hard at work again, laying rubber down a Southern French hillside for an interesting press pack shot.

quattro

During 1981 one source of road and mechanical noise was tackled, the lever and cable operation of centre and rear differential locks being criticised for transmitting transmission and road surface noise to the interior.

So the system was exchanged for a two-stage single knob on the fascia (replacing twin levers, one each side of the handbrake, between the seats) that allowed only the centre differential solo, *or* centre differential plus rear, not just rear. The theory was, and is, that the centre diff be used for poor road conditions, such as snow and ice, when it provides better braking force distribution. You then also engage the rear differential for successful escapes from snow several inches deep, or for driving over icy passes. The net result is always the same, traction that goes from effective to phenomenal on a scale that no other high performance car can approach.

The switchgear change for the differentials took its time coming through, arriving in Britain by October 1982, by which time the factory had made some

Original Quattro coupe dashboard with cable-operated differential locks and simple instrumentation comprising a 240km/h speedometer, 6500rpm-limit tachometer, boost gauge, time and fuel contents.

very important announcements regarding improvements to the latest LHD Quattro coupes. Externally we got the new quadruple headlamp look and the benefit of a beam spread enhanced from 40° to 60° on dipped beam, plus more effective main beam illumination in respect of range via bulb and reflector improvements. However some futuristic internal changes did not come to Britain, and nor did the previously announced ABS braking option: however this system was not available in Germany by Spring 1983 either. "Just no engineering time", said the smiling Bensinger; Quattro's "father" feeling that sensible use of the differential locks, an intelligent driver and Winter tyres were sufficient for the present. That may be so in Europe, where you prepare for Winter with a change of tyres in the knowledge of predictable snowfall during certain months, but British weather is so fickle that it is easy to find rain turning into ice, and such changeable situations, plus our crowded roads, probably make our writers and drivers demand ABS more vociferously than any other Audi market.

In August 1982, the traditional factory shutdown month in Germany, Audi

King Juan Carlos of Spain became acquainted with the Quattro when his country hosted the World Cup.

Franz Beckenbaur, West German footballing legend, takes over the keys of his post-August 1982 Quattro.

released details of the 1983 Quattro coupe whilst the small on-site factory was being readied not only for that more sophisticated LHD machine, but also for Quattro 80, which would be made in much larger numbers by a workforce that eventually grew to about 1000 of the 20,000 production workers at Ingolstadt.

The Quattro had always been notably light on informative instrumentation, even compared with the Audi Coupe at less cost. Now the factory strutted into the High-Tech eighties with a digital instrument panel, audible warning voice to monitor failures and a trip computer. The German language voice, based on a 128,000 bits memory, is that of Patricia Lipp, then the traffic information announcer for Bavarian road information service. All this six months before Maestro was announced . . .

quattro

New face. Larger, elongated headlamps came into production after the 1982 factory holiday and made for much safer night use of the Quattro's capabilities

The basic electronic dashboard provides road speed, with an instant switchover to mph, even on LHD, in large clear digital fashion not unlike the Maestro. To the left is the tachometer, a bar graph arranged in a 0-7000rpm crescent while the top right of the display is occupied by plain horizontal graphics with divisions to indicate water temperature and boost pressure. The bottom right corner is occupied by a digital fuel gauge reading in litres. To comply with German law a mechanical mile and trip-meter is provided, these twin displays below the digital speedometer.

The engineering department were not totally convinced about these displays,

Also new for the 198 model year was the elec tronic dashboard displa with a voice synthesizer British Quattros stuc with analogue instrumen tation until 1984, eve though the 1982 LH! model had mph capabilit at the touch of a switc . . . Differential locks ar now operated by a singl two stage knob on th centre console.

or the 15-warning voice, but they fell in with the motto "Progress through Technology" – and could largely be switched off! To be specific the dashboard display could be reduced to just speed indication as well as the mechanical mileage recorder, but you could also add information if required. The trip computer could be asked to show its findings in the bottom left-hand corner, beneath the tachometer, flashing up one piece of information at a time on request via a rocker switch. The computations included time of day; elapsed journey time; average speed; remaining fuel range; average consumption of petrol and instant fuel consumption figures. A zero set button will restart journey time, average consumption and speed on demand.

The spoken warnings were divided into three primary types. A reminder to fill the windscreen washer bottle would be given only once when on the move, but repeated at each subsequent ignition on/off movement. In the case of low fuel the whole shooting match goes straight over the top: first the fuel display starts flashing, then with some 50 kilometres range – about 31 miles – in stock, the whole blasted instrument display starts flashing on and off. Then there's the voice too . . .!

The second category of voice warning comes when the driver forgets to do something. A good example is within just one minute of moving off, for if he has not depressed the brake pedal to check that the rear bulbs are active, then he gets a public warning: Orwell's 1984, but two years early!

The third warning category is also safety related, but much more persistent. Any safety item, such as too little brake fluid, will draw the traditional *Achtung*! followed by a command to attend to the offending item that does not go away until the fault is rectified. No wonder the engineers shuddered when describing this on-board bully . . . As on many other "speaking cars" the voice emerges only after a warning chime has warned you that your puritan passenger is about to speak, which it manages through a priority arrangement via the usual radio/cassette sound system. German thoroughness is right up to the legend in this case because the beast also chimes after each announcement. As one morose Audi engineering ace said sardonically: "When I am driving, I just want to drive. When I am at a party then it's time to listen to a woman!"

Also new for the 1983 Quattro coupe was a revised suspension system that would be incorporated from the start of 80 Quattro output, with some minor alterations to take account of Quattro coupe's extra engine weight. The lower front wishbones were redesigned into a proper two-piece component. This was also prompted by complaints of tyre vibration as well as handling considerations, for the two-part arms were stronger than the original structure. The roll bar at the front was run up above the lower suspension arms and led back down to wide base arms by links, rather than a direct mounting, also a noise reduction step.

At the rear there was no anti-roll bar, and the position and length of the subframe-to-wheel upright link had been modified. The link was now mounted behind the rear subframe, and angled to run slightly forward over a greater length. The effect was to reduce toe-in/out variations and to remove a little of the over-the-limit twitchiness that some bold Brits had complained of: in Germany the increased motorway stability in crosswinds was judged a little more important. Either way the Quattro driver approaching a sharp corner at high speed was less likely to lose control if he suddenly decelerated or turned-in in mid-corner, than had previously been the case. For the 80 the system worked even better, thanks to revised spring rates, and you could be sure of predictable oversteer if the controls were correctly manipulated, rather than the turbocharged coupe's uncertain balance between heavy understeer and grudging oversteer. The bigger Quattro has a lot more weight in the nose, thanks to turbocharging and associated

quattro

Extended wheelarches and body-colouring for bumpers, with deep front and rear under-bumper panels, have become high performance hallmarks.

Pininfarina presented this Quattro styling exercise at Geneva in 1981 under the name Quartz.

intercooler plumbing, and needs a very cautious and firm rein when you first encounter snow or ice-coated corners: you can gain speed with astonishing efficiency, but the skill lies in getting rid of that speed and settling the car in said slippery curve. More about that later, for now it is time to look and see how some two years' production experience and the 4080 Quattro coupes produced prior to the December 1982 launch of the 80 Quattro had made it possible to virtually halve the cost of 4-WD motoring.

Part II: A Logical Development

When the Audi 80 Quattro was introduced, at a plush December 3-13 series of St Moritz press parties, its price was a major source of comment, for instead of Quattro coupe's 59,655Dm the tag read 31,000Dm. At the prevalent exchange rate corresponding to £7300 and £14,000. This was absolutely in line with Audi's wish to spread the 4-WD word; it is also worth noting that Volkswagen's first 4-WD road car, the Frankfurt September 1983-introduced Tetra version of the Passat Estate, used mostly Audi 80 running gear, with the exception of some rear end components vaguely described as "the rear axle".

Not the sleekest of shapes for the new Aero-conscious Audi, but better than the coupe. The 2.2-litre 80 Quattro possessed an Aero Cd of 0.41, slightly better than the first Quattro's 0.43, but not in the same game as the trendsetting Audi 100's 0.30

The 80 Quattro literally got away to a good start in snowy St Moritz, where the benefits of 4-WD − and the twin locking differentials activated by the same softly hissing two-stage pneumatic switch as for big brother − were immediately apparent. As were the advantages of the soft compound Goodyear Allweather tyres. Initial sales were restricted to the obvious candidates for 4-WD amongst European customers: Switzerland, Southern Germany and Austria, but built up swiftly enough to allow July 1, 1983, homologation of 80 Quattro into Group A; the competition category which admits vehicles produced only at the rate of 5000, or more, in each year. The 80 Quattro came to Britain officially in August 1983 at £11,268.56 by which time VAG could report, "production at the Audi factory in Ingolstadt increased from an original 33 cars each week up to over 300. So far over 6500 have been built."

Externally the 80 with 4-WD was subtly altered over the usual 4-door, front drive, 80 saloon. There were twin halogen headlamps under a larger single glass cover. The front and a new rear spoiler, the rear in a deformable plastic, were matched to the body colour, which appeared to be maroon, or maroon for the 25 pre-production examples offered in St Moritz. All of these cars carried the semi-chunky Goodyear 175/70 Allweathers on ex-Audi 100 steel wheels of 5½J × 14in, but neatly decorated with sleek wheel covers: alloy 6J spoked wheels of Quattro coupe parentage were optionally available. Even when the car came to Britain the Allweather tyres, officially HR-rated and thus a few mph short of the 80Q's near-120mph maximum, were retained.

From the rear there was the hint of extra 80 power via a twin exhaust system, but dimensionally the car was built on the usual modified 80 floorpan − with

quattro

You rarely see an 80 on these chunky tyres and wide wheels, but it looks terrific for press pictures! The 80Q with its coupe headlamps and deep front spoiler was subtly different to the ordinary front-drive 80 in appearance, and spread the Quattro principles to a much wider audience than the turbocharged two door.

its bigger centre tunnel and rear axle subframe mounting points − that also served the Quattro. Owing to the taller tyres, a slightly higher roof height was quoted than for the 80. Compared to the 4-WD coupe the 80 saloon rested on the same wheelbase (a millimetre different in the figures I have here: 0.039 of an inch!) but the saloon was 0.83in shorter, 1.6in narrower, 1.26in taller and weighed 1190kg, which equated to 242lb less than the turbocharged Quattro. The 80 carried less fuel, 70 litres versus the 90 of the production Quattro coupe, or 15.4 gallons compared to 19.8 if you are feeling Imperial.

Saving over 2cwt on body weight and a less complex engine ensured the fuel-injected five-cylinder could provide plenty of straight-line performance, something that was initially faulted by the press on the 80 (because we were operating at higher altitudes and spent most of our time ascending mountain passes). Once the car could be evaluated in Britain one could see that half price did not equate to a 50 per cent performance. Instead of the Quattro coupe's near-140mph maximum *Autocar* found a best of 121mph from the tired LHD machine loaned before VAG had their British RHD press fleet assembled. The same 80 Quattro provided 0-60mph in just 8.8 seconds: excellent when compared to the 7.1s of turbocharged Quattro. There was a fuel consumption bonus of 25.5mpg overall, versus 19.1mpg, when both cars were put through the same test routine.

The 80 Quattro utilised the same 79.5×86.4mm (2144cc) inline five-cylinder basic engine as had served Audi 100 and Quattro coupe, *sans* the turbocharging hardware and plus some detail development. The smaller American specification intake manifold − also used on the straightforward FWD Audi Coupe − was utilised for space reasons. Yet power output was 136bhp at 5900rpm instead of the Coupe's 130bhp at the same rpm. Why? Because the 80 Quattro compensated via three branch cast iron manifold and triple downpipes in place of the usual two branch design; this extra complexity not attracting any weight penalty according to Audi and providing a torque bonus. The comparative figures were: 80 Quattro, 176Nm (129lb.ft) at 4500rpm and 126lb.ft/171Nm at 4800rpm for Audi Coupe. Incidentally the same engine, also sharing the 9.3:1cr, is deployed in the Audi 100 "Aero Champ" where it is rated at 136bhp at 5700rpm and 180Nm by 4800rpm.

The non-turbocharged five-cylinder engine for the first Quattro 80 developed 136bhp from 2144cc, often officially labelled '2.2-litres'.

quattro

All these 2.1-litre fives used Bosch K-Jetronic mechanical fuel-injection, the 80 Quattro also utilising small air passages at the injectors to ''ensure good fuel atomisation at idle speed, which is now reduced to 800rpm''. Another idling refinement of this Bosch system was the fitment of a solenoid valve and a small control unit to ensure the engine breathed evenly during the changes in load that take place with the motor ticking over: changing electrical demands, such as those from the headlamps or the use of air-conditioning were what Audi had in mind.

Inside the 80 Quattro the instrumentation is predictably spartan, an econometer in place of the coupe's boost gauge and the later central knob operation for the vacuum assisted differential locks

These idle controls worked in association with a constant ignition advance, but instead of the previous 6° TDC timing was advanced to 18° TDC. This move was also beneficial for cold start emission performance: an important consideration when one of the 80 Quattro's first tasks was to tackle the emission-conscious Swiss market. In fact they used a further development on the 2144cc theme that went back to 130bhp at 5750rpm with substantially less torque (168Nm at 5000rpm) owing to further emission control work. As if the Swiss hadn't got enough to do, constantly yodelling and counting cash, without having to puff up all those hills with less power than Audi provided elsewhere . . .

The 4-WD system with the usual Audi assertion that it carried only 165lb weight penalty as against FWD was retained virtually intact from Quattro coupe although the driveshafts were slightly lighter than on the Quattro, the same as those used on the Audi Coupe 5E. This includes items such as the centre-jointed propshaft from the rear of the gearbox, and avoirdupois accrued via the rear differential, driveshafts and more sophisticated rear end suspension. In the case of 80 Quattro there was a substantial weight saving, as we have seen, thanks to the loss of turbocharging — this also provided an excellent service bonus with easier under-bonnet access to the engine and its ancillaries; also under-bonnet temperatures were considerably lower.

The Quattro 80 arrived in RHD for Britain belatedly after a Type Approval delay. Note the usual steel wheels and Good-year AllWeather tyres, instead of the wide, 60% low profile rubber shown originally.

There were changes to the gearbox of the 80 Quattro when set against Quattro coupe. Both five-speed units continued to take their mechanical parentage from Audi 100, but the ratios for the 80 Quattro were juggled with the emphasis on suitability for a less powerful engine working within an aerodynamic shape (0.41Cd) that was strictly from the past in Audi's 1982 terms. Thus both Quattros shared the 3.600 and 2.125 second, along with 3.500 as their reverse ratio. However the 80 Quattro used a 1.458 third gear instead of the turbocharged car's 1.360 and continued the theme with 80 Quattro selecting 1.071 in fourth (an overdriven 0.967 for Quattro coupe) plus 0.829 fifth versus the original 0.778. For 1984 Audi specified 1.458 third and a 1.071 fourth as common ratios on Quattro Coupe as well.

Final drives were sharply different as well, the Quattro coupe offering 23.55mph per 1000rpm from a 3.889 at either end. The 80 Quattro galloped at "only" 20.19mph per 1000rpm from a 4.111. Put it another way, at 100mph the turbocharged coupe is cantering along at around 4250rpm whilst the 80 Quattro needs almost 5000rpm. That is supposing both are wearing production wheels and tyres of 205/60VR 15 on the turbocharged car and 175/70HR 14 on the 80 Quattro.

The principles of raiding the Audi production bins for running gear remained in 80 Quattro, but they were not all the same components as for the more powerful Quattro original. Aside from the ratio within the differential the rear end was as per Summer 1982 Quattro coupe, which is to say minus anti-roll bar and plus the reduced toe-in characteristics. The front featured the anti-roll

quattro

That's why the gearchange baulks sometimes! Convoluted Quattro 80 shift mechanism and simple vacuum activation for the differentials, shown in St Moritz 1982 cutaway.

Quattro 80 shows off the 4-WD layout and revised rear suspension. As ever the five-cylinder engine mounts well forward of the front axle line. The hollow shaft ingenuity for transferring power forward without a separate centre differential assembly provides a very neat gearbox/transaxle installation.

New front seats and a leather-rim wheel sounds simple enough, but the bonus in comfort and driving pleasure during hard motoring is considerable, compared to front drive 80s.

quattro

bar links previously mentioned but also had a couple of features that differentiated 80 Quattro from the original. The struts themselves featured a deeper hold from upright to the bottom of the strut tube, however the important point about the 80 Quattro was its revised spring rates — employed as the result of a lighter front end; albeit one that still carried over 61 per cent of kerb weight as clear testimony to its Audi front drive heritage.

They worked on the principle of "hard back, soft front" spring ratings and came up with figures equivalent to 103lb.in front and 139lb rear justifying, on the road, Audi's claim that "the 80 Quattro has an even better overall balance" than the turbo original. The back springs were those of Quattro coupe, but the fronts were new, in line with steering geometry and negative offset as for the 130bhp Audi Coupe FWD.

As on Quattro turbos Audi raided their parts store for 80 Quattro and came up with 11.02in ventilated fronts and 9.65in solid disc rears. The fronts used Audi 100 calipers on fresh mountings, and the rears adopted Quattro coupe calipers as well. Unlike Quattro coupe's engine-driven brake hydraulics, the 80 used more conventional vacuum servo-assistance, although the standard power steering remained as for the Quattro with the servo-assistance dependent on engine speed: the effect is of lighter steering for parking and minimal assistance at speed. The effectiveness of the steering can be underlined by simply saying that it is quite sensitive enough to cope with downhill ice and hairpins. It is also interesting to note that in the 1983 Sanremo rally both Blomqvist and Mikkola had power steering failures, found the cars virtually undrivable and lost chunks of time. Power steering is no longer just for the weak!

At the rear a body-coloured spoiler, extended lower back valance, and twin exhausts told the 80Q story, along with appropriate badges.

Variations

As we have seen Audi 80 Quattro production built up very satisfactorily at Ingolstadt and led to exactly the widening of 4-WD appeal that Audi had prophesied when they made their pledge to offer at least the option of 4-WD on all models by 1985. Landmarks in the 80 Quattro's career, including its World Championship competition debut on the Swedish international of February 1983, where Stig Blomqvist was a stunning second overall with less than 200bhp, were to pass with rapidity.

Most modest 4-WD quattro package yet is the 1984 model year 80 with a redeveloped 2-litre version of the five-cylinder engine.

That Swedish rally feat of Blomqvist's was really a red herring so far as the 80 Quattro's 1983-4 works competition potential was concerned. Audi Sport were much too busy grappling with Lancia for the World Title to do more than make sure the car progressed from its original Group B recognition (200 produced) of early 1983 into Group A, as originally anticipated, albeit a few months late, in July 1983.

Most competition work went into the car via David Sutton Motorsport in the UK, who had backing from Audi UK and Pirelli primarily for Harald Demuth to tackle the British home international series, a tale that is told in a later chapter. Despite commissioning Terry Hoyle of Maldon, Essex (ex-Ford at Boreham engine builder of repute), the car rarely showed the form that was needed to match the dominant Toyota Corolla of Per Eklund, or the improving Escort RS1600i models run by MCD in Britain for Louise Aitken and Malcolm Wilson.

Variations on the 80 Quattro theme sprouted at the Frankfurt Show of September 1983, the first announcement predating the show as it was made in August to preview their intentions. In order to get down well under 30,000Dm Ingolstadt announced that the 80 Quattro would also be available with the 2.0 development of 1.9-litre inline five-cylinder unit, normally used in Audi 80CD and the straightforward basic Audi Coupe; both front drive models of course. However they opted for the 81 × 77.4mm shorter stroke motor in 115bhp injection form rather than the basic 90bhp four, because the 4-WD transmission bellhousing has yet to be machined to accept the four-cylinder power plants.

The scope of Audi's engineering and research activities for VW and themselves was reflected by the fact that Volkswagen charged the Ingolstadt engineers with the task of developing all engines over 1.3-litres in the eighties, an assignment that included four and five-cylinder units. The initial results were seen in the inline SOHC fours (coded EA 827) such as the 112bhp version of the Golf GTi engine at 1.8-litres, followed by 75 and 90bhp versions of, substantially, the same 1.8-litre four in Audi 100 and other VW-Audis. This work

quattro

Straightforward rec tangular lamps are used i place of the elongate units of the bigger c; pacity Quattros. Thi 115bhp version of the five cylinder engine wa developed as part of programme that als included the four-cylinde VW units.

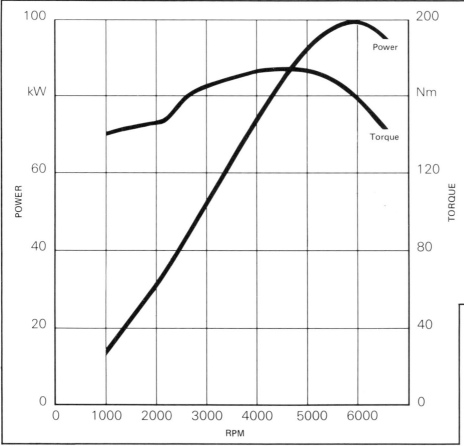

Power and torque curve for the 2.2-litre (left) an 2-litre Audi 80 Quattro: It is interesting to see tha it is the larger, olde engine design that feed on rpm with a power pea around 6000rpm an torque of 160Nm unt nearly the same rpm whereas the smaller un dips beneath 160Nr sharply beyond 4900 rev:

was important because the four and five-cylinder units became evermore closely interrelated, but to the Quattro it has always been the five-cylinders that were relevant for the transmission mounting point reasons mentioned earlier.

However, whilst the alloy five-cylinder with 20 valves would attract most Frankfurt show attention Audi also explained, via Dr Fritz Indra, a little more about the 2-litre five that went into the cheaper version of the Quattro 80.

Dr Indra explained that the EA 828-coded development of the fives owed a great deal to their earlier four-cylinder efforts, particularly the connecting rods. Moving from the 79.5mm bore of the 1921cc five to the 81mm of the 1994cc unit used in the cheaper 80 Quattro (both employing the 77.4mm bore) provided the opportunity to adopt the four-cylinder's 144mm con rods, which were 7 per cent lighter than the older design despite their 8mm extra length. Piston weight was also sharply reduced, each complete assembly going from 532 grammes to 434g; this 20 per cent saving and the new rods making the latest 2-litre five a lot smoother than the previous 1921cc fives.

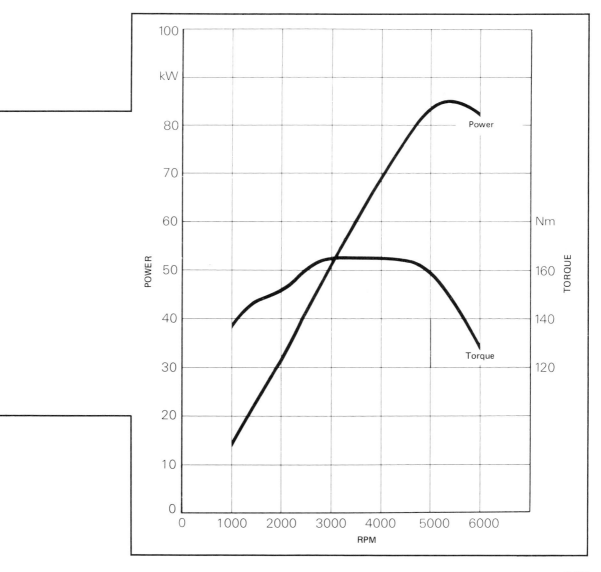

quattro

The Audi parts bin philosophy on four and five-cylinder engines culminated in the following common features: pistons, rods, combustion chamber shape, valves and their springs, valve timing and all principle internal dimensions, particularly bore × stroke in a variety of capacity variations that could be exercised simply by going from four to five-cylinders, and vice versa.

The 2-litre incorporated a number of other lessons from elsewhere in the Audi organisation too. There were the injector air passages noted in the original 80 Quattro and an alloy cylinder head with large valves (38mm intake, 33mm exhaust) which came from the 5E power plant and the 10:1cr was in line with current thinking on efficiency and economy.

Compared with the earlier 1921cc unit (which was an Audi Coupe, not Quattro powerplant) the 2-litre produced 165Nm instead of 154 at a peak of 3200rpm instead of 3700 revs. The 115bhp was as before, but was developed 500rpm earlier, emphasising that Audi see torque at lower rpm as a principle weapon in providing economical performance cars today.

Other features of the ''cheap'' 80 Quattro included manual steering as standard with revised front suspension to suit and a 400mm/15.75in diameter steering wheel in place of the power steered 380mm/14.96in unit that could be purchased optionally. In the latter case the front suspension reverted to exactly that of the 80 Quattro in 136bhp form. Incidentally, the big four spoke steering wheel came out of the Audi 100.

Inside the cheapest 8 Quattro for 1984 an Aud 100-style wheel and th usual basic instrumer tation, with a wate temperature gauge i place of the larger engined Quattro 80' econometer.

By this stage Audi could offer anti-lock braking as an optional feature on both 80 Quattros. Jorg Bensinger amplified on the reasons it had taken them so long, and the circumstances in which a Quattro 80, or any Quattro derivative for that matter, can use the system. ''Aside from the engineering manpower restrictions we had, there was also the problem that the Bosch system was engineered for 2-WD cars. It took time to adapt it to our needs. It was possible to reduce stopping distance to some extent by locking the centre differential. This overrides the brake balance which is specified by law to prevent any risk

of the rear wheels locking up before the front wheels (an EEC directive that ruins the brake balance on many modern cars − J.W.) Particularly on a slippery road or with a heavy payload, this unnecessarily restricts the braking effect at the rear, despite the action of the brake pressure regulator.

"When the centre differential is locked the rear wheels are forced to rotate at the same speed as the front wheels, so they brake better than when the differential is not locked. *If* the front wheels should lock up, however, the rear wheels will also stop revolving. This is not critical at the moderate speeds possible on slippery roads, but at higher speeds this can lead to instability and a spin in the hands of an inexperienced driver", said Bensinger in an English translation of his thoughts on the often controversial subject of Quattro braking. Bensinger's attitude to the question of stopping the Quattro safely on slippery surfaces can be judged from the following dryly-humorous appraisal. "In the Quattros a driver's subjective impression from a 2-WD car, namely that he can brake twice as well as he can accelerate, no longer holds true. The physical limits must be respected: four wheels are driven, but [still] no more than four wheels are braked!"

Therefore Audi had to co-develop what they refer to as a second generation in anti-lock braking, matched specifically to 4-WD. They say this version of ABS will, "shorten the stopping distance achieved by the normal driver, although it will not improve the absolute minimum distance also possible without ABS. Once again this is governed by the physical limits . . ."

Advising Quattro owners on when it's best for the differential locks to be engaged, the factory feel "at high speeds it is essential to prevent all four wheels from locking up, so it is better to leave the differential free. If the car is equipped with ABS there is no need to lock the differential since the wheels will always provide the maximum braking anyway . . . To maintain the high degree of steering control and stability with ABS even in difficult situations, it has been made impossible to use the differential lock and ABS functions simultaneously". Incidentally, if the driver does engage the differential lock the ABS system is electronically overridden and a yellow warning light appears on the instrument panel. It is also worth noting that the factory feel the rear differential lock is "only necessary in very extreme conditions, which are hardly likely to be encountered on normal roads". More about that in our chapter devoted to driving impressions.

The cheaper Audi 80 Quattro with the 2-litre engine was the slowest 4-WD development of the theme that Audi had offered prior to the Winter of 1983-4, but even then it was hardly likely to baulk other traffic. The factory claimed a top speed of 114mph, and acceleration from 0-50mph in 6.8 seconds, or 0-62mph in 10.3s. The equivalent figures for the 136bhp 80 Quattro from the factory were 120mph, rest to 50mph in 0.6 seconds less and 0-62 mph nearly a full second quicker, and firmly under the 10 second barrier at 9.1s. Naturally on fuel consumption one saw the advantages of the more recent small capacity power unit. Here are the Audi factory figures, translated from litres/100km, for the original 136bhp 80 Quattro with the cheaper 2-litre in brackets: constant 56mph, 38.7mpg (39.8); constant 75mph, 31.0mpg (31.7); urban cycle, 20.8mpg (20.9 or 22.78mpg, using the gearchange arrow warning light).

When this was written neither the cheaper Audi 80 Quattro or the VW Passat Tetra, with the same 2-litres, were being offered in Britain, which meant the cheapest UK way into 4-WD *chez* Audi was the £11,000 plus original 136bhp Quattro 80. So 4-WD had a long way to go before the masses could appreciate its poor weather reassurances . . .

The cheaper Quattro 80 made its first sales appearances towards the end of October 1983 at 27,000Dm: the equivalent of under £7000. When this was written it was too early to tell if Audi's move was simply spreading the word

quattro

— the adoption of 4-WD, based on 80 Quattro transmission, on the Passat Tetra Estate at the Frankfurt show could have been for this reason — or whether the initial novelty of 4-WD without an off-road application, in the usual agricultural sense, was beginning to pall.

The VW Tetra Passat also picked up this fuel-injected 2-litre version of the five in 115bhp injection trim, and offered it for public sale, using substantially Quattro transmission parts, from the start of 1984.

So the four-driven-wheels concept performed the full development circle and came back from Quattro coupe to the 80 in which it had been spawned. By the time the offspring were in evidence at that historic Frankfurt show of 1983, Audi were able to show a completely new Quattro approach, but one that had also sprung from a much earlier development programme. The short wheelbase (SWB) Quattro with unique no-cost compromise 20-valve engine was ready to steal a show that already contained a 186mph 4-WD Porsche. A rear-engined model emphasising Ferdinand Piech's original 80 Quattro launch claim that "every German manufacturer now has to work on a 4-WD variant."

Chapter 8

Short sensation

Unveiled late in 1983, even the basic road version of the shorter Quattro presented some stunning statistics — including a price tag equivalent to over £50,000 and a 155mph maximum for this exotic cocktail of Kevlar and plastic body with an all-aluminium engine rated at 300bhp. For competition there would be more, much, much more . . .

Show-stopper! Genuine visitor's gawp for the Frankfurt Show red Quattro Sport of September 1983.

quattro

Speaking to us over a snatched lunch in a comparatively quiet corner of the bedlam that enveloped the VAG Frankfurt Show stand during the multi-media launch of the 12.6 inch shorter Quattro Sport in September 1983, Hannu Mikkola recalled, "of course there had been shorter Quattros in the works and testing for some time — but I did not drive this shorter car until last year. The idea was to see if it was worthwhile — and today you can see the result! It is more nervous in a straight line, but quicker to turn in to a corner and a much better size for rallies like Corsica. Now, there will be no backing-up on really tight corners, where the old car could not go in one turn: you know, this car makes the first Quattro feel like a lorry, so long by comparison!

"For me the best rally cars are a bit unstable, so I do not mind the extra nervousness of the shorter car. For me it is better, I can change the course in a short time, even in the middle of a corner and this may avoid an accident." Mikkola tactfully did not mention the number of times that even he had careered the original Quattro coupe off the road, usually the result of the strong inherent understeer that can get the better of even the fabled left foot braking technique if a corner contains an unexpected hazard. Stig Blomqvist, Michele Mouton and many others like Mikkola had discovered that the Quattro did not like a sudden change of plan in mid-corner: sometimes they had simply been going too fast, but on other occasions (when Mikkola lost the lead in Sweden, 1983, in that snow bank) there was the feeling that snappier handling reactions could have avoided costly contact with the scenery.

Underneath its skin, the Quattro Sport allied proven rally car technology with a fabulous 20-valve version of the five-cylinder turbo motor.

Rumours of the short Quattro gained credence late in 1981 when some of the more persistent journalists snapped a visibly shorter chassis car underneath a dustsheet at Ingolstadt. Even as late as October 1983 they were still hiding short Quattros underneath the dust sheets at Ingolstadt, but when we rudely lifted the cape the reason became painfully apparent. Not secrecy, but a short coupe that had been brutalised by *terra firma*: it was even shorter one side than the other. So there's still a limit, and testing has certainly conscientiously reached it! Incidentally Mikkola confirmed that all the mileage he had done prior to Frankfurt in the shorter car had been with the usual 2-valve per cylinder (10-valve) rally engine, rather than the 4-valve per cylinder alloy unit designed specifically for the shorter Quattro Sport. The combination in 20-valve form did not receive its first testing from Mikkola until the day after that Frankfurt preview: further serious testing was expected in December, with the aid of new recruit Walter Rohrl.

In competition terms the extra agility and power of the Quattro Sport could not be brought into play until May 1984 at the earliest, because of the need to make 200 such cars for Group B and achieve homologation. Therefore the original Quattro concept went into its fourth season hoping it would not have to face the tight tarmac challenge of Corsica again in May! However, it is worth recording the fact that the Quattro Sport's competition potential was assessed within the secure confines of Porsche's Weissach research centre outside Stuttgart; fine facilities used by many manufacturers these days under conditions of maximum security. In Audi's case, of course, Ferdinand Piech had his status as a former Porsche engineering chief and current stockholder to ensure Ingolstadt made the best possible deals when it came to using Porsche's fabled facilities.

Almost a caricature of the original Quattro coupe, the Sport's lines are much more aggressive from any angle. Just how the wheelbase had been trimmed can be best judged from the abbreviated rear side window.

Engine Engineering

When the curly blond locks and infectious laugh of Dr Fritz Indra arrived at Audi from Alpina's Bavarian base in Buchloe (January 1, 1979), the forward engines engineering programme was one of the most exciting that could have been offered to an ambitious engineer with a competition heritage and proven turbocharged road car expertise. It didn't hurt that Audi's fellow Bavarians at BMW in Munich would now not be able to use the talents brilliantly exposed by Indra's seventies reign at the engineering helm of the racing (BMW would not have won the 1973 European Championship fight against Ford without Alpina) and road Alpina-BMWs either.

Fritz Indra recalled that one of the first priorities Ferdinand Piech handed him on arrival at Audi was the development of an alloy cylinder block for the 5-cylinder engines, and this work was central both to the use of such a block in the rally Quattro from 1982 onward, and to the development of the complete alloy engine found in the Quattro Sport. The order to provide 4-valves per cylinder came "about 1½ years before we show this engine at Frankfurt — and it makes sense for us to also make up the design for the 4-valves in the 1.8-litre VW engine that you have also seen in Frankfurt. This is the same as our Audi Sport 4-valver except that we make the VW have the hydraulic valve lifters for service reasons:

quattro

Dr Fritz Indra: from Niki Lauda's Formula Vee accomplice to Audi's new generation engine designer, via Alpina-BMW at Buchloe . . .

Grr! Plenty of negative camber applied to those special Michelin-shod front wheels, and 300bhp to be apportioned: 75 horsepower per driven wheel!

the Quattro is always being looked after in competition, so it can have the mechanical type.''

Dr Indra outlined the hurried, but thorough, engine development typical of Audi routine at present, surprising us with the low numbers of engineers drawn on at the heart of each project. ''For this Quattro Sport engine I am told I can make a no-compromise engine — and that is why it is so good . . . and so expensive!'' A brief burst of laughter and Dr Indra added, ''of course the basics are known: it will be inline five-cylinders and the alloy block will carry the bore centres we already have so that no new tooling is required. It must be lighter and more compact and have the strength for a lot more power than the basic 300 horsepower in competition.

''We make up the basic design and do the test bed work around no more than four vital people: if you get good people, you need no more — they just get in the way. On the test bed, for example, we must make a bearing test that takes three weeks with the engine running at 6300rpm. Then, again to pass the production standards at Audi, we run the engine at high speed for 24 hours. In this case that meant 7100rpm''. All this was delivered in deadpan engineering style, but we should remember that there are very few genuine production engines today that are capable of running reliably at a peak of 7100rpm, never mind for 24 hours. Also, we are talking about the least potent variant of the latest Audi five. Dr Indra and the small team (obviously augmented by mechanical and test staff where appropriate as the engines covered 150,000 test hours, and there was a complete production car to develop outside this department) were primarily occupied with the production variant of the Quattro Sport. However, previous experience with the 10-valve rally engine and some preliminary work

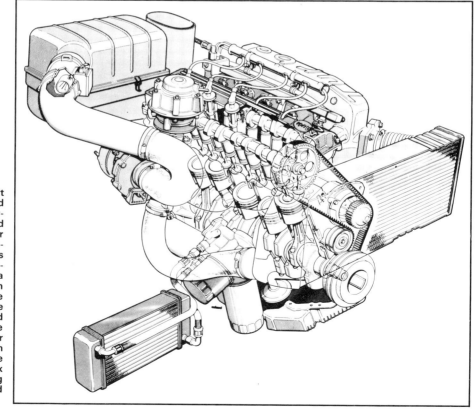

The 2.13-litre five with belt drive for the overhead camshafts, front intercooler, side oil cooler and four-valve-per-cylinder layout. The KKK turbocharger feeds cylinders with an 8:1 static compression to provide a basic 300bhp with an estimated 450bhp the likely rally figure for late 1984. With Ferrari and Porsche amongst the Group B newcomers for 1985, the figures quoted in the power race became more akin to Grand Prix figures when preparing for mid-eighties World Championship rallies.

on the 20-valve allowed Dr Indra later to outline the principle competition changes that would be made.

The alloy block descendant of those Audi 100 and rally car pre-production forays featured a new casting technique: aluminium alloy being cast directly around the thin-wall cast iron cylinder liners. As for the rally engines a weight saving of 23kg/51lb is quoted for the alloy block versus the original iron component. One of *the* design briefs was that the overall engine weight should not exceed 150kg and Audi claim 145kg/319lb for the complete turbocharged, intercooled, 20-valve Sport motor. This is remarkable when you consider that Cosworth quote 356lb as the original weight of their Grand Prix V8 power unit, reduced to "approximately 340lb" in the later lightweight versions according to John Blunsden's authoritative work, *The Power to Win*.

The principles of Audi five cylinder engine construction, such as the 6-bearing crankshaft (its dimensions as for the 136bhp fives) were retained, but the steel crankshaft provided a safe rpm limit of 7400rpm in production guise. "Beyond 7400 we must heat treat the crankshaft steel, but that is all we need for the 8-8500 that will be possible in competition", reported Dr Indra.

From the start the sub-3-litre capacity was specified, the crankshaft and bore combination providing 79.3×86.4mm, some 2133cc actual capacity and 2986 with the turbo multiplication factor. The Mahle pistons supplied 8:1 on a plus-or-minus 0.3 basis for the production 200 Quattro Sports of early 1984, but for rallying use where the turbocharger boost was likely to increase from the production 1.2 bar/17psi to 1.7 bar/24psi Dr Indra felt, "we must come down closer to 7:1. It is not possible to have such boost and stop the high speed knocking, but for the road this high compression is possible and the response is good . . . very good." Incidentally the old 10-valve motors started with 6:1cr and were still under 6.5:1 by the Summer of 1983, so the four valve layout and new combustion chamber shapes have provided tangible benefits already.

The cylinder head not only provided Audi's first four valve, double overhead camshaft, production head — but also the crossflow layout for the first time on one of their fives. This provides a much safer and more efficient basic layout for the Quattro engine bay as (looking from the front) the exhaust system and red-hot KKK-K27 turbocharger are on the left, divorced from the Bosch LH-Jetronic fuel-injection with its 7psi fuel feed to the right.

The head remained in aluminium but had nothing else in common with the previous SOHC Audi design. Dr Fritz Indra explained that the priorities had been to "make the head, like the engine, as small as possible so we can fit all the turbocharger components where we want — and also not have much weight in the front."

The result was exceptionally compact, for the belt-driven camshafts were geared together at the front of the engine, closer together than would have been possible with the traditional double pulley drive employed on DOHC engines. The valve layout reflected this desire for a compact head design too, the exhausts running parallel to the cylinder block line with the intake valves tilted outward at 25°. Incidentally it is the exhaust camshaft that is driven by the crankshaft belt, transferring motion to the intake cam via helical gears.

The shallow valve angle is complemented by smaller valve head sizes: 28mm exhaust and 32mm intake. Even in competition trim these sizes are not expected to increase by "more than a millimetre or so", according to Dr Indra. The four valve layout is completed by a 12mm central spark plug from Bosch.

Naturally the cogged belt overhead cam drive was also designed to drive some ancillaries, notably the water and oil pumps. Note that the homologation 200 Audi Quattro Sports had wet sump lubrication, as opposed to the usual dry sump competition system, and that the alloy baffled sump, with a special

Power and torque curves for the Quattro Sport's 2.1-litre power unit. At a leisurely 4300rpm, the equivalent of 188bhp is generated, while 1000rpm later there's almost exactly 10bhp more than a 3.2-litre Porsche 911 provided in 1983. Then, the Audi Quattro Sport's power curve still ascends briskly toward the 300bhp peak at close to 7000rpm.

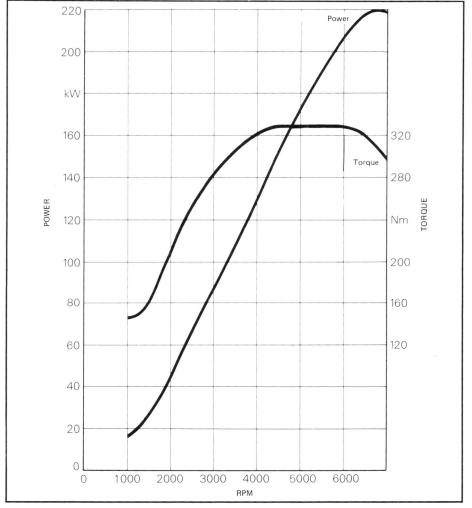

Sport's twin overhead camshafts are geared together, the lower shaft fed power via the cogged-belt from the crankshaft.

oil pick-up tube was sub-contracted to the Stuttgart's House concern.

Of the ancillaries and the general power-boosting methods used on the engine one could certainly say that lessons had been learned from competition. Not just from rallying, which provided both the basic larger Langerer & Reich intercooler and the bigger KKK turbocharger (model 27 instead of 26 in production Quattros), but also from Formula 1. Dr Indra explained: ''look at an F1 BMW, whatever, and you will see the lesson of a big turbocharger placed as close to the cylinder head and the intercooler as possible. The idea is to make the inlet tract as short as possible. Why? Because the throttle response is better. It loses maybe the last 20 horsepower, but it does not matter if the lag of the turbo is overcome . . . And, in rallying, this is even more important!'' Another no-compromise move which emphasised Dr Indra's claim that this production engine will externally look much the same whether it is in competition or road trim, was the provision from the start of individual throttle bodies instead of one guillotine slide, a move Lancia had to make as part of the evolution of their Rally model in early 1984.

The Langerer & Reich intercooler was of exactly the dimensions used in the 1983 rally Quattros, which meant it was capable of knocking 140°C back to 60°C when the motor ran at full boost. The intercooler itself was mounted forward of the engine while the production Quattro Sport mounted the engine oil cooler to the left (looking front to rear), low down in front of the roadwheel, while the water radiator lived on the right of the engine bay.

Inlet and exhaust manifolding was subjected to much research running, the inlet a one piece alloy casting and the exhaust cast in iron with the wastegate bolted neatly on top of the five branch union point. Fritz Indra commented, ''the 5-1 pattern of the exhaust is *very* important for competition''. Under Group B regulations you cannot change the production exhaust system, so it was vital to build the road car with a top manifold system that could absorb the gas-patterns created when 450 competition horsepower were being generated, rather than 300 within a roadgoing power band. As an aside, note that the water passages of cylinder head and inlet manifold are connected.

Lumps, louvres and inlet characterise the dual headlamp Sport.

The ignition remained the electronic computer-memory system of the Quattro with a flywheel sensor triggering ignition impulses, but the electronic Bosch LH-Jetronic injection system was new. Even the fuel-conscious over-run cut-off was supplied as part of Audi Quattro Sport's roadgoing spec: Audi claiming that "an all-electronic system is used here for the first time with a turbocharged engine. The air mass is registered by means of a heated wire, and with corrections for boost pressure, water and air temperature, the system assures the most efficient mixture at all operating points programmed in the data map". Fritz Indra simply said the whole concept is "wonderful! It's a new generation of electronics from Bosch and the same as Porsche use in F1, but Audi are the first to use this in rallying on the 10-valve engine and it is also good on the Sport engine. It is *so* simple, just one control box for injection and ignition."

Other salient induction features included a large air box behind the inline five and minimal pipe lengths between turbo and intercooler, thence from intercooler to injection with the accent throughout on preventing the pressure drops that are an inevitable hazard of piping air from the turbo via an intercooler with simple, Jubilee clip-secured, flexible piping.

A 155mph maximum speed claim and likely sub-5 second capability to whoosh from rest to 60mph occupied most in regard to the Quattro Sport's abilities, but economy was also claimed to be "very good". This was partially the by-product of an efficient engine — nearly 143bhp per litre from a road-legal motor is a mind-boggling performance on its own — with its high compression. However there was also the Audi idle volume control discussed for the 80 Quattro and the over-run fuel shut-off to show that performance blood lust had not totally overtaken all other considerations.

Whilst we awaited the 450bhp/8000rpm rally engine wonders of 1984, the Quattro Sport's power unit promised enough entertainment to keep those with £50,000 to invest in the early 1984 production examples ecstatic. At 1.2 bar boost on 98 RON petrol there was a promised 300bhp at 6500rpm and 330Nm/243lb.ft torque at 4500rpm. To give perspective you can absorb the fact that a 2-litre Formula 2 *racing* BMW motor of proven effectiveness gives little more than another 20bhp, and you would not try that as a production powerplant for the road. Or imagine the svelte Jaguar V12 engine of 5.3-litres: it gives 5bhp less from 3.2 litres *more*! However the sheer quantity of cubic inches do provide 318lb.ft torque at 3000rpm; vital when you must power a near-4000lb saloon effortlessly . . .

Quattro Sport: The Car

Slicing 320mm/12.6 inches from the wheelbase of the Quattro coupe and venting the front panels to correctly cool the rearranged engine bay left English Audi stylist Peter Birtwhistle with few options on how this functional coupe would appear externally, but the overall impression left by the sole road-trimmed red Quattro Sport on display at Frankfurt 1983 was certainly stunning, if not a front-runner in any *concours d'elegance*.

Versus the original Quattro coupe the Sport was 240mm/9.45in shorter overall on the chopped wheelbase. It was also 80mm/3.15in fatter and ran a track 95mm/3.74in wider up front and plus 34mm/1.34in at the back: roof height was quoted within a millimetre either way. Overall weight of the road car was not quoted, but *Auto Motor und Sport* quoted 1000kg/2200lb and another German magazine revealed that it was spread 55 per cent front, 45 per cent rear — a very large distribution improvement indeed compared with the original nose-heavy layout. In competition trim Audi expected to get comfortably down to the 960kg class minimum, a target Lancia had practically achieved by the close of the 1983 rallying season.

quattro

With lines drawn by a Englishman, one feels patriotic duty not to b too rude, concentratin on words like function ality for the 12.6 inc shorter Quattro Spor All-up weight of this roa car was less than all bu the most exotic ligh weight LWB originals fc competition.

Lightweight material were used for the exteric panels of the Quattr Sport, whilst Micheli developed some speci rubber to handle th 150mph plus Sport . . .

Since the original Quattro coupe weighed over 300kg/660lb more than the Sport, it was clear that some very fancy materials had been employed to save weight. Perhaps the most familiar in brand name but comparatively unknown in detail was Kevlar. This aramid — man-made fibre from the petro-chemical industry — is produced at the Du Pont factory in Richmond, West Virginia, USA, in a variety of golden threads which are weaved by specialists and used by designers in association with a number of composites and laminates for many different purposes. We may associate Kevlar with competition cars, but it has also been woven into cables that tow North Sea oil rigs, moulded into shields for space rockets and utilised as battle protection in such diverse roles as President Reagan's string vest and the superstructure of British warships!

Audi used Kevlar in association with laminate glassfibre for the wings, aprons and roof of the Sport and associated it with equally exotic carbon fibre to produce cowlings for the radiators. Composite plastics and glassfibre were also deployed upon the vented bonnet and bootlid. Carbon and glassfibre was used for the air intakes and some of the strength underneath those panels came from aluminium reinforcements. Unlike Lancia's Rally homologation 200 cars, no roll cage was provided on the Audi road car.

Former Ford competitions engineer Thomas Ammerschlager, now the engineer responsible for the chassis ride and handling engineering at Audi, told me how substantially different the Quattro Sport's suspension is to that of original Quattro. "In fact it is just like that of a rally car with round tubes fabricated for the lower arms and Boge dampers. We had to do quite a bit of ride and handling work to make it a comfortable road car and I loaned my top Quattro ride and handling guy to help it along". Thus the principles were really those of the rally car's evolution rather than the strictly production parts bin approach of the first Quattro. However the basic idea of upper strut/coil spring units and lower arms remains, sophisticated by location links and uprights of rally parentage.

ingle air intake in front
f the extended rear
wheelarch is reminiscent
f the evolution A1 and
2 competition Quattros
f 1983.

The massive four wheel ventilated disc brakes were also of clear rally lineage, four piston calipers to each corner. The handbrake operated via separate calipers to the rear of each back disc brake. The second generation ABS anti-lock system referred to extensively in the Quattro 80 chapter was also standard on the Sport, although optionally listed on its show debut. As before it would not operate if the centre differential lock was used, but as in other Quattros the driver could also override the ABS "by means of a switch. This allows rally drivers to set-up the car for a corner on slippery surfaces by deliberately locking the wheels briefly'', said Audi at Frankfurt.

The usual Audi power steering was fitted but the wheels and tyres caused a stir as Michelin had released some 235/45VR ultra low-profile rubber in place of the specified 225/50VRs recorded in the press release. The spoked alloy wheels were of the familiar Quattro optional style, but these five-bolt wonders measured 9J × 15 to fill those flared high-tech arches.

The 4-WD principle and the two-stage pneumatically-activated dog clutches for centre and rear differential did not alter for Quattro Sport, but the gearbox ratios did. The differences were (original Quattro in brackets): 1st, 3.500 (3.600); 2nd, 2.083 (2.125); 3rd, 1.368 (1.360); 4th, 0.962 (0.967); 5th, 0.759 (0.778); reverse, 3.455 (3.500). Final drives were altered too, the Quattro Sport carrying 3.875:1 versus the original 3.889 with the Sport geared for a very similar 23.16mph per 1000rpm. At the claimed 155mph Sport maximum, therefore, just over 6700rpm were demanded.

Walking around the show car it was hard not to be impressed, for it was beautifully presented. Instead of the double headlamp units of the post-August

Inside the show car you could sink into the seductive inlays of Recaro shapely sports from seats, or squat in the equally well finished rear equipped with a seat for suitably sized baby at its first public appearance.

1982 production Quattros, the front end of the Sport featured single rectangular units of the kind that have completed Quattro rally car front ends since the 1981 Acropolis. The red coachwork may have been in an enormous range of materials but it fairly gleamed beneath the show lighting and the complete machine had the air of a properly completed road car, rather than raffish rally homologation special.

Perhaps it was the interior that provided the illusion of respectability. The seats were sumptuously finished in grey leather with fabric inserts and the leather theme extended to the door inlays. There was no room save for specialist 2 + 2 dwarves in the rear, who would probably have cursed the provision of full competition Sabelt harness for the front ''crew'' anyway.

Instrumentation had been sharply improved, and about time too! The centre console carried separate water and oil temperature gauges (0-120°C and 0-170°C, the latter for oil), plus an oil pressure gauge reading up to 5 bar/71psi. The main dashboard display was not the latest Quattro electronic gimmickry but a stolid 0-300km/h (186mph) speedometer matched by the 0-9000rpm tachometer. A central boost gauge reading to 2 bar absolute was incorporated, along with smaller dials recording volts and the contents of the 90 litre/19.8 gallon fuel tank. A four spoke steering wheel carrying the Audi ring quartet, rather than the earlier turbo legend, was employed in an interior notable for simple ergonomics and multiple rocker switches for items like the electric front side window operation. The car depicted in the press photos carried a dashboard plaque with an indecipherable signature and a numbering system that was obviously designed to emphasise how exclusive those 200 initial production Quattro Sports would be.

Individually numbered road car layout for the Sport shows the properly rimmed interior, complete with switches for electric windows on the centre console. My! How homologation specials have changed . . .

Steering wheel is styled along the lines of that for the cheapest Quattro 80, but a 300km/h speedo and 9000rpm tachometer are ego-boosters. The Sport is also the first Quattro with comprehensive minor instrumentation, reading off water and oil temperatures, with oil pressure furthest right on the centre console. The turbo boost gauge is between the speedo and rpm-counter; the larger instruments flanked by battery and fuel content minor dials.

quattro

The Quattro Sport emphasised how committed Audi had become to proving the Quattro concept in World Championship rallying. It was an expensive solution to the tarmac rallying problem that the original car had always suffered, a sheer lack of pace that demanded a thorough solution against an opposition that grew stronger by the year in Group B international rallying. The Quattro Sport was not a car that either Audi's production engineers or Ferdinand Piech particularly wanted to offer for sale, but faced with the mandatory requirements of the Paris-based sporting authorities and a need to prove 4-WD most publicly over all kinds of terrain, the Quattro Sport was the logical answer . . . and it would do the company's recent sporting image no harm either, in a technically-conscious German market.

Planning ahead. Whilst the short Quattro broods at Frankfurt, in the background Roland Gumpert and Audi Chairman Dr Habbel discuss its future.

Chapter 9

Contagious Quattrophobia

Four-wheel-drive Audi-style may have taken a while to cross the channel and the Atlantic, but the enthusiasm for its sporting and everyday road capabilities has been consistently high. We pick out some British and American highlights and talk to some of those responsible for the success of Audi Sport UK.

Double champion style! John Buffum took the 1982 and 1983 SCCA Pro Rally titles with his works built Quattros: this is the 1982 car. In 1983 Quattros also took the South African (Sarel van der Merwe), Austrian (Franz Wittman) and British titles (Stig Blomqvist) for champion rally drivers.

quattro

"Do you realise there are nine, yes *nine*, national teams operating Quattros now?" enquired the entrepreneurial dynamo they call David Sutton, at the effective heart of Audi's UK sports programme. Sutton spoke from one of the two plush sofas that threatened to burst the walls of his compact office when we called. With customary pugnacious zeal David Sutton swerved from pot roasting motoring press reputations, to expounding on the remarkable record of the teams who now deal with Reinhard Rode at Ingolstadt. The 1983 season was a particularly good year for Audi Sport customers with Sarel van de Merwe

John Buffum (left), and Neil Wilson.

massacring any South African opposition, John Buffum winning a second successive American title; never mind Sutton's own Audi (UK) and Pirelli-backed Quattro for Stig Blomqvist, which had scooped the British Open International Rally Championship. There were many more Quattros running, and winning. Quattros tackled everything from European rallycross to national contests in private hands of the kind typified by Daryl Weidner's double British Championship tally in the ex-1982 British Championship Quattro. This Quattro won both the Shell Oils and BTRDA British national titles for a driver few knew before his astonishing Audi-mounted 1983 season began.

The factory went rallying in 1981 with few 'foreigners' able to join the Quattro club, save by invitation, while competition-prepared Quattros were scarce — but 1982 had been a different story. Harald Demuth's Konrad Schmidt-serviced factory coupe took seven of nine possible victories and dominated the *Deutsche Rallye Meisterschaft.* The 1982 Swedish series went to Stig Blomqvist and John Buffum, the boldest of the bold after his performances in Triumph's bumbling TR7 V8, bumped his way to that first American title against very stiff opposition from Rod Millen's now-4WD Mazda RX7. With three national titles under their 1982 belt, plus the World Championship of Makes for the Ingolstadt team, you would have thought the Quattro's second season was sufficiently well-rewarded, but one finds that they also won the Austrian national rallycross series with a win in all eight rounds. Even better was the competition to beat the best in 1982 European rallycross, for the opposition included men like Martin Schanche with his terrifying 400-horsepower-plus Escort relying on Zakspeed Capri turbo running gear. Franz Wurz emerged on top from this tough sport, winning three rounds and becoming Champion, while Quattros for former DAF driver Jan de Rooy

and Ole Arnsson won another two of the eight European Championship qualifyers.

David Sutton, team manager, multiple sponsorship wizard and high profile headman of the companies that bear his name and carry out everything from a routine road car service to World Championship duties on Ingolstadt's behalf, is not typical of the men who represent Audi outside Germany . . . But, since

David Sutton, owner of the team that won the 1981 World Rally Championship for Drivers, former driver, current publisher and the fastest dealer in the West! No private team owner has accumulated so much success, and there are many works teams that cannot match the Sutton Equipe's Championship record or global enterprise.

all are pretty rugged individuals, with differing organisations behind them, our fair-haired friend of former Ford Escort World Championship fame (Vatanen won the 1981 title in a David Sutton Cars Escort RS, funded by Rothmans) could explain the basics of running not only the Quattro coupe, but also the 80, outside the factory walls.

How did the liaison begin? Sutton thoughtfully replaced a pen in the *Audi: Rallye Weltmeister* container on his plain wooden desk and relaxed on the large sofa. A wistful grin spread gradually as he recalled the day that a driver, and long-standing friend, had replied to a request for a loan car on the 1980 Finnish 1000 Lakes with a counter deal. For when Mr Sutton approached Mr Mikkola for said car, Hannu said: "Fine, OK, but will you take my boss for next year along with you, around the rally?"

Thus David Sutton and Walter Treser, then Audi Sport's recently-appointed competitions manager, set off around the route of the 1000 Lakes in company

quattro

with a Rothmans executive who was also along for a Sutton education: how not to miss a trick whilst appearing Laid Back. Naturally the Treser-Sutton dialogue eventually covered possible co-operation, but DS was actually more interested in owning one of the road Quattros at this stage (1981 was already scheduled for a maximum British and World Championship final fling with Rothmans' Escorts). Even whilst Ari Vatanen was illustrating that the Ford could win the driver's title once more, Sutton was taking delivery of his Quattro, which appeared on his premises in the Summer of 1981.

Although there had been press speculation that Sutton would be with Audi as early as the 1981 season, there was little real ground for this assumption as the factory were in no position to supply another car and VAG in Britain really needed a sponsor at this stage to go ahead. The VAG spirit was obviously willing, but 1981 was too early to test the flesh's resolve . . .

Minds Made-Up

Sutton vividly recalled the turning point at which "a lot of minds were made up"; it was very late in 1981. "The 1981 RAC was a critical time for us: Ari had to fight Frequelin for the title right down to the wire. On the eve of the event starting I went along with senior Rothmans personnel to some evening presentations, one honouring Vatanen by an Italian magazine — and the other the Halda Golden trophy co-drivers award, which had been won by Ari's co-driver, David Richards. At one of these 'do's' I remember Ford's competitions manager Peter Ashcroft was standing at the back with us.

"Peter tapped me on the shoulder and said, 'we shall *not* be here next year'. That was tremendously significant, because it meant we would not be having a new Ford RS1700T during 1982. Now, we previously hoped to have it sometime during 1981, perhaps early 1982. We hadn't been too bothered when it had not shown in 1981, because the old car had shown it could still win some events like Sweden and Acropolis, early in the 1981 season. It was hopeless in Britain, where the Opels were just running away from us, so we knew we *had* to have a new car in 1982.

"That simple statement from Peter Ashcroft made up a lot of minds: Rothmans went with Opel and we went to Audi", Sutton summarised. Why not Rothmans-Audis with Sutton? It was, and until Autumn of 1983, continued to be, a valid question, although by 1983 Rothmans were negotiating direct with Ingolstadt. Still, the reasons for a lack of alliance appear to have remained the same. Neither side wanted to lose corporate identity — and if a deal could be done, then the price was not right. It is often said that Audi would not be prepared to lose their Audi Sport colours, but we know that if the budget demands it,* the colours can and have been muted or replaced by that of a cigarette company: Marlboro in Africa, for example. On the other hand one industry insider told me of working with Rothmans' sponsorship "it can take a bloody Act of Parliament to get a tiny sticker on a Rothmans' car!"

A week before Christmas 1981, David Sutton flew to Ingolstadt to close the deal for Audi UK to run in the British Championship using Sutton-built, serviced and administrated Audi Quattro coupes. "In six weeks we went from a blank sheet of paper, and an outline, to a full-blown team that appeared on the Mintex in February 1982", recalled David Sutton.

"On the first working day of January 1982 four mechanics from our workforce [which had sadly been reduced by redundancies in the weeks following that Rothmans Escort Championship victory, and was once down to five mechanics although late 1983 saw Sutton's operation with eight in the workshops

— J.W.] were out in Ingolstadt building the first works Quattro by outsiders. We built a brand new car to 1981 specification — and we built it there because all the parts were to hand and we could learn by example".

Back in Acton, West London, David and his tiny team prepared to move from the well-known cramped cavern at 11 Colville Road to newer premises, literally just around the corner. Here separate factory units could look after customers bread and butter servicing needs, while a small workshop across the road, with administrative offices and a compact stores, tended to the rally cars. At that point "David Sutton Motorsport Ltd" was founded to look after all Audi business, leaving David Sutton Cars "alive and well", having disposed of all the Rothmans Escorts only 11 months after that 1981 RAC, with the last of the spare parts for the defunct team slowly clearing the premises one year and two months after that historic RAC. Thus the need for clearly separate companies . . .

n the clag as usual! Germany's 1982 national champion Harald Demuth gets the 80 off to a lively start with Mike Greasley on the 1983 Mintex. Note the Fuchs wheels on the BBS-backed saloon . . . !

Sutton selected Mikkola without hesitation. "After all it was Hannu who got me into Audi — besides which he is the finest driver I could have . . . And I still believe he's a lot more to offer in 1984, and beyond. Look at that sensational drive on the 1983 Scottish and the 1000 Lakes. Magnificent! No other word for it. Hannu could also teach us how to service the thing. The Quattro is relatively easy to build — in fact it's even quicker than an Escort to assemble now that it's got those bolt-on plastic and Kevlar outer panels. Just work on a bare car, all round, then pop the panels on afterwards.

"But the problem I could see was in the field. How would our lads get on servicing the Quattro? That's where I thought Hannu's experience would be so important. After all, we had been involved with the Escort for 13 years. We'd got used to 9 minute gearbox changes and all the rest of it". On a personal front it is also worth remembering that David and Jill Sutton's links with the Mikkolas are of the closest kind, for David and Jill are "godparents to the Mikkola's first-born child."

Whilst the Quattro was being constructed in Ingolstadt, January 1982 also saw Sutton move into those twin premises in Acton and Maldon, Essex-based engine expert, Terry Hoyle flying out to Bavaria for two days' engine tuition.

quattro

Ferrari fanatic and the top source of Ford-Cosworth BD-series engines, Mr Hoyle was the ideal man to learn the intricacies of turbocharged inline five-cylinder rally engines. Hoyle could keep Sutton and the inevitable demand from private customers satisfied whilst the factory suffered no extra hassle.

British Engine Parts

The first engine for the Quattro that became "LYV 4X", Mikkola's 1982 British Championship mount (it won the Welsh for Waldegard and contributed toward two 1983 British Championships for Darryl Weidner) was a factory five, but thereafter Terry Hoyle has regularly rebuilt four and five units, including all those used in the Sutton Quattro coupes, and some of the British 80 Quattro engines too.

By 1983 Hoyle had also built up two brand new Quattro five cylinder units that had both joined the Weidner collection — the Clearlite-sponsored Quattro driver needing two cars for his 1983 season: the ex-Ron Hudson car "VRP 675W" and the ex-Sutton machine "LYV 4X". In both cases Hoyle supplied new engines and these featured a very extensive British supply element: Cosworth pistons, Hoyle-cam profile and nitrided crankshaft, new connecting rods and replacement flywheels by G.A. Farndon in Leicestershire. The cylinder head casting was by Audi, but the head's modified porting was the result of British work, including a contribution from Weslake. Incidentally the Hoyle British-sourced engines tended to run 6.7:1cr, instead of the factory's normal 6.3 to 6.5:1, favouring higher compression to reduce turbo lag.

Inside Darryl Weidner's Newcastle upon Tyne workshops, the Team Clearlite Quattro collection seems to breed! Darryl's 1983 RAC coupe is in the foreground.

It should be emphasised that the Sutton Quattros for the British Championship remained faithful to the factory philosophy and parts supply; Hoyle rebuilding them along the strict factory lines and using the British sources to satisfy his own creativity and to reduce costs for private customers. In Britain in 1983 a new factory engine unit would have cost the equivalent of £17,000,

or £9500 rebuilt: Hoyle's last engine for Weidner cost around £10,000.

Power? Hoyle and Sutton stayed with the mechanical Pierburg fuel-injection system as a matter of philosophy, even when the factory went Bosch electronic on the A2, because the mechanical system gave better bottom end response on Britain's 'blind' rallies. The A2 Audi Sport Bosch electronic injection/ignition specification likes to live only above 5000rpm, whereas they reckon maximum torque for a Hoyle-rebuilt Pierburg motor occurs at 3600 to 3700rpm. "Don't ask me how much torque it's got", said Terry, "we just found it banged off the end of the scale at the equivalent of 305lb.ft . . . so we've got to get another machine in to find out!" Power? On 1.7 bar/24.2psi they find about 340 to 350bhp. Certainly Michele Mouton was *very* complementary about the low rpm power characteristics of the Pierburg-Hoyle five she had when demoralising all trace of opposition, male or otherwise, in winning the October 1983 Audi Sport National over stages well known to her rivals.

Another divergence in specification from current factory thinking has been the British team's use of Pirelli tyres. Sutton said, "we needed an additional source of revenue, and Kleber in 1982 could not really cope with us. In 1983, when the factory [Audi] went to Michelin, we stayed on with Pirelli. Also we have been with Duckhams and now BP, while the factory have a Castrol contract."

The 1982 Season

In four of five qualifying rounds to the 1982 Rothmans RAC British Open Rally Championship the white Sutton Quattro with its distinctive red Pirelli "noseband" was driven by Mikkola, partnered by Arne Hertz. When Mikkola had to contest the Corsican World championship round for the factory Mikkola's former team-mate at Ford, Sweden's Bjorn Waldegard, slotted into LYV 4X for the Welsh International Home Championship event. Navigator Phil Short became the first Briton to win an international rally in a Quattro. The hard-worked Quattro also appeared in one rallysprint and for the Tour of Cumbria plus the RAC. The latter two events tackled with gritty style by a youngster Ford had groomed for stardom, Malcolm Wilson.

Results? In the home international series Mikkola finished third amongst the drivers — 35 points to the 47 of Champion Jimmy McRae in an Opel — and Audi were runners-up in the makes section, nine points behind Opel. The Mikkola season started well enough with a 3m 43s win over Toivonen's Opel on the boggy Mintex, but the tarmac Circuit of Ireland saw the Quattro struggle home sixth.

"One of the lessons we learned from 1982 was looking after the driveline, which gave constant problems", David Sutton recollected. "We used to get front diffs breaking; at the best this means taking off the sump guard and a [very hot] exhaust system. This car's not like the Lancia, a purpose-built competition machine. It uses the standard floorpan and suspension pick-up points for example, and you simply have to learn to live with some aspects, such as the time to change transmission components. For instance we now have three bolt-fixing for the driveshafts, whereas the original was a six bolt, so that's three bolts that don't have to be fiddled with anymore! So far as the gearbox is concerned, that has been simplified in 1983 with the shorter gearbox, and we have learned to change it faster and faster. I reckon we need to be under 20 minutes to stay in a World Championship rally effectively. We started off at over 30 minutes on the 1982 Circuit and our last change, in the 1983 Manx, was 25 minutes, so we're getting there."

quattro

The 1982 Circuit of Ireland brought little joy to the UK Quattro team, but Mikkola and Hertz finished the season with Mikkola third in the points after winning two rounds outright.

After Easter in Ireland, Waldegard took over the car in Mikkola's absence and, co-driven by the paradoxically lanky Phil Short, the British-based Quattro toddled to a 1m 58s victory in Wales. "The first international victory for a British co-driver in a Quattro", Sutton proudly recalled — along with the British drivers used in both Quattro and 80 Quattro on occasion — to vehemently reject any charge that he and Audi UK "Shun the Brits" as one sporting magazine headlined a story days before we met.

The 1982 Scottish looked as though it would be a Mikkola disaster: "you know, if there are three identical works cars lined up ready to go, brand-new, Hannu will *always* draw the one that breaks early on", expounded Sutton with feeling. "He just has to be the unluckiest driver in World class rallying". However, as the skilled rally correspondents often pointed out at the sight of yet another mechanical misfit staggering down the order, it is a lot better to suffer trouble early on, when competitors are comparatively closely bunched, rather than later. Then the time deficit, which is what matters, rather than the number of places lost, is minimal.

In the June 1982 Arnold Clark Scottish Rally, Mikkola's Quattro suffered a broken steering arm on the opening stage. This left the right front wheel flapping to-and-fro with no sense of direction, but Mikkola was able to finish Strathclyde Park anyway — in a series of backward, patiently-judged, lunges! There were 49 stages on that year's Scottish and it was hard to find anyone apart from fellow Finn Vatanen (MCD Ford Escort RS) getting much more than a peek at the fastest times thereafter. Mikkola simply tore away at the deficit and emerged with 35 fastest stage times, and a half minute lead over McRae's Opel: a win achieved only in the final stages of the event. As when Mikkola had flown a Ford Escort through a disbelieving field a decade previously on the same event, it was the stuff legends are rightly made of; Hannu finally emerging in the lead only three stages from the finish.

quattro

Long distance ace Andrew Cowan gave the Quattro 80 of Audi Sport UK an outing on the 1983 Scottish with Alan Douglas alongside, making a film for Scottish TV! They were seventh overall, one place and 12 seconds ahead of Weidner's ex-Hudson coupe; some 24m 36s behind Winner Blomqvist's Quattro coupe.

A new factory aluminium block engine was installed for the Manx that year, the team looking for the ultimate in power from their charge on what promised to be a difficult event for the large 4-WD. Even Mikkola's talents could squeeze no more than two third fastest, four fourth-quickest — and nine fifth-fastest times before the engine slowed, a piston ring failure eliminating the Quattro.

Mikkola was in a factory car to dominate the 1982 RAC Rally, so Wilson was given a chance to warm-up on the Tour of Cumbria (leading comfortably until a last stage rummage in the undergrowth!) and then contested the RAC in LYV 4X. Sharing with motoring writer and then keeper of a Quattro on the

Darryl Weidner in one of the two Quattros he used to secure both British national championships in 1983. This is the ex-Ron Hudson machine — originally RHD — and Weidner also used much of Mikkola's 1982 machine (LYV 4X) on the championship trail.

171

road, Michael Greasley, the pair of Brits started slowly. Once Malcolm had given the fabled left foot braking "the elbow" they progressed steadily upward, finishing tenth overall. This wasn't really the result MW was looking for, as Russell Brookes was "Best Brit" in sixth overall with a Chevette. Yet Wilson had the sense to get the car safely to the end — not an easy driving task for someone raised on bravery and simple Escort handling — and he had more fastest stage times (four) than any other British driver, so the potential for greater things was there.

The A-Team

Whilst LYV 4X went to Darryl Weidner to begin his astonishing assault on the British National Championships of 1982, the Sutton team regrouped with new machinery. I wrote "the Sutton *team*" and that is exactly what I meant, for it is easy to overlook the men behind the personable glamour of David and Jill Sutton, men who make things happen in the field. For example there is the quiet expertise of Ron Lumley, chief engineer. The kind of man who can look at a dying competition engine, scant stages away from victory, speedily examine and rectify what is essential to its survival, and send it on to a win that otherwise would have been an out-of-time non-finish.

Lumley's longest serving co-conspirator on the mechanical front has been John O'Connor, but these full-time Sutton survivors were also augmented regularly on events by mechanical freelances of the stature of Alan Clegg (ex-Boreham, now a partner in Pace Engineering) and former Talbot team member Paul Ridgeway. The Quattro's complicated electrics demand inside expert help and David Sutton is fortunate enough to have attracted voluntary assistance from VAG employee John Bevan.

Much better known Sutton team men have been Graham Rood and Allen Wilkinson. Rood has the kind of expertise that makes his employment at Farnborough's air research establishment seem natural, but his Sutton part-time skills have been connected with ensuring that the team is properly co-ordinated on-event. Graham's skills, earned over 13 years with Sutton teams could be interchanged with those of a professional co-driver, but he has remained outside the helter skelter of competition itself. Level-headed judgement delivered concisely but with a smile from a bearded countenance that has seen mechanical and human folly and its worst consequences — but within remains a strong rally enthusiast.

Allen Wilkinson was a much higher-profile member of the team. An outspoken engineer with a forceful talent that was aptly rewarded by winning the Escort Mexico Racing Championship whilst at Ford Advanced Vehicles. Wilkinson worked not only for Ford Competition during their World Championship zenith, but also for Toyota in Cologne. Allen returned to Britain to set up on his own as a consultant design engineer in time to join Sutton's Quattro effort for much of the 1982-83 seasons. He left "officially" in July 1983, but was persuaded out for the final Championship round of that season, the Manx. By which time he'd confirmed his reputation for engineering that worked, with an alternative tarmac suspension system for the Sutton Quattro that saw the 4-WD win its first all-tarmac international in 1983. By the time this is read Wilkinson will be better known for his project work on the Mitsubishi 4-WD project, being replaced at the Sutton works by Wynne Mitchell. Wynne was one of the engineering forces behind the creation of the Sunbeam Talbot Lotus formula that won the 1981 World title for Talbot and ended eight years of Escort victories on the RAC Rally. Prior to joining Sutton he had been assisting W.B. Blydenstein's Datsun and Vauxhall rally programmes.

For 1983 the Sutton mechanics ventured once more to Ingolstadt to construct two brand new Quattros. These would become MVV 44Y, Stig Blomqvist's regular British Championship coupe, and VMN 44 — a registration of Manx origin needed because the 80 Quattro to which it was attached (usually driven by Harald Demuth) was not then type-approved on the British mainland.

The coupe was simply a big-winged A1 of the then-new Quattro Group B 1983 breed, and it stayed faithful to Pierburg mechanical injection throughout the British season. During the season it could have gained an increasing number of British parts, as Sutton arranged alternative sources for some customer cars, and his own team. For example roll cages could come from Safety Devices, fuel tanks from Premier and all those external lightweight plastics were eventually made in the UK too. Of course the engines were rebuilt by Terry Hoyle, and David Sutton acquired all the tools necessary for his outfit to become the first outside the works capable of maintaining the transmission systems of a competition Quattro; gearboxes and differentials included.

Sutton was proud of the amount of British parts sourcing for practical reasons: "in 1982 we had people trailing to and from the factory all the time. In 1983 we made just one trip per rally". Incidentally the bodyshell of a works Quattro can benefit from an old Sutton liaison with Gartrac at Godalming, Surrey. After seeing the work they could do on the coupe body, Ingolstadt sent a total of three shells for complete preparation by the English experts, who found working on the Quattro body "quite straightforward. You just have to watch that all the mounting bracketry is absolutely right and that the roll cage is also fitted absolutely right to do its job as crash protection and a second chassis", opined Gartrac co-founder David Bignold. When I researched a little further I found that Gartrac had made extraordinary efforts on detail quality and finish work to meet German standards, whilst retaining a lower cost advantage over Matter owing to the obvious differences in British and German labour rates. Coals to Ingolstadt!

As to the time taken to build each new Quattro Sutton insisted, "it was really much the same as the Escort, four to five weeks, or less for the Audi if we had all the parts to hand. We've noticed that, unlike the Ford, you had to do less of the little fiddly bits of fabrication — such as a 50p bracket that takes a man three hours — and that speeds things up. And, as I have said, the access to work all round the cars, is much better with all those plastic outer panels to just bolt in place afterwards."

For 1983 Audi wanted "to broaden their rallying appeal to Joe Public. After all a factory Quattro is the equivalent of an F1 car: you can't play unless you've got £75,000. So the 80 Quattro made a lot of sense and it's a car we and the factory see as the right one for customers — so we'll be doing more on that front in 1984, along with a Clubman's Audi 80 Sport, front drive", revealed David Sutton.

The 80 Quattro was basically along the lines of the car Blomqvist used on the Swedish, so it was entered in Group B but had all the equipment it would carry in Group A. That meant it was very heavy by competition Quattro standards: whilst Sutton's A1 coupe with its Kevlar panels and lightweight doors weighed 1130kg with over 330 turbocharged horsepower, the poor 80 had most of its steel panels in place and 1260kg for "185 to 190bhp at 7500rpm", according to engine builder Terry Hoyle.

Incidentally the 80's engine spec could change from event to event as the chronic lack of straightline speed — more attributable to weight rather than deficiencies in the 2.1-litre five — led them into trying German, Kolb Tuning, engines. Whichever unit was used, rally correspondents did not receive warm and glowing references to the power and reliability of said non-turbocharged

quattro

units — and the car started the year with better British placings than it was to achieve later in the season, by which time Toyota and Per Eklund had Group A, UK-style, wrapped and tied in a pretty corporate ribbon!

Charged with a lack of British driver sentiment in a line up that included Bjorn Cederberg co-driving Blomqvist in the coupe and Harald Demuth, 1982 German Champion, with Michael Greasley (later Arwed Fischer, when Demuth returned to the wheel after a bad German Quattro testing accident) Sutton said, "we approached two Britons to drive the 80 Quattro. And they both turned us down flat! So we had to ask the factory to fill the 80 seat as well. We tried . . ."

I understand that Mikkola could not drive in Britain during 1983 because of his extensive, and successful, World Championship challenge. Blomqvist was a logical choice: he had appeared in Britain pretty regularly with SAAB and, to a lesser extent Talbot, and Audi wanted to keep him as busy as possible in 1983. Thus Stig's Audi contracts for 1983 initially included six British Championship rounds (Ulster had been added to the schedule after a long absence: a very tight tarmac event, compressed into 23 hours) and six World title events, plus the Swedish series.

Stig Blomqvist began the UK season at home in the snow with the first of four 1983 wins in Britain, scored on February's Mintex.

The 1983 Season

As ever, February, in and around the Yorkshire moors and forest, supplied the kind of going that any 4-WD machine laps up. Some snow and fog added to the fun so far as Blomqvist was concerned and he motored away from any trace of real opposition, settling for 6m 6s victory margin over McRae's Opel. Stig's former SAAB soulmate, Eklund, was an astonishing third, but Demuth debuted the 80 Quattro honourably enough in England, finishing fifth.

The Circuit of Ireland yielded nothing but grief, although Blomqvist in the Wilkinson-revised Quattro started in stunning form and led until a gearbox failure away from the service mothercraft eliminated the Swedes. The 80Q went astonishingly well over mostly dry tarmac, inside the top ten, but ended its rally against (in succession) an Alfa Romeo Course Car and a dry stone wall. Sutton dryly told me how they had managed to rebuild the car around the existing shell, although the front section was completely new.

Blomqvist's second win of the season came in another crushing defeat for the RWD brigade over the Welsh International's unique combination of first class forest and the nerve-tingling secret tarmac twists (to some, more secret than others!) of Eppynt military ranges. This time Blomqvist left the winning margin

Classic Welsh forest action and precision motoring from Blomqvist in the BBS-wheeled A1 Quattro. While Blomqvist and Bjorn Cederberg dominated the Welsh with an 8 minute victory, Audi were facing a tough time in the World Championship qualifyer on the island of Corsica.

Bjorn Waldegard/Phil Short took over LYV 4X for the Welsh and won on Waldegard's debut in the car! Here they attack Eppynt military ranges on a run that took them to victory by less than two minutes over Toivonen's Opel.

quattro

slightly under eight minutes: he wasn't beaten on stage time until they got to tarmac and the 16th of 24 stages, by which time his lead was enormous anyway. Also appearing on this event was Lasse Lampi's LYV 5X, a car re-shelled from Mouton's Monte Carlo house-hitting wreck, and that finished third. The 80 Quattro was crewed by Weidner and Greasley following Demuth's testing debacle; it finished just over a minute outside the top ten after a run that saw some alarm about the engine's oil pressure.

Stig Blomqvist in Scotland displayed a mastery of the loose that left the chief opposition from the GM pair — a Chevette for Brookes and an Opel Manta for McRae — 4m 35s adrift at the end, McRae second. The Quattro coupe was now well in its stride, and heading toward the British title; Blomqvist sharing the Championship lead with Brookes at the end. There were other Quattros out in Scotland too: the 80 was given to Andrew "Marathon Man" Cowan with BBC man Alan Douglas, while Weidner had the ex-Hudson coupe out in LHD trim, also with an engine from Hoyle. Cowan was seventh and Weidner eighth, his Quattro co-driven by Greasley and just 12 seconds behind after four days rallying.

In 1984 more international forays were on the menu with Phil Short in a coupe as well as a very special turbo 80 (whose Acton premises and star quality appearance we also show).

Super Stig in action. The Sutton-prepared Quattro revelled in mainly wet Scottish conditions to lead from start to finish.

Now the terrain was unlikely to favour the Quattros in the remainder of the British series, for both Ulster and the Manx events concentrate on tarmac stages. Undaunted, Wilkinson and the Sutton team had revised steering castor angles and installed hardware reflecting their own ideas on spring rates and damper settings to provide a car that clearly could cope with tarmac efficiently. Of twenty-five stages Blomqvist was through fastest on eleven and the Swede only relinquished the lead briefly when a driveshaft failed and demanded replacement. Although that was almost a minor problem, compared with the constant worries over fuel pressure — or lack of it for the injection system — that Wilkinson eventually traced to a fuel line blockage. By then the fuel pumps had been replaced at least four times! The Quattro burst back into the lead, and kept it until the end: Blomqvist rather relieved that the trouble had been cured, both from a British Championship viewpoint and the fact that such problems had often cost World Championship Quattros more than a temporary loss of competitiveness.

Not so lucky in Ulster was Demuth, who covered but eight stages before an engine failure eliminated the 80 Quattro.

The final British Championship round provided multiple use, in daylight, of the classic Isle of Man tarmac tests. The Audi UK team arrived with Blomqvist in an almost secure Driver's Championship lead that could only be eradicated by Brookes and the Chevette winning. The 80 Quattro was also on hand for Demuth/Fischer, now running in Group A, as it had been on the Ulster.

It rained heavily in the initial stages and the Quattro proved an embarrassment over puddles, aquaplaning badly on the broad rubber used for tarmac, so that Blomqvist had to allow "a little bit of space, wherever there was standing water". At the end of the first section Blomqvist was seventh, a brace of Finnish-driven Opels dominating proceedings to prophesy Toivonen's first international victory since the 1980 RAC.

quattro

Flying today: the Rothmans Manx was unlucky for Blomqvist in 1983, but he still grasped the British title, despite an engine failure late in the event.

Blomqvist fought back as conditions got a little dryer and was third at the close of the second leg, 1m 26s ahead of Brookes. However, as the battle between Blomqvist and Brookes literally reached the final stages the Quattro's engine let a connecting rod liberate itself. In theory Brookes might have done some kind of deal with the two GM Manta drivers ahead to let the Vauxhall through, to be rewarded with the British Open title (for Drivers; the Makes series was pre-destined for Toyota), but all the background politicking failed to produce any kind of fix. So Stig Blomqvist, driving a David Sutton Motorsport Audi Quattro A1, annexed the 1983 Rothmans RAC British Open Championship title, by three points over Brookes.

Incidentally the 80 also finished in the Manx top ten, tenth behind two Group A Toyotas.

Throughout the British season Blomqvist had shown all those qualities that make him such a formidable competitor at world class level. "A complete professional", was David Sutton's summary, and you could say the team behind him was also composed of Complete Professionals, except that some of them are there courtesy of other employers "on holiday" and unpaid! That is the exception rather than the rule, but it shows you the kind of magnetism the Sutton-bred Quattro has brought to British rallying's premier series.

To emphasise the professional team point, be reminded by David Sutton of "the rather flattering thing that happened within three months of us signing with Audi". Sutton Motorsport found themselves looking after Italian Quattro charger Michael Cinotto and that led to co-servicing arrangements on both the Acropolis and San Remo of 1982, plus solo responsibility for the works entries in New Zealand and Brazil that year. There is no higher mark of respect from a German factory team!

* * *

So, in both Britain and America rallying was used to promote both the Quattro and the overall image of Audi. How much success did it have?

In 1982 VAG at Milton Keynes began their Quattro rallying association in the UK with David Sutton under the Audi Sport UK banner. The Group 4 car was crewed by Hannu Mikkola/Arne Hertz at most British championship rounds. Here it is on its way to Yorkshire for the opening round, stopping off at Milton Keynes for display on roadwheels and tyres.

To discover the commercial answer to that query I went along to the Milton Keynes HQ of VW-Audi in Great Britain. Within a cool office of greenery and swooping chrome lamps Managing Director Michael Heelas asserted, ''it's

Michael Heelas.

quattro

The 1984 specification Audi Quattro arrives in Britain with its 8 inch wide Ronal wheels and P7 tyres, plus ABS braking, digital dashboard and many other features. Ray Hutton, editor of *Autocar*, looks from the cabin of that magazine's 53,000 mile LHD long term test car, at the scarlet newcomer. As of March **1984** this Quattro retailed in Great Britain at £20,401.77p, compared with £17,721.98p for the previous RHD model.

definitely been good for us and for Audi in Great Britain. Before we started this motorsports programme people were not quite sure what Audi stood for: not quite a Mercedes or a BMW — not even a Ford in Britain. Now that image is much crisper and we have leap-frogged past Ford. People have seen in the Quattro programme that we can not only make four-wheel-drive to win competition, but that it also works on our road cars for sale to the public.

"We now sell about 100,000 VWs and Audis in Britain. Some 30 per cent of that total are Audis, and that percentage is increasing. Why? I think motorsports have played a part — in fact I am so convinced of that, I can sit here in late 1983 and tell you that we will definitely be back in 1984. The drivers are not decided as we speak, in fact it's possible we may even run two Quattro coupes in addition to the 80 Quattro that Darryl Weidner will use in 1984, but I can tell you that other commercial concerns view the Quattro in rallying as very good news indeed. In fact we have three oil companies offering sponsorship and outfits such as Hella obviously feel that the TV exposure is very worthwhile with their lamps well displayed in each head-on shot."

Most MDs are pretty reluctant to discuss what motor sport costs, but Mr Heelas agreed that a figure of a quarter of a million pounds was a reasonable 1984 season estimate. "You must remember that sponsorship is offset against this first cost — and we can sell the car at the end of the year, so it is a very cost-effective way of getting a message, and an image, to the public.

"I would say that those small paragraphs you see in the *Express,* or any other daily paper are worth much more in advertising and publicity terms than you might think. Remember that each paper is likely to have something in, and you'll see that if a headline says Mikkola's Audi wins, then backed up in a number of papers and the specialist press, it is worth the same as a full page advertisement.

"Yet the *World of Sport* twenty minutes on a Saturday is worth most of the lot. Imagine, twenty minutes TV with the sort of success we've had this year . . . the costs are really peanuts beside that", felt this experienced manager

Centre of attention. Since David Sutton started running the Quattros in Britain, they have created this kind of interest. This is Blomqvist's 1983 A1 tended by John O'Connor, Terry Hoyle, Graham Rood and Pirelli's UK motorsport manager, Andy Hallam. This atmospheric picture, like most of the Sutton Quattro in this book, is by David Bryant at VAG.

quattro

This winter, you could have the only high performance car on the road.

Permanent four wheel drive gives both the
Audi Quattro and Audi 80 Quattro twice the grip of other cars.

Pub ammo on the Audi Quattro:
0·60 in 6.7* seconds, top speed 137mph,
2.2 litre turbo-charged fuel injected
engine, 200 brake horse power, 5 speed
gearbox, permanent 4 wheel drive.

Official government fuel consumption figures: urban, 18.3mpg (15.4
1/100km); 56mph, 34.9mpg (8.11/100km);
75mph, 27.4mpg (10.31/100km).

Brochures from Audi Marketing,
V.A.G (UK) Limited,
Yeomans Drive,
Blakelands, Milton
Keynes MK14 5AN.
*What Car?

Quattro advertising, like
all VAG advertising in
Britain has been full of
original thought and
frequently pugnacious.
Responsible for these
examples were BBH, who
were appointed in 1983 as
Audi's UK advertising
agency.

with a wealth of motor industry experience behind him, including Ford's biggest
retail vendors (Bristol Street Motors) and Mercedes-Benz in Britain, when that
concession was owned by Thomas Tilling.

* * *

Sales Story

So what has been the effect of two years rallying in Britain and America,
combined with the overall high profile publicity that the Quattro attracts? How
many Quattros have been sold in these major markets, and in what specification?

The American model had the most obvious differences from the usual
European LHD Quattro coupe. Sales started in January 1982, and 154 were sold
in 1982, whilst Buffum scored their first 4-WD North American victories after
years of playing with various modified front drive USA derivatives. In 1983 some
235 Audi Quattro coupes had been sold by September.

By comparison the British market received its first supplies of the Quattro
coupe in November 1980, although these cars were destined for evaluation —
sales beginning Spring 1981. From the initial chassis (85 BA 90099) onward just
163 LHD Quattro coupes were sold in Britain; a sizeable percentage of these
now converted (sometimes disastrously in terms of poor brakes) to RHD.

quattro

Snow on the hills, it's spring in the moorland above Torquay! The Quattro arrived in Britain as an LHD-only machine but a number of RHD conversions finally convinced Ingolstadt it was better to offer this facility ex-factory.

August 1982, and chassis number 85 DA 900556, saw the commencement of RHD imports to Britain of the Quattro; just a year and two months later 366 had been sold. Which tells you a lot about how the British dislike LHD . . . Incidentally the 80 Quattro had only been on sale for a month when this was written and over 100 sold in that time as a result of orders waiting whilst the Type Approval was sorted out.

Naturally the American models had the most detail differences, suiting them to life in emission and crash-conscious USA. Externally the obvious changes included the impact-absorbing front and rear bumpers, and unique headlamps to comply with local laws.

Internally there was American instrumentation and a fuel system adapted to run unleaded fuel, including a replacement fuel filler neck and appropriate adjustments to the electronic ignition.

John Buffum is normally partnered by Doug Shepherd in the American Quattro, but here Buffum is out on his own scoring a win on Pike's Peak in the 1983 A1 car that also visited Britain for the RAC Rally.

The five-cylinder engine included a catalytic convertor layout (called the Lander Closed Loop Centre). The effect on power compared with Europe was predictably dire. A June 1982 *Road & Track* test showed that the 3115lb Quattro had 40bhp less than the European models. The official total was 160bhp at 5500rpm coupled to 170lb. ft torque at 3000rpm. In test form this had to power over 3200lb, distributed 58 per cent front, 42 per cent rear.

R&T discovered gear speeds of 33mph in first, 56mph in second, 88mph in third and 125mph in fourth. In the land of an overall 55mph speed limit and where many speedometers are curtailed at 85mph, this popular American monthly magazine discovered that 5500rpm, instead of 6500 in the lower gears, was the maximum revs they could attain. That meant a maximum speed 9mph down on Europe: 128mph. Acceleration? The American model returned a respectable 0-60mph time of 8.2 seconds and took just over 23 seconds to reach 100mph from rest. Full specification of all production Quattro types, including that for DSA, are supplied in the appendices.

"Audi's all wheel, all weather assault weapon. A legend in its own time, and the most sophisticated machine man knows how to make." Those words come from America's *Car Driver* monthly magazine and describe how they feel about the 160 horsepower Federal version of the Quattro coupe shown here in 1984 trim. A full specification of the US Quattro is given in the appendices.

In the English-speaking export world it was what the Quattro said about Audi and high technology that mattered rather more than sales performance graphs. We look at some of the printable memories the Quattro produced in the next chapter.

Chapter 10

Quattrophenia

The headline is one that got rejected the first time I tried it on an editor, but has since been widely used and I take to mean a complete mania for four-wheel-drivers of the Ingolstadt kind. Here are some memories of notable Quattros from the standard 80 to a testing ride in Mikkola's machine, prior to the RAC Rally, and a driving session in the 350bhp A1 that won the British Championship for Blomqvist in 1983.

These experiences are at the heart of why one should write a book about the Quattro, for money certainly is not a priority reason for any motoring book on a royalty basis! The Quattro is not a beautiful car at rest, but see one striding away from a hairpin up a loose RAC forest slope, stones, dirt and water spray in its wake, and the sight is striking enough to stay in your mind's eye. The worse the weather, the better Quattro-spectating becomes. The slides become ever more exaggerated as the (frequently) misted-up interiors allow pale-faced crews much the same visibility as the enormous man-made forest of Kielder in North Eastern Britain provides at anything after midday on a November day: minimal! Even when the factory fitted front screen heaters, *a la* sixties Mini, for the 1982 RAC there was a special spectating memory.

I had, unwisely, stepped out of the car at the appropriately nicknamed Kielder service area of Splashetts in what appeared to be the final downpour before Noah set sail in the ark.

As my companion's unseemly laughter at my floundering form was shut off by the closing door of our snug (and borrowed) £17,000 plus Quattro, I thought of

"Grip" it says — and that's exactly what you do when the David Sutton equipe let you climb behind the wheel of an A1 Quattro . . .

Just needed an excuse to wheel out the *ooh la la* cliches: Michele Mouton came to Britain before the RAC of 1983 to mop up the Audi national, prior to a rather disappointing outing on the Lombard RAC international a few weeks later.

all the places I would rather be than watching Quattros prove that motoring to the end of the world in a deluge is no problem, if you are a world class crew in the most technically advanced rally car yet.

Moving into the service area like a salmon forging upstream, I homed-in on the open passenger door of Mouton's coupe. Inside, the glow of instruments and Mademoiselle frantically rubbing down her high-tech heated screen with Gallic curses. "Is no good, uh?" she greeted the wet invader, "I get no 'eat, see nuzzing

quattro

— and Fabrizia, she can see all what is 'appening. She sees the accident before me. It's crazy!'' The giggles followed frequently as I sat and surveyed the comfortable hot cockpit and listened to this modest miss describe setting some of the fastest times ever seen in this daunting complex, a forest that's reckoned to summon all Mikkola's considerable British experience. I swam back to my now slumbering companion in our ''roadie'' considerably warmed by the humanity within a Quattro that eventually went on to finish second. By which time I was an even more respectful fan of both the Quattros and the crews who inhabit them, for it is not a car from which it is easy to extract the full potential; but, if you are brave and skilful enough, the rewards over loose going are spectacular indeed.

The Quattro love affair for me started with a brush-off. Geneva 1980 and the world's press was clamouring for details whilst the German press walked out in protest at *Auto Motor und Sport* having scooped them all; apparently with factory co-operation. My own concern was to get details of the new car back for a front page item in *Motoring News:* gently letting them know that a colleague would be driving the car, whilst I sat out this first encounter. Nothing rankles in the motoring memory like having been left off the select invitees list when your playmates return with ecstatic stories of amazing traction and a new standard in transportation — so, when the car came to Britain, I approached it coolly, to say the least.

Audi UK had the first supplies of LHD Quattro coupes at £14,500 each ready for the British press to assess in March 1981. By then the car had won its first World Championship event in Sweden and had shown demoralising potential wherever else it had competed, so there was little chance of anyone overlooking Audi's newcomer, even though it was introduced with the visually very similar Audi Coupe to the UK market.

German-registered silver Quattro coupe made up the numbers on the English press launch in 1981. Here it provides comfortable and capable thrills over Dartmoor, and bears evidence that Peter Newton (editor, *Cars & Car Conversions*) and myself had been re-searching the loose surface grip over a track laid on by VAG.

The interior was functional but in no way outshone price rivals of the time such as the BMW 732i at £14,325 or Jaguar's £13,100 XJ6 3.4, or the Lotus Esprit at £13,461. In fact there was not even as much instrument information as on a Capri 3.0S at under £7000. The big white on black dials suggested speeds beyond the highest indicated (140mph) and recorded safe rpm to a recommended maximum of 6000. Minor dials included only a clock and a boost gauge − the latter marked so that the maximum 0.85 bar boost looked like nearer 2 bar and could have caused a flutter of anxiety for the engine's health because + 1.85 bar would equate to far beyond what the World Championship cars currently use as full boost! There is a simple explanation. You have to remember that 1 bar is ambient atmospheric pressure, Audi pedantically indicating this as well as boosted pressure, where most manufacturers use a scale that shows only the boost *above* atmospheric pressure.

The seating was somewhat gaudy in sports checks, and none too durable in *Autocar's* 40,000 mile plus experience, but it was very comfortable and held you tight even in the most awe-inspiring moments. The latter were unfortunately common for British journalists who did get a lot of miles on the early cars: it later transpired that some of the cars the UK received were not adjusted within the rather fine factory limits of suspension tolerance. In fact, after the Summer of 1982, Audi were able to incorporate the revised linkages discussed in our Audi 80 Quattro chapter, which eliminated much of the on-the-limit twitchiness that three of my respected colleagues complained about. I came to the conclusion that I simply wasn't trying hard enough, or that the cars I drove were absolutely right, for I experienced nothing but handling pleasure at the Quattro's four-spoke, leather-rimmed wheel. I subsequently found things a lot dicier on the loose or on ice, but even then I didn't end up entering the weeds, backwards, as two friends did . . . at *very* high road speeds!

The original launch Quattro I shared over Dartmoor was German-registered, and had already been timed in its Fatherland at the equivalent of 136.62mph: a speed it reached for with startling eagerness, despite that rather restrictive clanking gearbox with its barely 50mph second. Reverse was not easy to select and the view backwards was awful in the finest tradition of high-tailed, heavy hindquarter coupe sheet metal.

The inline five-cylinder turbo engine had a truly distinct note, much gruffer than the 170bhp Audi 200 Turbo in which I had covered a wet, wheel-tugging, week in 1980. I said at the time in *Motoring News:* "feels like a 3.5 litre V8 (sounds a bit like one too from the twin pipes) in response to the throttle between 3000 and 4500 rpm. Then it gets its second wind and just flies to 6000rpm". I can see no reason to change that quote, although it was at low rpm that the five had the most pronounced V-burble, thereafter having more in common with a four than an inline six.

Outstanding early impressions were of a car built to give road pleasure and normal standards of civility and service. This came as a rude shock to those, like myself, who were used to British homologation specials of the Escort RS type. Here was a 200bhp machine that rode so smoothly over the Devon bumps, power steered its way adeptly over standing water or city junctions and had the engine manners of a Ford V6 in production trim. Yet it really did go! Until then we had been used to a fair bit of pain from rally-related road cars − in my experience only the Renault 5 Turbo was as well developed, and that was inevitably noisier with 160bhp drumming through a lightweight metal and glassfibre body from a mid-engine position.

This original Quattro had the cable-operated differentials and I tended to use the rear one only for wet roads, feeling that the extra rear traction under power might help me induce final oversteer on each corner's exit, instead of the car's

quattro

natural understeer which gets worse on slippier surfaces. On the muddy field provided to test the Goodyear 205 section-shod Quattro, both differentials were utilised, but I did try the first run without the left foot braking that had been instilled within me by a succession of loose surface or ice racing encounters in front drive hatchbacks. The Quattro rumbled away from the line with exhortations from companion, and *CCC* editor, Peter "Go For It" Newton to *attack* said muddy track, or forever be branded a wimp. The first corner saw us run straight off under conventional braking, skirt the shrubbery and rejoin a few yards further on. The mud still flew from under Quattro's four arches with great vigour so we pressed on, each subsequent curve an adventure literally beyond the beaten track.

By the second and third runs I had resorted to applying brakes and power at the same time; making some sense as the turbocharger is thus working at full efficiency and the front turns in without washing out in understeer. I must emphasise that I only find this necessary on mud or slippier surfaces, but that at very low first and second gear speeds it's not necessary at all . . . If you're name is Stig Blomqvist. Said Swede demonstrated an 80 Quattro in standard form to me on an ice circuit of mainly sub-40mph curves and simply drove conventionally saying "it's not worth it at these slow speeds", and proving it as we went along. However, the next passenger got dumped straight in a snow bank, so maybe even immortals change techniques during a day!

Those cable-operated differential locks worked with some delay before the green light indicated they were home, but I must say I preferred having a choice of which end was providing greater traction than is available with today's two stage centre, or centre plus rear selection. As to the centre differential being used to give additional braking security at low speeds and being unlocked at high speeds, I can only say that I prefer not mucking about with buttons at all whilst in serious action, so the present ABS option would appeal strongly — I have had my share of travelling ever onward in Quattros of all kinds with the wheels locked up under heavy braking at speeds from 30mph downhill on ice to 80mph on mud, all with the differentials locked. The problem is exactly as Bensinger said, you can accelerate at twice the pace, so your mind assumes you can stop equally quickly. By any standards outside 4-WD the Quattro stops eminently safely and is not likely to worry the sensible driver, but let the enthusiasm switch on your personal turbo over slippery going, and you had better be sure there's plenty of run-off space and no oncoming traffic!

In respects apart from its docile performance and astonishing stability — over cambers or in crosswinds it was particularly impressive, ideal for motorway travel on a wet and blustery day — the Quattro was similar to any other Audi to live with. The boot was cramped, particularly in Britain where compact spares were not allowed (they still were not *definitely* legal in late 1983 and VAG were therefore not installing them on UK cars), but the ventilation, prompt electric windows and neatly laid out rocker switchgear, three per side of the instrument binnacle, were all unobtrusively efficient in top teutonic style.

I later used one of the launch cars for a long racing weekend that involved going backwards and forwards between Snetterton and the Thames Valley and found these original impressions augmented only by annoyance with the gearbox. It really did clank from ratio to ratio and second gear was far too "short" for comfort, demanding swift upchanges on the way out of roundabouts, or some subtle third gear motoring in its place. The Quattro could be almost outpaced at lower traffic speeds by machines like the fleet Lotus-engined Sunbeam Talbot 2.2, but as soon as the Audi was on boost it would float away with marvellous ride and interior comfort, whilst the Sunbeam beat along with the owner crouched over the wheel in a 6000rpm rhapsody. Truly different eras.

Generally these early Quattros proved pretty durable, but spares prices were

One of the LHD 1981 press test fleet, WNH 53W had a very hard life, tackling all sorts of missions — including a sporting trial. I used it to commute to a Fiesta Championship race at Snetterton, the particular Fiesta I raced having a damaged gear linkage that made the Quattro change feel good by comparison!

right in the BMW league if *anything* required replacement. For instance *Autocar* recounted the tale of spark plugs at nearly £46 for five, and service bills close to £200: the latter not an unfamiliar level to other German car owners I suspect. Indeed some may even wish their prestige machinery was as cheap to look after! In 35,000 miles *Autocar* paid £488.58, major repairs confined to a warranty-replaced gearbox and the need to renew seized-on rear handbrake calipers just before 34,000 miles. Naturally that was out of warranty and amounted to the best part of £150 at London labour rates. Don't think body parts will be any cheaper either: another colleague nearly fainted when he realised that his wife's slight traffic bump and consequent bruised front wing was going to cost over £400. A Quattro demands a top class income even if it's bought at today's tempting sub-£10,000 second-hand prices . . .

Deep in the Forest

My next Quattro encounter was the most exciting, and reason enough on its own to write this book. I had always been an unashamed Hannu Mikkola fan since working in a junior capacity at Ford Competitions whilst he was driving the Escort during his first contracted Ford period. When Michael Greasley, then editing *MN*, asked if I could travel to Wales and interview *the* Flying Finn and take a ride in the 1981 spec Quattro I did my best to *yump* at the idea.

It was a midweek session on the sub-3 mile loop of Nant yr Hwch forest that sits in the pine-populated hills above Llantwrd Wells in mid-Wales. It was pouring with rain when I rattled into town in my then lightly abused Escort. The session was held behind locked gates, whose location I did not know, so I wended my way to that fountain of journalistic knowledge, the local pub, and found Audi Sport's mechanics topping up food and liquid supplies as well as fuel from next door. It really was a surreal sight, quiet Welsh gossip counterpointed by staccato German phrases and a collection of white Audi jackets that stood out sharply against the gloomy brown walls.

quattro

Up in the hills I found a lot more rain and a little mist, but very little testing going on as four laps had eaten the new RAC camshaft profile, and the team were busy rebuilding valve gear around a Sanremo shaft providing "a minimum 320 horsepower", according to the bearded figure huddling within the rented Audi 80 nearby. We got chatting. Roland Gumpert, then a diffident technical partner to Reinhard Rode in running Audi Sport, and I took stock of the test session's resources: two VW LT vans, four fitters and tyre men from then contracted Kleber, although both Michelin and Pirelli were assessed in the awful conditions too. The test car is IN-NU 81, later used to win the Donington Rallysprint prior to the RAC Rally itself, for which Hannu had a different mount.

Up on Nant-yr-Hwch with Audi Sport in pre-1981 RAC Rally testing. Roland Gumpert breaks cover from the convoy of UK-loaned Audi 80s and an old-style 100 to confer with Mikkola in the beak-nosed rubber-tester.

As the engine work drew to a successful conclusion I had time to study the cabin. I found, "it's a gloomy day outside and almost dark within, surrounded by a spiderwork roll cage in black and clasped tightly by a four point harness. There is the irony of an Emerson Fittipaldi-branded Personal steering wheel". Other first impressions included: "that dash starts on the left with a tiny 200km/h speedo then talks through its dials of fuel pressure (a sore point; the system is now mounted on a quick-release panel for fastest possible replacement after their Sanremo aggravation), oil pressure, turbo boost. All these measured in bar, the turbo allowed up to 1.6 in our damp and cool conditions.

"In the centre is the large tachometer, redlined at 7000. 'I can go maybe 8000, but we use 7400 most of the time', Hannu says. Gumpert quietly confirmed that maximum torque will now be around 3500rpm. Next to the rev-counter is a small oil temperature gauge to a maximum 150°C and a water temperature dial with a similar maximum. 'There is just too much to look at in a rally — so we have this light for emergencies. If there is too much water temperature, or too little oil pressure for the engine, then it tells me', explains Hannu stabbing a finger at the enormous orange beacon between us. It is about the only cheerful thing in an area of matt black aluminium sheet that houses the systems which monitor this complex car.

"As the order comes to start, and Hannu begins the protracted wrestling match with the switchgear to stir the cold and wet five-cylinder to life, I cinch the belts up another notch. I try to anticipate what is obviously going to be a ride even to eclipse Munari in the Stratos on home ground, but the growling and *very* lumpy 2000rpm of the Audi banishes memories instantly. In fact they have to stop the motor and get the fifth-cylinder to co-operate before we can go, but the engine is still in every beat a character. There is almost the ragged beat of an American V8 in the exhaust emissions, which seems to veer toward a more conventional four-cylinder note, and a hint of vibration, above 2500rpm.

"We trundle onto a 2.5 mile lap of Nant-yr-Hwch. Familiar territory to RAC regulars, and a track at which Hannu holds the unofficial record — according to our supervisors from the Forestry Commission — at 2m 51s. That was achieved in as dry a condition as a Welsh hilltop can ever attain, but today it's all squelches and spray.

"The Boge rally dampers are not having to work as yet. We pitch listlessly from rock to boulder, Hannu gesturing at the inert water temperature gauge needle, while I get a chance to see the kind of terrain that we'll be averaging over 60mph upon. Naturally there are a couple of first gear corners, but the most exciting sequence is a downhill straight with three or four crests. These followed by a sequence of rights and lefts that look as though they will demand second or third in a good Escort driven by somebody such as Mikkola. That sequence is followed by a long left-hander that leads into a double apex, tightening left, and back to the start. Just after the start of the test circuit there is a right followed by a first gear left and then a yumpity bumpity section on which it looks as though just touching third is going to be a problem in a conventional Group 4 car, such as the old Escort.

"The stones patter off the best Rhine steel floor, but the car is just grumbling along while Hannu explains some of the year's misfortunes. I ponder his usual lack of even a helmet for testing, never mind the racing overalls which are replaced by casual jeans and sensitive footwear. Then I wonder if he will be able to see enough out of the honourably mud-clotted side glass when we go in for some of that famous Finn broadside approach? Or are the bar-room pundits right? Is this a car you drive fairly straight, just taking advantage of the phenomenal traction and accurately transmitted power?

"The gauges tell the right story. Hannu flows from Captain Nice to Demon Driver. The elegant black casual flattens the massive, heavily-drilled accelerator pedal to the floor. Outside one would just say that the white and two shades of brown Audi is accelerating efficiently. It does not look dramatic, as any TV viewer will tell you. Inside, the idle clattering and banging with the patter, patter rhythm changes to the sound track from *A Bridge Too Far*. The turbo whistles and starts dumping excess gas just before every gear change. The engine grunts with the sudden effort. Suddenly four-wheel-drive takes on a new 90mph meaning, far from the Range Rover crowd.

"Compared with any other rally car, the acceleration is in the Formula 1 versus Formula 3 category at least on the loose. The Audi really does lunge forward, its power harnessed to the ground by a man who is not going to feel a single missed heartbeat in driving you faster than you have ever covered a rocky, rutted, forest trail. The trees and mud streak into a dull multi-coloured blur in your side vision as you try to keep faith. Look ahead and see what a magnificent job this machine makes of destroying time and muddy space in this soaking hillside forest. I managed to watch ahead for 10 laps before I had to seek a brief respite looking at Mikkola's feet. My eyes were just too frightened to transmit any more messages to my brain!

"Every little crest becomes a yump. Every 70 yard straight becomes an

quattro

80mph motorway. The safety belts suddenly seem loose and I loll about in my seat like some plump doll, banging my head against the roll cage. Not hard, but enough to remind me that the ride inside is not what I had been expecting. Memories of Pentti Airikkala over a very rough private track in the Group 4 Chevette in comparative comfort were instantly replaced by the surprising amount of punishment you take inside the Audi. Naturally Arne Hertz will just relax against the back rest, but the combination of my tenseness, an admittedly more rutted RAC stage than usual (akin to some of the rougher parts in Kielder that afternoon) and the stiff damper/spring rates needed to support over 1220kg of competition car; all played their part.

"My notebook comments regarding the car's speed are mainly obscene, but I think my overwhelming impression of superiority from the Mikkola/Quattro combination came over those downhill yumps. Naturally the Audi wanted to fly. So would you if somebody demanded full power just before a 90 to 100mph brow, one that is followed by an evil mud-wallowing dip. Hannu brakes so hard the engine actually stalls on landing, but that's no drama. It instantly decides to live again, and we wallop right with Hannu somehow having found the time to brake, select a gear (third) and left foot brake again, this time balanced against the power. All in 0.3s as far as this passenger can tell.

"The inspirational bit comes next. The speed just grows with all the shocking surprise of a BMW garage bill. While the Quattro turns sandy mud and flinty stones into high-speed mousse, your brain cannot believe the speed at which Hannu approaches the next left. By now the Quattro is wedged firmly in fourth gear, veering toward 100mph. There is a little dab of left foot braking on the tiny (by comparison with the macho throttle) centre pedal. The Quattro rears out sideways, as intended. Instead of the Escort-style gradual slide at 70-75mph, with little traction, the Audi goes on gaining speed at a terrifying and simultaneously exhilarating rate. That long left-hander steps back aghast as the maestro contemptuously keeps the Quattro in a long motorcycle dirt-racer's slide. Now the tachometer is reading close to 7000rpm in fourth, and fifth is an imminent possibility in mid-curve. Then it's time for an even sharper kick at the brakes. Second gear selected, the Audi literally flies over puddles and back into view of the huddled personnel in the Audi encampment. Another leap and we are back in third again. Now the track tightens up.

"As the exhaust belches flame to backlight the bleak scene, Mikkola's left foot braking technique has done its work well. The Quattro is plunging left, the bewildered passenger looking out of the side windows at the rugged road ahead. Another tap dance and the Quattro lunges into the air again, beating its way down the track in a succession of rapid, but totally fluid, twitches from its fine driver.

"The balance of power against left foot braking on some of the slower corners provides all the oversteer an ex-Escorteer could want. Yet the slide disappears very rapidly when the brakes are released, which is usually immediately after a corner's apex. Then the car just takes off down the next semblance of a straight like it was a ground-to-ground strafing mission. The Quattro feels 10-15mph faster on to, and along, any straight; but it is marginally slower than a conventional car, if extra power is needed in a hurry, or if the corner is very tight."

I have cheated a little with the exact wording of that 1981 *Motoring News* original account to make some of the slang a little more understandable, but 95 per cent of those quotations were as written at the time. I still haven't enjoyed a more exciting ride and found it very interesting to read about the feelings of former *Evening News* motoring columnist, and now TV personality, Sue Baker after her October 1983 ride with Michele Mouton to an easy victory on the British Audi National Rally. Amongst other things the honest Susan recalled, "during the day, however, I wondered what the hell I was doing here . . . The stages were very

quattro

End of a ride to remember. Mikkola wheels in IN-NU 81 (a rebuilt machine from the 1981 Acropolis, where it was disqualified whilst Mikkola and Hertz were using it to dominate proceedings) to the waiting wet mechanics in traditional Welsh weather.

slippery indeed but these Welsh roads are superb. The car just flowed through them and Michele was a joy to sit with''. The car's considerable performance took even the former regular club competitor and ex-Tony Fowkes co-driver by surprise and she did not feel very well at all for some of the event, a condition I can understand all too well after my briefer – and low profile – ride with Mikkola. It really is one helluva competition car, it sets new standards of adhesion and traction that demand that little bit extra of the occupant's bodies – particularly if it is hot, when 45°C has been the reported cabin temperature within this turbo cooker!

quattro

Now it can be revealed. In Switzerland, Audi had to transport the hacks by train in order to ensure that they found the generous fleet of 80 Quattros, merely by falling out of the goods wagons onto them! Peter Newton of *CCC* (right) and Toucan-touting author prepare for another adventure into the outer limits of credibility . . .

Road Impression: 80 Quattro

My first sight of the Quattro 80, a car I felt had to challenge the proven smooth power of BMW's 320/323i with an added measure of road security, was at Chur railway station in Switzerland. Audi had lined up over 20 of them , all in a kind of metallic plum shade, ready for us to drive over the conveniently snow and ice-surfaced passes that separated us from St Moritz.

I do not suppose we covered more than 250 miles in all, even taking into account the amount of snow-packed deviations my partner and I managed to take in after the inspirational second day rides with Mr Blomqvist. Yet the car left just as strong an impression as Big Brother, lacking only the thrill of turbocharged top end power and compensating with instant throttle response and far more predictable handling on ice than any Quattro coupe I have driven under the same treacherous conditions.

Everyone of driving spirit complained that these 80s didn't accelerate like the Audi figures implied they would, and quite a few suggested that ABS braking was vital. In fact it seems as though the altitude and constant pass-climbing route may have dulled the responses of the 136bhp machines considerably, for *Autocar* certainly found no cause for complaint when they borrowed a machine from VAG that was not intended for press demo purposes. Following my own later acquaintance with the 80 Quattro in Scotland I felt the same way: the 80Q was capable enough in a straight line. Yet there was no denying that in Summertime Britain it was irritating to have the Allweather Goodyears braying for mercy as those fellow-Bavarian BMWs slipped away at slightly greater pace in their revised 1982 shells.

The five-cylinder engine is no smoothie, unlike the BMW. It has some odd thrumming periods, and revving it to 6500rpm while utilising that fine chassis and balancing it on those four wheel disc brakes is only enjoyable; not the ecstacy that might be demanded by the owner of a BMW that cost the £11,000 plus of an Audi 80Q in the UK. It might well be that the cheaper 2-litre engine presently confined to the home-market might be a more rev-worthy companion.

Scotland in Summer was the venue for the British announcement of the RHD 80 Quattro and provided some superb scenery as well as the complete opposite in weather conditions to the Swiss shindig. The All-Weather tyres coped well with hot tarmac and sun-lit country roads, but I came away convinced that you need two sets of tyres to enjoy the Quattro concept to the full in Britain's predominantly mild climate. Most dangerous moments came with Honda's incredible All Terrain trikes, which were either cornering on two wheels, or suffering from an airborne front wheel, particularly accelerating uphill. I finally rolled my mount in combat with VAG's Tony Hill, who had elected the Croquet Lawn perimeter as a suitable "track" within the manorial grounds of this temporary press HQ. Braver souls slithered round this courtyard with a trike wheel permanently airborne . . . At the end of the week the hosts had more bruises than the press, who were lured away from the trikes to drive the cars at regular intervals.

quattro

At 7493 feet on the Julier Pass, the Quattro 80 from the December 1982 LHD launch fleet displays the Goodyear AllWeather tyres and Audi 100 Aero wheel covers that would become familiar as the most common equipment.

No, generous torque is the forte of the 2.1-litre in non-turbo trim, particularly between 2700 and 5000rpm, where the engine is relaxed about delivering the goods. No fault could be found in the pneumatic two-stage differential lock operation and its ability to extracate us from snow up to the centre line of the wheel hubs was appreciated in Switzerland. The gearbox still had the occasional baulk and clonk to let you know its linkages and selectors were better, but not the best, as yet. The gear ratios seemed poorish in Switzerland, where you would wind it up in second uphill only to feel that the wick had spluttered its last when the lightning change to third plunged rpm from 6500 to barely 4000 revs. In fact *Autocar* found that usual Quattro curse of a second gear was worth only 51mph at maximum rpm, third providing 75mph and fourth 100. However fifth was neatly chosen to provide maximum speed with 500rpm to go before the 6500 limit. A 'legalish' 80mph motorway amble at 4000rpm was certainly a pleasure on dry Scottish roads, but you did notice the tyre noise of the Allweathers and the squirm from their well-treaded carcasses when pushed, by that fine chassis, through the Highlands. I would try and fit the optional ex-Quattro and 200 Ronal 6J alloys with Goodyear NCTs or Fulda's equivalent for all but depths of Winter use in Britain.

As an everyday city car with some weekend use covering rallies or otherwise making use of its exceptional traction (*Autocar's* weighbridge revealed 61.5 per cent of the kerb weight concentrated on the front wheels), I rate the Quattro 80 as a better bet than Big Brother. Why? The engine picks up instantly and its flexibility masks some of the gearbox ratio deficiencies, compared to the turbo which emphasises any sudden rpm drop. So the 80 Quattro's five is a better bet round town, and not a lot slower outside: 0-60mph takes just under 9 seconds, compared with the Quattro coupe's average 7 to 7.1, and 120mph may sound marginally less offensive to the magistrate's than 137mph!

A ride with Stig
Blomqvist in the 80Q was
entertaining . . .

quattro

More seriously the 80 Quattro offers 25mpg even under duress, the coupe will drop slightly below 20 under the same circumstances. Then there is the question of visibility in the 80 saloon shell, which is excellent by any standards and makes the car a lot easier to park than the coupe in difficult circumstances. To illustrate this point I opted to take the saloon around the 1983 RAC Rally after completing the same route in 1982 with the coupe. There's no doubt which was more exciting — the turbocharged coupe, of course — but for superior vision, swift parking and good accommodation of occupants and luggage with that wonderful feeling of wet weather security that is common to both cars (and which is 4-WD's strongest safety argument), I think the 80 Quattro has much to recommend it over the more powerful machine.

November Bliss

For the 1982 RAC Rally I had the most appropriate transport it has been my pleasure to drive in the 2000 distinctly odd miles that are involved in reporting the event for the organisers. A nicely run-in Quattro coupe in the then new British RHD specification, with the larger headlamps, was provided by VAG. I spirited it swiftly away to the York rally base of that year's event, which was to witness squadrons of Quattros running in the top ten and a final 1-2-5-10 finish, only 20 of 69 special stages failing to provide a Quattro with the fastest times!

We covered considerably more than 2000 miles by the time the rally had been reported and I had hung onto the car greedily for as long as possible afterwards. I logged fuel consumption over 1389.1 miles of a route that covers England, Wales and a slice of Southern Scotland, the majority of the mileage in pouring rain and an intensely pleasurable minority pounding through places like Kielder's Forest Drive. The result was an overall 19.76mpg, with a low of 17.9 and a high of 21.73 of the eight tank-fulls gargled in that distance. The only problem we had was that the gear linkage stiffened beyond its usual piggy self and made fourth to fifth gear selection laborious and occasionally brutal.

Otherwise complete contentment from the two cynics aboard. Rain, snow or the comforts of an underground car park all saw the injected turbo engine beat its unsteady rhythm immediately on cold start request. The seating and ventilation coped admirably with the often soggy occupants, though the tendency to mist up did demand constant use of the electric rear screen. Add in the already limited rear vision and you can see that we were in more potential danger reversing out of parking slots than in some of the irresponsible Quattro-combats that took place between the loan car fleet in dank corners of the forest . . .

As a load carrier the coupe was sorely tested beyond all reasonable limits. Rallying is a highly social sport . . . when it's wet outside, or there's been an accident, the cream of the superstars suddenly find they want to share your life. Thus we found ourselves carrying Ari Vatanen and Terry Harryman back from Wales after Wales had bitten their Opel back, and one service area saw the crews of at least two Quattros crammed in the back — and anywhere else out of the rain — while we trickled them from their refreshments van to *Parc Ferme*.

While the Quattro performed such tasks with complete civility, the memories are of fleeter two-up motoring. Of the Quattro disdainfully paddling through Wales at astounding speed over soaking roads, or grumbling away from an icy early morning start in Scotland and gathering speed so surefootedly over the slickly-coated tarmac to the Lake District that the occupants literally felt as safe as if the roads were basking in Summer sunshine. A new dimension, and one that suited even the Quattro's brakes at these slowish speeds with the differentials locked.

On rarer dry roads, a trip across from the Lakes toward Beedale on the Northern Yorkshire moors, gave us a chance to relive that enthusiasm created by the original car on the Dartmoor test route. The power-steering provided much of the pleasure, always weighted correctly to transmit cornering demands that varied from 10mph hairpins to 110mph swoops. Still the Quattro behaved impeccably, rewarding the least sign of enthusiastic competence with a .faint whistle of turbocharged thrust and roadholding standards that I still rate in the Lotus class. That is to say bumps are absorbed without deflecting the car from line and where you point the car is where it goes on dry roads − an act it will repeat on 95 per cent of slippier surfaces. Of course, if you plough into a slow wet corner too fast the Quattro wants its nose to nuzzle the scenery, but it really is only a matter of responding in classic front drive manner, easing the power and lock, to retrieve all but the worst-judged situations. The Goodyear tyre choice is particularly effective on a drive like those encountered on the RAC.

The NCT (Neutral Contour Tyre) cuts through standing water in the manner I remember of wet racing tyres ten years ago, whilst in the dry they seem to protest less than other brands and provide positive feel and a lack of on-the-limit squirm that is refreshing, especially in a durable road tyre. Durable, after the life *Autocar* reported? Yes, for *Autocar* conducted a series of handling tests that provoked the very worst in wear possibilities, largely around a tight slalom course. They paid nearly £136 per cover to replace those tyres too, whereas the trade ads in the back of *Motoring News* suggest that 205/60 HR-15s are freely available from a number of sources at £71.25p to £77.50 or in VR (as specified in the *Autocar* long term test) from £87 to £89.40p. It may be worth noting that various tyres suitable for high performance motoring *are* offered FOC to motoring journalists but, for my own car, I buy discount NCTs from local specialists. No, Goodyear *do not* contribute to my freelance earnings . . . !

When I tried the Quattro coupe again in November 1982, the price for RHD was £17,052 without the digital instrumentation package − which did not appear in Britain until 1984; by which time the price of the pre-digital model in RHD had risen to £17,721.98p. Equivalent prices in Germany were a guesstimated £51,282 for the Quattro Sport, which was not in production, £16,723 for the Quattro coupe and £8473 for the 2.1-litre Quattro 80, (which was £11,474.13p in Britain from October 1, 1983, onward!) All prices courtesy of *Auto Motor und Sport* at the prevailing exchange rate of 3.9Dm to the Pound.

These prices reflected a closing in the gap between German and British markets that was marked compared with earlier comparisons I had made. Of course the exchange rate played a strong part in reducing the attractiveness of personal import of prestige cars such as the Quattro coupe from Germany, but it was also obvious that VAG, like many other German-based manufacturers, has met the problem by raising German market prices closer to UK levels. The large discrepancy still existing in the 80 Quattro cost is officially attributed to the extra equipment and RHD, but also has a lot more to do with Audi wishing to meet BMW's 3-series head-on in Germany. Thus the car is marketed at slimmer profit levels in the Fatherland and as a fully equipped luxury model in Britain.

Stig's stunner

That was the headline *Motoring News* used to top my November 1983 test of the A1 Quattro that had brought Blomqvist the British Open Rally Championship title. MYV 44Y was built by British-based David Sutton mechanics at the Bavarian factory to the original Group B evolution recipe and ran in all six British home internationals that year, although it did not take in the RAC Rally as the later 44

quattro

Loose surface paradise: a Quattro and ten gallons of fuel to burn . . . .

CMN to A2 specification was by then available for Blomqvist to take to victory.

The car certainly was stunning, and one could see exactly why a top driver such as Blomqvist had managed to win four of the six qualifying rounds. Indeed a Quattro had yet to be beaten over British international forest going since the January 1981 RAC, when this book was written! Even more impressive than a two season domination of the premier loose surface British events, was the fact that Blomqvist had also managed to win the Quattro's first tarmac international, July 1983's Ulster, with the same Quattro.

Compared with the Ingolstadt Championship Quattros the David Sutton machine had some major differences in approach. Gone was the electro-hydraulic clutch operation, and Sutton had installed their own wiring loom, Premier's 26 gallon safety fuel tank and had sourced the Kevlar and plastic lightweight components in Britain. The engine was maintained in Britain by Terry Hoyle, and used the factory 6.3:1cr with 1.7 bar boost (340bhp at 6000rpm: over 305lb. ft torque at 3500 revs) and factory parts, rather than the British-sourced crankshaft and pistons that Hoyle had developed for UK privateers.

The A1 engine bay with Pierburg fuel-injection, exhaust system and KKK turbocharger, all to the left of the Terry Hoyle-maintained five-cylinder engine.

In keeping with their contracts, the Sutton VAG UK Quattro wore shiny composite alloy wheels by BBS, their 6J × 15 dimensions centrally cheered by natty gold paintwork, and their rims more functionally decorated by Pirelli SG35 M + S tyres of chunky forest tread pattern.

The cockpit was right in the space shuttle league for instrument and switchgear complexity, but the large 10,000rpm rev counter (I was allowed to use 7000) and 200km/h speedo were clear and informative enough. The ASS high-sided seats, Klippan six-point harness and Momo Grip steering wheel conspired to boost confidence via a first class driving position. Yet the stark open rod linkage connections of the conventional H-pattern plus fifth gearchange were not so inviting.

quattro

Inside the David Sutton Motorsport-prepared Quattro, a Matter cage and deep cloth-covered seats provide reassuring comfort whilst the dashboard, with the usual 200km/h speedometer and large central rev-counter, offered a welter of information that was hard for a stranger to digest quickly. Above the shiny alloy footplate for the passenger on this LHD machine, can be seen the spare ignition and injection packs that demand only a quick swap of electrical plug-in points to activate the supercar's back-up systems.

Guided by former Sutton mechanic Peter Holley, I went through the start routine, culminating in a protracted push-button finale to the accompaniment of the throttle one third open. It had taken patience to wait whilst the fuel pressure increased after the ignition circuit had been energised, before trying to fire the engine up. However, what followed was the most satisfying test drive of 16 years infiltrating myself into various sports machinery.

The bare figures of independent tests relay that 60mph will be reached from rest in under 5 seconds, even with this comparatively outmoded Pierburg injection example, and that 100mph will take under 14s. The striking impression is that the Quattro will return this 5-litre V12 acceleration level over a ploughed field, with outstanding traction and comfortable stability! In fact, I tried just putting one set of wheels over bumpy grass and mud from the equally rugged runway that the Boge dampers were so easily absorbing, and this astonishing competition coupe just pounded remorselessly closer to 90mph.

The interior noise was a unique experience in itself, the five grunting up to 5000rpm with all the charisma that led one prominent rally engineer to dub it with a charming Welsh lilt, "the electronic tractor". Pass from 4900 to 5000 revs and "Mr Tractor" transformed instantly into "Ms Turbo Terror". The revs recorded on that large tachometer seemed to show that 5000 had been swapped for 7000 "just like that", with the turbocharger whistling chirpily just before each high rpm gearchange.

Perhaps the biggest surprise was the handling, for with full boost in a low gear — anything up to the 68mph offered in third at a snorting 7000rpm — the Quattro would slide its rear wheels out of line in traditional rear drive Escort style. Obviously the 4-WD tended to drag it straight under full power, but it was certainly not the porcine understeerer that one might have expected. A degree of rear brake bias on the superb four-wheel discs helped set the Audi sideways before very slow and dry corners too.

Slow loose surface corners presented the truth of the old racing cliche, "slow in, fast out". Unlike a conventional 2-WD, you have the means to accelerate

General A1 engine layout is well displayed here with the shrouded water radiator closest to the camera. The large bore tubing across the engine's rocker cover, in a diagonal path from the front-mounted intercooler, feeds the lowered temperature air to the injection system. Farthest tube is the air feed to the turbocharger from the collection point in the rear bulkhead. Both tubes, the camshaft drive cowling and the radiator fan cowling are in lightweight materials, mostly Kevlar or carbon fibre composites.

rapidly uphill over stones from a slow hairpin. You can see, as well as feel from the driver's seat, that the Quattro may draw four to five seconds over conventional opposition under such circumstances — or away from a loose surface standing start.

The famed left foot braking technique, in which you use the brakes to produce oversteer, whilst building turbo boost with an open throttle, made sense on the Quattro. For example there was one point on our mile long route (provided courtesy of Silverstone-based Rally Racing Ltd) where the Quattro hurtled toward a gateway with fifth gear briefly engaged, having used up the 87mph offered in fourth. To thread the Quattro through the gateway, from fast tarmac onto 30mph clag, demanded that there be plenty of boost ready to power slide the car left, and away along a subsequent straight. The sequence provoked the tester into such a clumsy impersonation of tap dancing the pedals during the change from fifth to second, with full braking also required, that the nerveless photographer alongside could be seen misting his glasses in mirth and putting his pants in peril of a warm shower!

Executed with some semblance of accuracy, the big coupe would arc lazily out of line over the loose and straighten up on a turn of lock, to streak down the following loose 300 yards beyond 80mph. Then came the hardest section in which to even begin to understand Quattro. Just a simple right, left, right chicane through tyres with hidden concrete centres. Again you needed to work down the gearbox and preserve some boost ready for the slow turn that followed heavy braking. First gear would be used in an instant flurry of wheelspin, all 37mph of it. Whilst in second you had a job to pull anywhere near the 5000rpm power band opening, never mind its 50mph maximum.

Thus the choice was a bumbling second gear, which made sense of the middle section and exit, or a spectacular shuffle through first and into second, often well off the course as you endeavoured to complete several tasks in triplicate simultaneously! Certainly it proved that, once the engine was above 5000rpm, the left foot braking would produce exactly the slide you wanted with only minimal

quattro

Inside the UK-prepared A1's boot, the left-hand section is reserved for the circular dry sump oil tank, with the white semi-circular mass of the safety petrol tank carrying fuel measurement in gallons, ready for easy reading from a transparent display tube that is hidden by the oil tank. On the right are the petrol filler and floor-level battery.

Getting the British-based Sutton Quattro for Stig Blomqvist in 1983 to turn right, left, and right again at slow speed called for a lot of pedal pushing and power steering manipulation, usually simultaneously.

skill. The trick is to do all that on a dark Welsh hillside after four days rallying, in sheet ice, at treble the speed. Thanks Stig, you show us how!

Aside from the consistent brakes, the greatest of pleasure came from the power steering's consistent information service over any surface at anything up to the 100mph the test track allowed. Clambering to 7000rpm in the first four gears, the Quattro still bounding forward with all the enthusiasm of an unleashed Doberman Pinscher, and much of that beast's growling excitement, was another highlight. You just want to go on doing it, and the large single plate clutch never seems to object.

I summed up in *MN*, ''overall the Audi UK Quattro A1 provided more sweat droplets and more grins per yard than any test car I have encountered. Every minute behind the wheel gave a gripping insight into the realities of life behind the wheel of a Group B supercar, convincing me that very few can extract the potential offered by this specification − never mind the short wheelbase monsters of 450 horsepower that we are promised in 1984.''

I think I'll ask my son to drive the Quattro Sport!

Of the road miles I have covered in Quattros I would say the sheer traction and handling pleasure has been the outstanding impression. The interiors are not pretty, but in all cases I felt they were comfortable and I particularly appreciated the seats and variable power assistance steering. I can't say I like the five cylinder 2.1-litre engine anything like as much as a BMW 2.0 or 2.3-litre six, but then the 80 Quattro offers its fabulous chassis and commanding traction as compensation. I cannot, offhand, think of a mile on the road I did not enjoy in any of the Quattro coupes, although that does not mean I find the handling of the big coupe always predictable on snow, or that the gearbox should not be taken out and cremated along with its loathsome linkages. However, press a spare £17,000 into my palm and watch me ignore the blandishments of Porsche and the like on my way to the VAG dealer for a coupe I can enjoy every day in greater safety and stability than any other car I have driven in the past 19 years.

didn't manage to get the Quattro to do this for very long, but it certainly was satisfying while it lasted!

quattro

Right a bit . . . left a bit . . . and suddenly heading for the hills! Author, J.W. getting all crossed up in a moment of over-enthusiasm.

Chapter 11

1983: The tough one

The 1983 season brought technical changes to Quattro with bewildering rapidity, and a regular three-car turnout on World Championship rounds. Once again Audi and Mikkola looked safe Championship bets: for Lancia, Rohrl and Alen close the gap with wins just where they were not expected, as well as on tarmac . . .

"Small things mean big results", said Audi Sport's chief Roland Gumpert in summary of a season that had seen the Quattro make enormous technical strides, and improved significantly by detail pre-event testing such as had provided a comfortable, progressively-sprung ride to victory on the 1000 Lakes in just the kind of 1-2-4 and 7th overall finishing order that Quattro team management dreams were made of in 1983. Unfortunately the quote about "small things" could just as well have applied to the compact Lancia two-seaters that provided *the* Championship opposition that year, carrying off Audi's 1982 Manufacturer's title by October. It was also largely "small things" that tore apart the Audi season, such as sunshine in Monte Carlo and a number of mechanical details that triggered off incidents such as the major rear end fire that literally melted Mikkola's definitive Quattro A2 evolution coupe in San Remo. A2? What had been going on in Ingolstadt in 1983? Read on, join the curiouser and curiouser Quattro Club . . .

To understand the cars Audi Sport presented in 1983 for the regular trio of Mikkola/Hertz, Mouton/Pons and Blomqvist/Cederberg, and why they seemed to change "before our very eyes" at every event, we must go back to 1982. Away from the Championship battles, Audi Sport were busy readying for a 1983 in

quattro

ACTION 1983! Audi were either flying high or down in the dumps. Despite the altitude of *Mme.* Mouton's New Zealand Quattro, and the fact that she set 12 quickest times this was one of the bad times — both works Quattros retiring from the fray. The arresting picture is from Colin Taylor Productions.

which they would have no option but to switch from their original Group 4 international recognition to the Group B category. When Group B was introduced, for the 1982 season, with a waiver that allowed companies such as Audi to continue for one year with their cars in Group 4, it was thought that the only way to gain Group B recognition was to build 200 highly competitive cars and, with comparatively minor modifications, to rally them. In other words the only way to make a competitive rally car was to have a high basic specification on the 200 examples sold to the public. Audi had no real problem with that route, there were plenty of Quattros made and the basic specification of turbocharged five-cylinder engine and 4-WD was enough to at least ensure a competitive basis, providing that the vital competition components could be carried over into Group B from the old Group 4 status.

From the 26th of July 1982, Audi satisfied the Paris-based FISA sporting authority that the Quattro was eligible for Group B and the 1982 car, complete with most of the Group 4 rallying equipment, became a Group B machine. It wasn't enough.

While Audi had been going through this process other manufacturers, notably Lancia and Opel, were busy proving that the smart thing to do was make 200 cars featuring the basic components of your competition mount — *eg:* Lancia's supercharged, mid-engine 037 Rally — and then evolve a further 20 red hot flyers with the skimpiest body work possible (in the most exotic materials) and extra power. As an example the Lancia was perfect: from July 1 1982, it could appear with Bosch fuel-injection and forced induction by a supercharger that incorporated water injection, whereas the original layout was a Weber carburettor sucking air and feeding mixture to a straightforward supercharger. Also the Lancia's competition body weight went down from over 1000kg to the class

quattro

minimum for under 3-litre cars of 960kg — and with the aid of carbon fibre panels and titanium roll cages, this could be achieved. Opel ran into a lot of trouble trying to convince the authorities that they had made sufficient Manta 400 coupes, and were forced to run the heavier Ascona 400 into 1983, but Lancia had shown what could be argued through and Audi started to think how they could improve their lot with lighter bodies. Of course, there was always the short Quattro in the background, but Piech had already said that he didn't want to use that unless forced — and there was nothing much to be gained unless Audi started working on another engine size, the traditional 79.5mm × 86.4mm producing 2144cc that had to be multiplied by the 1.4 turbo factor to make 3003 or 3002cc, according to which calculator you used. Either way it meant Audi were marginally over 3-litres and therefore had to comply with a FISA minimum weight of 1100kg. A marginally reduced engine capacity — one of Gumpert's pet "small things" — would bring Audi into the Lancia sub-3-litre domain with a 960kg minimum.

However Audi's first step, recognised from January 1 1983, was to improve the existing 2144cc Group B Quattro in time for the Monte Carlo rally through the official inspection of 20 lighter machines, formally known as Quattro A1. Each of these had regained the alloy block that was lost in the earlier transfer from Group 4 to Group B and also boasted great fat wheelarch extensions, made from Kevlar, and a carbon fibre bonnet. Those arches carried rear air intakes that served the brakes only and there were pages of suspension alternatives for the model, all duly photographed for official recognition purposes.

Monte Carlo 1983 and dust rather than the required snow was the menu for the Quattros, which finished third and fourth in their new A1 evolution bodies.

211

quattro

Upright and stone guard protection for A2 Quattro disc brake assembly.

As for Group 4, the Quattro gained additional leading links (also to be seen on Quattro Sport road cars) that ran from underbody to outer suspension arm mounting points, front and rear, one per suspension "corner". However Gumpert's, November 1982 engineering recruit, Hans-Peter Gassen, four draughtsmen and the 42 other members of Audi Sport (including 28 mechanics by Spring 1983) had gorged themselves on alternative suspension systems. "Altogether we offer four choices", smiled Gumpert at the recollection, "and these have all been tried, but not all in competition. They were in steel, plastic, aluminium or titanium. No, I don't joke! We really did try these other suspensions, all based on the lower arms with bracing. Altogether I think, we had the choice of six wishbone types. We find that even the titanium does not save much weight for this application, in fact we have to build it up so much we don't save weight at all . . . and it's *very* expensive!" After crawling round the workshops twice during 1983, I would say that: a) every rally Quattro appears to differ from its neighbour (the 50th rally Quattro was Blomqvist's unlucky San Remo mount); b) the most common wishbones scattered around the shop, and underneath the cars, were hybrid steel triangulations with aluminium outer mounting points into the Quattro's hub/upright assemblies.

Front and rear disc brake and strut assemblies for the 1983 Quattro, with the backing plate protection clearly shown, along with unattached leading links for the unfitted suspension arms.

However, we haven't understood anything yet, for in 1983 Audi Sport really attacked the weight and engine size with awesome and expensive energy. By May 1, 1983, we could read the results upon the Quattro A2 homologation form, which was the result of two production moves. First a run of 200 sub-3-litre machines with alloy blocks. That meant 79.3mm bore, instead of 79.5, allied to the usual 86.4mm stroke: 2135cc or 2989cc with the usual FISA turbo multiplication. Gumpert actually giggled at the next calculator answer, for he'd worked everything out on the maximum permitted tolerances for this engine and come up with 2999cc after turbo multiplication.

As usual, it was not enough for the restless Audi engineers. Not content with that 200 run they officially stopped production and made 20 further evolved flyers from that base! These were the true A2 Quattros, ultimate derivatives of the original concept ready for battle on the Corsican Championship round of 1983. For these 20 cars the official capacity dropped further, for Dr Fritz Indra and the men of R&D had come up with a new short-throw steel crankshaft that worked in conjunction with the standard stroke. Thus the Quattro A2 engines for the majority of 1983's wars with Lancia measured 79.51mm × 85.0mm, a fact I had to elicit from friendly Dr Fritz. An official 2953cc after the turbo multiplication factor but up to 2999cc with the maximum bore allowed, 80.11mm. Based on Dr Indra's dimensions for this unashamedly "racing" version of the engine the actual capacity appears as a minimum 2110cc to a max 2142cc without multiplication by the 1.4 turbo factor; some 2954cc minimum and 2998.8cc maximum after multiplication. Confused? So were all of us at the time!

The important points to recall from the Quattro A2 homologation form were the sub-3-litre capacity with the shorter stroke crank doing the competition work in alliance with a new large bore exhaust manifold and a new generation of

quattro

New era. The A2 Quattro is primarily identified by the twin intakes in front of the rear wheels, but beneath the lightweight bonnet was a smaller capacity version of the five to bring the Quattro within the 3-litre international class, once the turbo multiplication factor had been added.

electronic Bosch engine management for the fuel injection and ignition (using one common brain). The Bosch system then coded MS2 and previously hidden away from the public's gaze as Porsche engineers at Weissach worked on the TAG Turbo Grand Prix V6 for McLaren, although they were by no means the only manufacturers working with the latest in Bosch electronics.

Audi spoke only of 360bhp at 7000rpm and 450Nm/331lb. ft torque at 4000 revs as the principle results from this demon development of the SOHC 10-valve engine, but feedback from the main engineering side of the company spoke consistently of 400bhp with the bigger KKK 27 in full 1.9 bar/27psi Corsican cry. Even with 1.6 bar/22.8psi boost for the Safari over Easter, a minimum of 340bhp was quoted as most likely. In fact, after they had proved how well the larger turbo and high boost overcame the traditional lag problem they tried out the combination on Mikkola's Acropolis testing routine and discovered that what felt good, subjectively, in the car — small turbo with good low and mid-range response — was not necessarily fastest. In fact they could provide a meaty 362lb. ft of torque from the SOHC 2.1-litre at 3500rpm after trying "a lot of camshaft profiles" as well as juggling with turbo boost and an eventual 6.5:1cr.

Besides the engine — which had many other detail competition improvements for durability and the other glamorous items I have mentioned at this stage — the A2 specification also wrought other worthwhile benefits. Externally you could seize on the double vented intakes before each rear wheel arch and know that these now served the differential as well as the brakes. The front Matter tubing that contributes so much to the engine bay's integrity under stress was cross-braced with vertical tubes.

The choice of suspension wishbones was severely curtailed but new steering arms were specified on the A2 form, primarily to fit in with an engine bay already crowded by the latest in large intercoolers (from Behr or Langerer & Reich). Service needs and those of the drivers had also produced what Gumpert described as "a better gearchange mechanism: now it has fewer parts, is lighter and uses straighter runs for a good change".

The engine bay looked like this for most of 1983 with the Bosch-Pierburg electronic fuel-injection system for the A2 small capacity motor. Externally the layout was much as for A1 so far as the turbocharger air supply and intercooler to injection tubing was concerned. Note the wide use of lightweight materials, particularly for the raised bonnet.

quattro

The front can be identified by the two exhaust pipes curling into view and the sump pan in front of the crossmember! Underneath a works Quattro the cross-braced bottom suspension arms can be seen linking into the subframe with their links running forward into the lower section of Matter's front end tubular construction. At the back the suspension arm and link layout on the A2 and A1 looks similar, although there were plenty of alternatives in materials and the fundamental length change for tarmac or forest road use. The anti-roll bar mounts behind the subframe at the rear. (C11-22 & 22a)

Non-stop activities characterised the A2, for the extra 30, or so, horsepower was also accompanied by significant gearbox internal changes. Gone was the central differential casing of original Quattro, replaced by a simplified outline. This made the gearbox both shorter and lighter: minus 10cm/3.9in and saving 6kg/13.2lb were the relevant figures. Another weight reduction was made by lighter door panels made from Kevlar, a saving over the previous plastic and alloy specification of 4.5kg/9.9lb per door.

Beautifully finished light-weight cowl moulding for Quattro electric fan and radiator: used in both A1 and A2 Quattros of 1983.

The only negative effect of the engine capacity change was to reduce maximum permitted rim widths from 12in to 11in, really only relevant in Corsica as the only all-tarmac event on the World Championship calendar.

Audi Sport are always willing to give a new tweak a try. Here's the tarmac racer look applied to the 80 Quattro, along with Fuchs wheels and an uprated interior.

quattro

Summary

Audi's slogan "Progress through Technology" was sorely tried in 1983 and the engineers, both from Audi Sport and the main company's R&D centre, certainly came up with more answers than any World Championship rally constructor I can recall. In fact the engineering thoroughness of making what amounted to four complete Quattro derivatives in 10 months and then making an intensive eight week effort prior to Frankfurt to produce a convincing road/rally basis in the Quattro Sport, can only recall the Mercedes approach to racing and rallying. As we all now know Mercedes found late seventies and early eighties rallying too much to totally dominate, and withdrew at the end of 1980. They hadn't failed totally, for there were World Championship wins in the more rugged loose surface events, but they did not match the Audi Quattro record.

Even in 1983, a season which was far from fulfilling Audi's ambitions, there were four victories against the five of Lancia when the title was decided in October — and Audi looked set to notch up a further two wins on the remaining loose surface events. Clearly Audi had not achieved their 1983 aims, which were not just confined to retaining the Manufacturer's World title, but also sweeping up the driver's equivalent. This was impossible after Lancia's Rally, which remained in much the same sub-1000kg/305bhp mechanical trim throughout the 1983 season, collared the Manufacturer's Championship. Yet, to judge 1983 a failure for Audi would be too much of a generalisation: the Quattros were still capable of devastating wins and the 1984 prospect of a shorter Quattro and an appropriate quartet of drivers, including Walter Rohrl as well as the 1983 pool of Mikkola, Mouton and Blomqvist, was enough to send any rival scuttling back to their boards for extra funds!

We shall never accurately know what the 1983 season cost Audi. Informed rivals in Germany reckon the equivalent of £6.25 million is a fair estimate. Gumpert states the obvious fact that it is very hard to truly know, because so much R&D work is carried out for the team that has development as well as competitive importance, so how can the overheads be divided fairly? To back up that judgement he pointed out: "one year of our budget is equivalent to 1 per cent of Herr Piech's development budget!" Since there are 2800 people working at that R&D centre that is not too much of a surprise . . .

That's what I call a works hack!

Cockpit contrast. Mikkola at rest and Blomqvist in his snowy element.

quattro

The 1983 Season

Having cleared at least the complicated bulk of the intriguing 1983 Audi technicalities away, we will look at how that expertise fared in action.

As ever the glamour of Monte Carlo in January pulled a representative initial turnout of the faces and machinery that would become familiar through the season. Lancia, having failed to win a World Championship event in their first three-quarter season with the 037 Rally, had three near-960kg cars for Markku Alen, Walter Rohrl and Jean Claude Andruet. Now minus the lubrication problem that had knocked out their engine bearings at medium rpm on tight tarmac corners these Lancias looked a lot more formidable, especially as Pirelli were making a comeback after two years and had brought along some 1500 tyres in six basic types to support their effort! Meanwhile Audi had "Switched to Michelin" for 1983 . . .

Also expected to offer serious opposition on the second successive dry Monte were 1982 winners Opel — who had three of the outdated Ascona 400s in Rothmans colours for Ari Vatanen, Henri Toivonen and Guy Frequelin to drive. These carefully developed rear drive reminders of another rallying age provided 255bhp from 2.4-litres and weighed about 1050kg: the Quattro used on Monte 1983 averaged 1130 to 1140kg.

Renault defended home honours and the fading memory of that unexpected 1981 victory with three directly factory supported Group B Turbo 5s (using enlarged front wheels and untested front suspension left them largely off the pace) and one privateer who was allowed an extra 20bhp (totalling 285bhp from 1.4-litres) in the 900kg bodywork. Like Opel and Audi, Renault were favoured Michelin users, adding to the strain put on the French tyre company's 1983 Monte resources to the point where teams had to provide their own tyre transport in many cases.

The Japanese were represented by European preparation, Mazda relying on former driver Achim Warmbold and Nissan-Datsun presenting their new 2.3-litre Silvia RS of 280-claimed-horsepower for ex-Vauxhall specialists W. B. Blydenstein to run on Japanese Dunlops.

Against this crowd Audi had the most powerful and sophisticated machines — not quite so sophisticated as envisaged because FISA changed their minds about the legality of electric clutch operation as seen at the 1982 RAC, and the Bavarians had to remove said switchgear from the Monte Quattro trio. However FISA did change their minds again before many months had gone by and we saw the electro-hydraulic clutch operation back in the 1983 cars . . !

New Quattros were provided for Mikkola and Mouton but Monte Carlo debutants — they were better known as expert ice noters for men like Bjorn Waldegard on this event — Blomqvist and Cederberg had Mikkola's RAC Rally winner in rebuilt trim; it being the only factory entry that had survived the British event with unsullied coachwork.

Basically the 1983 scheme was that Audi would use BBS racing wheels for tarmac and continue with Fuchs on the loose, but at Monte Carlo one could also see Ronal and Tech Del Minilite pressed into action.

The season literally started with a bang for Gumpert, his Quattro rudely rammed in the rear by an errant Ford before even the first stage had been run! When they did that 27 mile opener, Mikkola lost over two minutes "trying too hard, too soon", as he freely admitted to *Motoring News* reporter Michael Greasley whilst Mouton had terrible trouble getting gears, particularly first and second, so that only Blomqvist featured amongst the top six.

It was swiftly clear that this edition of the Monte was not going to provide the kind of weather that would suit a 4-WD car in battle with a mid-engined two seater

Uphill struggle. Mikkola wends his fourth place A1 over the diet of mainly dry tarmac that constituted the 1983 Monte.

and lighter, rather more agile, saloons. Some mixed conditions on the way down to Monte gave Audi and Blomqvist a brief lead after six stages, but when they restarted in clear conditions from Monte at midnight, Rohrl's Lancia supercharged into a lead it would hold until the end, marking the Great German's third win in the World's best known rally.

Mouton's Monte ended with an accident − she had yet to finish in any of three Audi-mounted Montes when this was written − and Mikkola's engine developed a hairline block fracture that required an external brace. However Blomqvist's first Monte was a triumph under such difficult conditions for the car and he came away with third overall, 3m 47s ahead of Mikkola. Third and fourth place behind the two Lancias of Rohrl and Alen was really not a bad result on a dry Monte, for neither Finn nor Swede had managed to record more than two fastest times.

The Swedish, in February, saw Audi Sport domination with a 1-2-3-4 finish and a most successful World Championship debut for the 80 Quattro in Stig Blomqvist's skilled hands. The 80 appeared at "over 1100kg" with 194bhp officially claimed from the unturbocharged 2.1-litre five at around 6000rpm. In this period it appeared in Group B − moving into Group A recognition on July 1 1983 − but it should be noted that the factory 80 made its debut two years after the original coupe. Franz Wittman putting in his traditional first Austrian Championship round appearance with the coupe in the Janner Rallye and completing a hat-trick of wins, whilst rallycross ace Franz Wurz took the 80 Quattro to its first international result: eighth.

quattro

In Sweden, counting once more only toward the Driver's series in the World Championship, Mikkola led all the way. Blomqvist started slowly, the engine reportedly down on power in the manner that 80 Quattro drivers find traditional (perhaps because of excellent traction and instant response?). When Blomqvist realised that even a Golf GTi was ahead, he used his favourite Swedish stages to maximum effect and re-learned his old Saab front drive technique — the normal Quattro coupe's 300bhp plus means that there is always surplus power, where the 80s "don't have power. So if you get into a corner sideways there is not enough power to stay sideways. So now, with the 80 Quattro, I have to go even faster into the corner, like I would do with a front drive car. Flat out into the corner, sideways from the beginning, so that it gets less and less towards the end of the corner. You go sideways to drop the speed so then you have the line — because if you go too slow into it, you will be understeering", said Blomqvist in a masterfully-directed interview from Peter Foubister for *Autosport* after that debut.

Neither Mikkola nor Blomqvist had any serious car troubles throughout the event and it was widely felt that they finished 47 seconds apart in that order, under team orders, although this was denied by Gumpert. Finn Lasse Lampi with an ex-1982 Michele Mouton Quattro fettled by David Sutton Motorsport (LYV 5X) was third, little over a minute ahead of Mouton, who suffered an early parting in the injection throttle mechanism that cost four minutes. Thereafter she drove with true grit, setting five fastest times over the icy terrain. Incidentally they did use Michelin tyres even on this specialist event, the French having learned enough to produce a very effective, narrow, ice tyre to compete with the usual choice of Scandinavian rubber for this event.

Perfect Quattro paradise! Ever since 1981 and its first ever World Championship win, the Quattro and Sweden have gone together — and this shot says it all about the reasons for Quattro's supremacy. In 1983 Quattros finished 1-2-3-4. This is the third-place Quattro of Finn Lasse Lampi, a machine supplied by David Sutton.

quattro

The **1983** Swedish saw the 80 Quattro arrive with stunning snow speed, Stig Blomqvist taking this factory example to second overall. Then it was run in Group B, because too few had been made to qualify for A-grouping, but a year later the same 80 was winning Gp A on the Monte with a Frenchman at the wheel.

This time Mikkola made no mistakes and won the Swedish for the second time in three years with a Quattro. He is also the only non-Swede to win this qualifyer in the World Championship for drivers.

quattro

A fabulous Audi *versus* Lanci duel in Portugal was settled with Audi first and second; Lancia third to fifth. Mikkola and Mouton tied on the number of fastest times set, but second-place Michele Mouton set four more quickest times than either of the men and finished less than a minute behind Mikkola, who is shown in this picture.

The Port Wine Portuguese World Championship qualifyer in both title hunts ran to its usual entertaining formula of constantly changing fortunes. This is partially the by-product of using both tarmac and loose surface stages, but also because this first class event with only its death wish spectators to mar an otherwise perfect plot, attracts a first class entry. Unlike Sweden the opposition was substantial, Lancia sending three factory Rallys and Nissan two of their 240RS models: only Opel were absent of the significant opposition.

Audi came armed with a Quattro quartet for Mikkola to defend his Championship lead, supported by Blomqvist and Mouton. All three were in the Quattros used for the Monte, Mouton's practice coupe going to Wittman.

As ever fortunes fluctuated with the road surfaces and lady luck's dealership on wild cards like punctures and damaged dampers. Lancia were 1-2 after 11 stages, the Pirelli-shod machines showing surprising loose surface speed as well as their usual tarmac flair, but the first long and rough stages soon saw the Quattros comeback. Unfortunately Blomqvist's belligerent assault on the lead was blunted by mechanical maladies in the damping department and he eventually belted the countryside sufficiently hard to bend the rear bodywork, and damaged both driveshaft and rear differential. The car was rescued in the stage and had its propshaft disconnected to take Stig back on front drive only, but by that time it was simply out of the running.

On the longest, 35 mile, Arganil stage both Mikkola and Rohrl suffered punctures whilst fighting for the lead, allowing Mouton to close right in with a fastest time, 1 second quicker than Alen's Lancia and 1m 13s faster than Rohrl, who was over a minute faster than Mikkola. The German had a rear tyre puncture on the Lancia and did not have to stop and change the wheel, whilst Mikkola knew that his front-end tyre deflation must mean a wheel change, as it is all too easy to damage a Quattro differential or driveshaft under such circumstances.

Despite this setback it was Mikkola who increased his and Audi's points totals with maximum scores, winning by 55 seconds from Mouton with Rohrl third and Alen fourth in a magnificent battle quartet that left the rest, headed by another Lancia, long behind. Incidentally Wittman managed a finish too, seventh after clutch slip slowed his progress a little in the later stages.

Hannu Mikkola/Arne Hertz led a Quattro A1 assault in Portugal that brought them first place with Michele Mouton second. Look at the sheer number of background spectators . . .

Trailing Lancia by two points, but with Mikkola in a firm 18 point lead of his World Championship, Audi paid their first factory visit to the Safari Rally, Kenya over Easter. Drawing on their African Ivory coast experience they built three brand new Quattros for Mikkola, Mouton and local former Ford Escort contract driver Vic Preston jnr. Power was the lowest on boost seen all year, but the cars fed from enormous 200 litre/44 gallon fuel tanks that almost invaded all the cockpit accommodation too! Extractor fans, as used in their earlier African sorties, were

Altogether six works Quattros were shipped by Lufthansa Cargo to Nairobi for Audi's first assault on Safari, three used on the event and the others to practice. Mikkola's second place machine is on the left (IN-VC 17) with Preston's crunched Quattro centre and Michele Mouton's third place coupe coming out, beneath the Boeing 747's uplifted side door.

quattro

also fitted where the rear seat backrest would normally be, making the cabin a little less dusty.

Opposition to Audi lacked Lancia, but Opel and Nissan could be expected to provide a formidable fight because the Safari is an event that seems to respond primarily to suitable mechanical specification and driver experience. For example Nissan's Shekhar Mehta had won the event five times for the Japanese, and Opel had been trying for a win over several years, finding that it's easy to lead, but more difficult to drive at a pace that gives low mechanical and accident worries for eventual victory.

Mikkola lost over 1.5 hours early in the event when his car's water pump pulley was damaged and upset the camshaft drive. Mikkola pulled up before the engine was irreparably wounded, but even the helicopter-born Roland Gumpert and his mechanics could not put this humpty Quattro back together again in less than 100 minutes.

Tough task. 4-WD may be ideal for Kenya's Safari Rally, but Michele Mouton had all sorts of dramas on her way to third overall. Note dust-laden screen and large background crowd.

Thus Mouton led the first leg, three minutes ahead of the first Nissan Datsun with Preston sixth and previous multiple Safari winner Mikkola charging back up the running order. Mouton suffered the sort of service problems that African inexperience can bring: a bonnet flapping loose in the first leg and a wheel following the bonnet's example on the second. Eventually the wheel broke loose and the girls were unable to fit a fresh example to its place, Mouton driving over 8 miles on three wheels and losing over 40 minutes. New rear suspension for one corner and associated driveshaft was eventually installed when the service crews could get to the ladies, but by that time — even with the large spread of time between competitors that is a feature on Safari — they had dropped back to seventh.

Salonen went into the lead but was no match even for the frequently badly-suspended Quattro of Vic Preston, which swept back from a cannily-judged opening pace worthy of a local into the lead by the time they returned to Nairobi at the close of the second leg. Preston's lead was 11 minutes over Salonen, with Mouton now in third place a further 23 minutes adrift and Mikkola placed eleventh.

Preston continued to lead for the majority of the event, having 14 minutes over Salonen and 59 minutes over Mouton at the finish of the third leg, Mikkola now fifth. Preston then literally hit trouble in the enormous dust clouds thrown up by slower competitors and clumped a rock with enough spinning force to immobolise the Quattro with curly front suspension and a dead front differential.

Mouton scrapped with Salonen until an alternator started starving the Audi's electrics, while Vatanen and Mikkola — old Escort team mates — battled for third overall. Believe it or not Mouton lost another wheel — a rear, the nuts having loosened — and that was another hour gone in consequent clearing up activities, dropping the now rightly fuming Michele down to fourth. She suffered further

Worth all the setbacks. Fabrizia Pons (left) and Michele Mouton stand at the finish of the Safari with their heavily-armoured Quattro beneath.

quattro

alternator troubles on the final run-in leaving a clear path for the Vatanen-Mikkola clash to be resolved, for Saloon's Datsun destroyed its engine.

Although Hannu was removing great chunks of time from Ari's advantage in the Opel it was not enough: Vatanen with Ulsterman Terry Harryman made it by six minutes over Mikkola with Mouton a rewarding, and fitting, third following a drive that might be described as very much in the "character-building" top rallyist's tradition.

Thus with four rounds of the Driver's Championship completed and three of that for Manufacturers, Mikkola led his sector by 65 points to 37 of Michele Mouton, 34 of 1981 Champion Vatanen and 32 for the absent Rohrl. On the manufacturer's front Audi had 48 points to 37 accrued by Opel and 32 in the Lancia corner. Audi had the new A2 weapon to draw on for their least suitable impending Championship round: Corsica. With Lancia's record, via the fabulous Stratos, or using much the same Abarth personnel when running the Fiat 131 to World Championship success in the seventies, Audi would need a buffer . . .

The Corsican opposition was both numerous and experienced, Audi losing one excellent chance of success before the event got underway — shades of 1982 — when Bernard Darniche crashed his Quattro and crushed his heel. It was a serious road accident of the kind that is all too easy when topline competitors are forced to practice on public roads, and Darniche looked far from recovery even when he limped into action during October's Sanremo — never mind taking any further part in the Corsican proceedings.

So Mikkola and Mouton returned to the Mediterranean island as sole Quattro representatives against four factory Martini Lancias, two good semi-works Rallys, a single Manta 400 for Guy Frequelin. The coupe shape and liberal use of Kevlar panels took the Opel down close to 980kg while a Cosworth-built four-valve per cylinder engine of 2.4 litres had now been persuaded to give 275bhp. Also on hand were Renault, only 1982 winner Jean Ragnotti appearing in the official work's yellow, Nissan were represented just by Corsican expert Tony Pond and Bernard Beguin had the fabulous BMW M1 in GpB trim, the obsolete Bavarian machine a

Neither of the new A2 Quattros that actually made the start of May's Corsican Championship qualifier got to the finish. However Hannu Mikkola, seen here in the fat-wheeled tarmac Quattro, was in amongst the slower factory Lancias and looked likely to finish within the top four. In 23 stages he set two fastest times and was in the top six on 15 occasions.

hangover from the fabulously rich ProCar series and offering a good 430bhp from 3.5 litres.

As ever Corsica was unkind to Mikkola and just as brutal to Mouton, who has a much better record on this event. The A2 derivative did show more promise, Audi timing making it considerably faster than the Lancias, wherever there was more than a car's width to be used in road space. Unfortunately that is not how the notoriously twisty Corsican roads are mainly built — they tend toward the tightest of UK lanes with harsh rock faces and armco as the main "run-off" areas. So the Quattro continued to lose chunks of time where jinking manoeuvrability should have been the order of the day, tortuous hairpins and acute road junctions causing particular problems.

From 32 stages Mikkola massaged two fastest times. However both Audi cars managed to run in the top half dozen pretty consistently and looked likely to finish fourth and sixth at the conclusion of the penultimate leg. On the event's longest stage, the 50 mile plus Lianone-Suaricchio, Mikkola brushed the Corsican countryside hard enough to buckle the back suspension and remove a wheel.

That was bad enough but Mouton's similar ultra-lightweight Quattro (using wire for the door pulls and mirror adjustment, and a cellophane reflective strip that carried the usual Quattro legend across the rear in place of the usual plastic, plus the flightiest plastic panels you have ever seen) had been consistently in turbocharger trouble. As the casing on the turbine allowed vital pressure to breeze away the exhaust system and water started to make their presence felt. Michele had to give up when the engine's internals escaped through a neat hole in the block, two stages from the finish.

Corsican battle cry. Mikkola's new Quattro A2 sprints past the lens of one of many camera crews recording this scenic event, aided by a probable 400bhp. Mikkola eventually brushed with the local terrain and Lancia filled the first four positions. (C11-15)

Result? Lancia 1-2-3-4 and not an Audi in sight. Ingolstadt fell to third in the points table, just two points behind leaders Lancia, and one behind Opel. Mikkola hung on to series advantage, but by 65 points to the 47 of Rohrl, who had finished second to Alen in the grand slam, a somewhat surprising result for all three of the front-running Lancia drivers — Andruet, Rohrl and Alen — had led at various points.

June should have applied Audi's revenge, for the rocky heat of Greece with its dusty loose going was made for Audi to pound Lancia into oblivion. Ingolstadt presented three new Quattro A2s with the electrically-operated clutch, now made legal by FISA, much in evidence for Mikkola, Mouton and Blomqvist: the fourth car was for Wittman, his national Austrian Championship mount brought up to the latest specification. Opposition embraced a Lancia trio — Rohrl, Alen and Attilio Bettega — and Opel had three Manta 400s there for their biggest European effort, driven by Vatanen, Toivonen and McRae. Renault had a single works turbo and there were three works Nissan Datsuns, including machines for Salonen and Mehta.

The kind of event Audi had can be simply judged from the *Motoring News* heading on the front page: "Audi: apocalypse now?" Indeed it had been a wipe out. Mikkola led from the twelfth to the 39th stage when, with three minutes in hand over Rohrl, Hannu found the orange oil pressure light had blinked on. A flapping boot had allowed an oil line to pull away in the complex boot plumbing and that was that.

Mouton had rolled on the first stage (!) and although the inversion was not a serious problem, those vulnerable boot oil lines to the huge rear wing-shrouded coolers had fractured, and the five-cylinder was feeling very poorly by the time the car straggled into service, well out of time anyway.

Blomqvist? The saviour once more, despite the limited-slip front differential tried on his Quattro alone. This device seemed to work well, with Blomqvist returning the fastest times on 17 of the 46 scheduled stages, but the pump that is used to provide hydraulic pressure played up and that upset steering, braking and the electronic clutch action. When the mechanics replaced it the ignition timing was disturbed and it was a few stages before Blomqvist could start motoring hard again, taking fastest times on three out of the four final stages. Stig Blomqvist, the professional's professional, emerged third, Lancia taking first and second with Rohrl heading Alen's troubled Lancia to an unexpected 1-2.

Although the gap at the top of the points table was not insurmountable for Audi and Mikkola — Hannu was now two points adrift of Walter R and Audi had the same disadvantage against Lancia — one could sympathise with experienced observers who reckoned Audi were snatching defeat from the jaws of victory. The servicing erred toward erratic, the company putting greater emphasis on pre-event preparation for this complex car rather than in-field service and using a rota of mechanics, some drawn from areas unfamiliar with the sport, and Lancia looked increasingly professional as they sensed the chance of victory. Contrary to popular British opinion, the Italians had been moulded into unmatched service expertise with excellent organisation born of over a decade's winning experience with Lancia and Fiat. The kind of team that would change even fumbly five-bolt wheels in midstage if they thought surface variations demanded it — and accomplish such high pressure tasks with non-Latin aplomb.

New Zealand ought to have saved the Audi bacon, but 1983 was not a season in which Ms Luck dealt kindly with Ingolstadt's aspirations. As is almost Audi tradition, things started going wrong before the event. Not with the trio of cars, all basically of Safari specification and over 1200kg, but with a later entry for Blomqvist to join Mikkola and Mouton down under. Lancia didn't like this one bit — they were running just two cars — and kicked up a fuss that lasted the best part of 20 days. Horrendously mismanaged between appeal and final judgement, the result was that Stig Blomqvist completed eight stages of the event extremely competitively, despite an absence of pre-event preparation and the need to use Mikkola/Hertz recce notes, and then found himself excluded through no fault of his own.

Adding to Audi's woes Mikkola had one of those starts. On the first stage a camshaft pulley let the belt escape and that was nearly 21 minutes lost to Rohrl while repairs were completed, although fitting the belt in such a hurry allowed no time to refit the intercooler and Hannu had to tackle the second stage *sans* turbo boost. This Audi five had about 260bhp less than intended, albeit temporarily. By stage four Mikkola was in the belt wars zone again, this time an oil pump was getting zero drive after an attack by the debris from the earlier incident. Once again Gumpert and the Audi helicopter literally flew to the rescue.

Eventually Mikkola lugged the Quattro back up to fourth overall, only to be eliminated by an underbonnet fire that owed its source to fuel leaking from the injection's engine plumbing on the intake gallery. Blomqvist had noticed a similar seepage on his car and it was by no means the only time that such an incident occurred in 1983 . . . A problem traced later in the season to a Y-branch in the fuel-injection petrol delivery plumbing, adjacent to the hot engine, and rectified. yet fires continued to haunt Audi for different reasons in 1983.

Mouton? Going very well indeed, despite an engine that loved to guzzle oil. On the 28th of 36 scheduled stages the Audi ladies were defending a lead that approached five minutes over Walter Rohrl's Lancia. Then a connecting rod bolt sheared and let the rod escape through the alloy block, preventing what should have been a thoroughly deserved victory by a significant margin. Lancia now had 86 points to 62 accrued by Lancia and Rohrl had 87 against the 65 of Mikkola, with Alen in touch on 60.

It was time to take the medicine, swallow and produce the maximum effort. An Audi army went to Argentina for an event that covered over 1860 miles of frequently muddy and icy going in the first six days of August. Their tenacity was rewarded: a quartet of Quattros dominated the proceedings to reduce Lancia's points potential to that of scooping up fifth place. In such slippery conditions the Quattro coupes excelled, even Mouton losing a wheel (is there no end to these dramas?) did not interrupt a tidy team formation arriving in the order Mikkola,

Argentina was the scene of the fastest Championship round ever with averages well over 100mph on some sections. Mikkola led the Audi rout of the first four places and a Quattro 80 was sixth as well.

quattro

Blomqvist, Mouton and Marlboro-backed Shekhar Mehta in the fourth works coupe: Mehta within 10 seconds of giving Alen a 10 minute hiding. To complete Audi's happiness it might have been nice to see local lad Ruben Luis di Palma take the fifth Quattro coupe to the finish, but he inverted it after four stages! However, European rallycross Champion Franz Wurz confirmed his early season Audi 80 promise by taking sixth overall in the now Group A Quattro derivative.

Score? Mikkola was back to within two points of Rohrl and Lancia's Makes lead had shrunk to 16 points. With the 1000 Lakes imminent, Mikkola almost airborne for Finland and the chance of a record-breaking seventh win as Argentina finished, it looked as though Audi might still have a chance of a championship double in 1983.

Against twin entries of Opel and Lancia, plus a trio of new Group B Toyotas and single cars from Mitsubishi and Nissan, Audi entered three factory Quattros with Lasse Lampi and Per Eklund, the latter Blomqvist's front drive sparring partner in Saabs, appearing in factory-supplied but privately serviced Quattro coupes. Eklund had Blomqvist's training car and Lampi Mikkola's, whilst the factory drivers used machines of Corsican ancestry with the progressive rate springs Gumpert discussed with us earlier in this book — which were a great success, minimising the Quattro's tendency to dart unpredictably following a heaving landing of the Finnish yumping kind. Only Mikkola, Mouton and Blomqvist were serviced by factory mechanics.

As had almost become tradition Mikkola was in trouble straight away. A heavy landing on the first spectactor-orientated stage devoured the front differential. Getting off the stage on rwd, setting second quickest time *en route*, was no problem: changing it for a new unit fast enough, definitely was a problem! The works mechanics managed the change in the kind of 30 minute style that had been expected, but there were still heavy penalties: arriving 11 minutes late at the next stage dropped him to 143rd. It was a situation Mikkola had almost become familiar with over his Audi years: at least the driver then has the maximum stage mileage to overcome such an initial problem.

After 11 stages Mikkola was back to seventh, Alen's Lancia leading Blomqvist's Audi and messrs Toivonen and Vatanen in the Rothmans Opels. Eklund was an excellent fifth and learning Quattro technique with some genuine respect for the turbocharged power provided; Mouton was eighth and not over-awed with the handling, progressive springs or no progressive springs. Certainly on Blomqvist's Quattro they wound on extra camber during the event to fine tune its yumping manners.

Blomqvist had a fraught start to the second leg, a rear differential failing even though conditions were actually rather nice for Quattro rallying: typically British downpour plus a nice slippery loose surface. It didn't take too long to change the back differential and the Swede incurred no time penalties, enabling him to concentrate on slicing back Alen's advantage. They had only completed 16 of 50 scheduled tests when Blomqvist moved ahead, trading fastest times with Mikkola as the Finn hurtled ever forward . . . and, apparently, backward, on occasion, when the sideways stuff reached its ultimate!

From the eleventh stage to the twenty-second it was war between three of the world's finest. Mikkola and Blomqvist set all the fastest times, score 6-5 in the Swede's favour, but neither were totally trouble free. Blomqvist spotted a fuel injection leak that had obvious hazards and Mikkola had the computer chip brain for ignition and injection die twice, so that Hertz had to switch them into the back-up unit. After those 22 stages Blomqvist had just over 50 seconds on the magnificent Alen, with Vatanen just holding Hannu out of fourth overall. Eklund was fifth and Mouton continued eighth in a contest characterised by personal bravery and enormously experienced expertise from the front runners.

The third leg saw Hannu go for it. He took nine consecutive fastest times, an almost impossible feat in such competitive company, and it promoted Audi's World Championship leading driver into 2nd overall. Not bad from 143rd!

After 34 stages, the Audis had moved into command; Mikkola leading Blomqvist by a second! Alen was third but Lancia were well aware that Audi had their troubles, particularly the curse of under-bonnet injection fires. Mikkola suffered a minor outbreak but both Eklund and Mouton were worse affected, the lady lying down in 35th place after smothering a fire in mid-stage and losing over 20 minutes. The cause? Audi said at the time that it was simply the severity of the jumps pulling away fuel lines, but it is also true that there have been material changes in the way that the injection was plumbed, substituting metal for plastic on at least one connection.

Audi Sport wanted Mikkola, their leading points scorer as well as their number 1 from the start of the Quattro project, to now drift away to an unchallenged win over Blomqvist, but the best laid plans . . . on test 36, Ohtinen, the sheer yumping pace of the 1000 Lakes showed up when the lead Quattro's engine keeled over on its shattered mountings and pulled the intercooler plumbing apart. Effectively without turbocharged boost pressure the motor lost the best part of 150bhp and Mikkola lost over half a minute to the front-runners. Now he was second, 19 seconds behind Blomqvist, but they were still not confident of the car's turbo plumbing, for Hannu and Arne had somewhat apprehensively re-connected the pipework and it was another stage, losing perhaps a dozen seconds to the leaders, before they could have the car serviced by the factory mechanics. Even then there was a leak in the intercooler itself that later demanded attention before the car returned to its normal ultra-competitive pace.

Another August win for Mikkola. This time the background is Finland and the maestro is on his way to an unprecedented seventh win on his home event, even though there were some severe set-backs to overcome.

quattro

Just five stages to go. The weather was better than it had been all of the short (two-day, 906 route miles containing nearly 300 stage miles) event. Blomqvist held 24 seconds in hand over Mikkola, who had only 13 seconds lead over Alen's Lancia. There were 20.27 stage miles left, none of them of the lengthy kind where big hunks of time can be sliced away from an opponent at this level of international competition.

Gumpert went in search of Blomqvist to underline the result the factory wanted. At a subsequent press conference the Audi team boss explained that the result was not a fix on team orders, the result had been in doubt right to the end, and that Lancia was too close for comfort. This was Gumpert's logic. The times spoke of yet another occasion when Stig Blomqvist had been forced to give best to Mikkola, for the good of the team. Consider: the first stage after the Gumpert-Blomqvist chat, 5.38 miles of it, saw Mikkola pull eight seconds back from Blomqvist. On stages of similar length earlier in the event, the gap between Mikkola Blomqvist, or vice versa, had been largest at two seconds. That brought Mikkola to within 16 seconds of Blomqvist with four stages to go. Over the next 3.38 miles, another five seconds were removed to Mikkola's credit. Another 2.65 mile test slashed another seven seconds away, so that, with two stages left, Mikkola was only four seconds behind. It was duly done: Mikkola was nine seconds quicker than Blomqvist over the penultimate stage's 4.73 miles and an incredible 16 seconds separated the Flying Finn and Swift Swede over the final fiftieth stage's brief 4.14 miles.

The official results showed Mikkola 21 seconds ahead at the finish, a fit reward for a fine drive and one that took him to 105 World Championship points. Rohrl remained on 87, not competing on this specialist event, while Alen's Finnish flair and sheer persistence had acquired 80 points and third overall in the series for Drivers. With hindsight one can only feel sorry for Blomqvist in that it was far from the first time that he had obviously had to slow and hand over event leadership after a superb drive, but it was thought that 1984 could provide a fitting Championship crown for the Swede as the rest of the Audi driver quartet had already publicly said they wanted to do fewer World Championship rounds than previously.

The 1983 Rally of the 1000 Lakes provided Eklund with fourth overall and Lampi with seventh as well as those leading places, but Lancia still held a twelve point lead in the Makes title chase — and the next round was in Italy.

The Decider

Lancia-Fiat competitions director Cesare Fiorio knew that the 25th Sanremo Rally could provide their eighth Lancia or Fiat title since 1972 and a fleet of battle-ready 037 Rallys lined up on the Mediterranean sea-front start to face four Audis. There were actually eight works-built cars in the flower-conscious city of Sanremo, all ready the night before the off so that the mechanics could get their rest for the drawn out contest ahead. The Sanremo event sprawls from that Italian answer to the nearby coastline attractions of Southern France and Monaco down to Pisa and Siena in five distinct sorties. Over six days, 1659 route miles they tackled only 480 stage miles, divided into a first, fourth and fifth leg with tarmac tests totalling 212 miles and the middle two legs of loose gravel going and 268 miles total.

Therefore it was vital that the Quattros not only deliver the expected pounding to all opposition over the loose, but also at least hold the Lancias on tarmac if they were to have any chance of securing a second World Championship of Makes. To make sure they had the right engine and gearbox spec, Audi ran a number of preliminary tarmac tests and settled for a very peaky motor with

associated close ratios (the gears themselves thickened and a new gearbox mounting homologated) which gave the best results on the fast test stages they selected.

Blomqvist and Mikkola had brand new Quattros, Stig's the 50th complete competition car constructed at Ingolstadt (many of the rebuilt cars equate to the same amount of work but are not usually allotted new numbers). Mouton and the now fitter Bernard Darniche were allotted ex-1000 Lakes machinery, Mouton in Mikkola's winner and Darniche, the great Lancia Stratos ace for Chardonnet in France who won that classic's last Monte in 1979, drew Blomqvist's 1000 Lakes mount.

The exotic location brought further excitement in machinery too, Opel's two Manta 400s for Vatanen and Toivonen joined by three Ferrari V8 308GTBs, these four valve exotica each offering over 300bhp for a team that included 1979 World Champion Bjorn Waldegard.

The signs that a monstrous miscalculation on engine and gearbox specification had occured in Audi's pre-event testing was evident after the first six twisty tarmac tests in the hills behind Sanremo: the highest-placed Quattro was twelfth! Furthermore it was not Mikkola or Blomqvist that were shining — their power steering had packed up thanks to faulty pump drives and reduced the maestros to survival rather than swiftness — but Mouton struggled with her Quattro to that twelfth place, Darniche well off the pace throughout.

The power steering pumps on the new cars were replaced by older units from the practice cars, but it was obvious that, even with this problem fixed, the Quattro had actually regressed in its tarmac competitiveness. Why? I asked Jorg Bensinger this question as he was preparing to drive back from Sanremo at the end of an event on which he had been joined as an observer by Audi Chairman Dr Wolfgang Habbel. "It was just the wrong choice of engines and gearboxes for this event. When we did the testing it was on very fast tests so the engines we had were no good for low down power. That meant the drivers were always changing gear, and on these slow roads where the Lancias were in second gear we had to take first gear, and that was much slower. Too much power in the wrong place. It was terrible".

Indeed it was. The first loose stages flattered to deceive with the Quattros of Mouton, Blomqvist and Mikkola moving into second, third and fourth despite Blomqvist caressing a tunnel wall in the prevalent dust.

The third leg, running from Siena to Pisa, emphasised that fortune and Audi don't belong in the same sentence. "The car just took fire", explained Mikkola, his fair hair soaked, along with the inevitable Audi T-shirt, in sweat and the usual faint smile of regret accompanying the words recalling their ordeal with typical understatement. "The back was burning completely. It was not the same as in 1000 Lakes: it was bad this time, and of course we did not know. We did not notice the flames before we had done many kilometres. Then the fire was so bad we could not get it out. It was too late, the whole car burned". It certainly did, even the alloy block returning to molten metal under the heat of those lightweight materials blazing.

Because the wreckage was so charred it seemed unlikely that we would ever discover the cause of the conflagration, although Audi themselves would obviously have to investigate a lot further as fire, for a number of reasons, had haunted the car's career, particularly in 1983. Looking at the cars in action you can see that the usual turbo over-run flame-outs come from two sources, the usual rear pipe and underneath the front engine bay, so that any stray fuel vapour being dumped or leaked stands an exceptionally good chance of being ignited. The reason one could see turbo "flame-outs" at the *front* of a works, or works-backed, 1983 Quattro, was because an ingenious sliding plate was fitted to the engine

quattro

What was left of Mikkola's Quattro after the 1983 Sanremo fire. Frightening, but also interesting as a revelation of the basic sheet steel frame that supported the late A2 Quattros beneath those light exterior panels.

exhaust downpipe. Closed, it provided a scrutineer-proof road-legal Quattro: open it gave 5-10bhp extra for ultimate speed. In Mikkola's case the spectators had seen a fire at the rear long before the crew, and all reports indicate that the rear end was well alight from causes unknown before the crew could react. A sad affair that added to Audi's 1983 Sanremo gloom.

Mouton was no ray of sunshine either for she was in real trouble with a sick engine that meant "we can go, but it is very difficult. The sensor for the temperature of the air in the turbo is broken from 1 kilometre of the start of the stage — and of course it was the longest one!" At the close of the third leg Alen continued to lead for Lancia with Blomqvist second, although a sideways moment had seen the Swede bruise the Quattro further, requiring masses of "racers tape" to bind together the wounded rear bumpers and associated lightweight panels. Rohrl was third in his troubled Lancia and Toivonen had taken fourth from Mouton's banging and popping Audi. With only tarmac mileage left and Audi's engine choice in mind it was now obvious that nothing short of wholesale carnage amongst the Martini-liveried Lancias could save Audi's Championship chances.

In fact things just got worse. Blomqvist dropped to third and Mouton seventh after the fourth leg, both former Sanremo winners for Audi totally outpaced despite trying even harder than in their victorious years. The fifth leg proved the final insult, Blomqvist slowed by a clutch change and a puncture before it all proved too much even for this top pro and he knocked a front corner sufficiently hard to bend the suspension and retire on the 53rd of 58 stages actually run.

Mouton did make it to the end despite repeated injection sensor maladies, 18m 3s behind the victorious Alen, who headed a Lancia 1-2-3. More than enough to grasp the Makes title from Audi. Incidentally Darniche did finish, ninth and over 14 minutes behind Mouton after he had suffered two fires, one definitely attributed to a power steering leak being ignited by the exhaust.

Having secured the Makes title at considerable extra cost beyond that originally budgeted, Lancia were reluctant to attend the final pair of World Championship rounds, although drivers Rohrl and Alen clearly had a good chance of pulling off the unexpected if they could get rides in the Ivory Coast and

Lombard RAC. For Mikkola had only 105 points to Rohrl's 102 and Alen's 100, almost as close as the three-cornered title fight amongst the 1983 Grand Prix contenders. Unlike GP drivers the rallyists might well swap cars and continue their challenges, although the odds were on Mikkola as he had almost made the RAC his personal property — and had yet to be beaten on the event in a Quattro.

Mikkola made sure of the 1983 Driver's title on the penultimate African Championship round, but he did not win the event. That honour fell to Bjorn Waldegard's turbo Toyota and the very experienced team that ran the Japanese machine, giving this Group B newcomer victory on its second Championship outing. As ever the organisers had a job scraping together the minimum of 50 entries that are required for World Championship status events, Audi and Toyota the only works teams, each with two entries. They were Mikkola/Hertz and Lasse Lampi/Otto Harsch in Audi's case, the second factory Quattro simply Hannu's recce car crewed by the resourceful Finnish driver Lampi, who demonstrated his driving prowess with a subsequent fourth on the RAC, accompanied by one of Ingolstadt's best mechanics in the African rally.

Additional Audi support came from two light aircraft (helicopters were specifically banned) and a third Quattro for another innovative and mechanically aware Quattro driver, John Buffum. The American champion was not entered and his car was notable for the three seater layout, another competition seat

The Audi workshops in September 1983 had few management personnel present because of the Frankfurt Show introduction of Quattro Sport. Here we can see A2s being readied for Sanremo and the RAC with a three-seater Ivory Coast support Quattro in the middle of the shop.

quattro

placed in the rear, that I first recall seeing at Ingolstadt in September. It is a perch to provide a bird's eye view of the front, but not the most comfortable room in the house!

Audi's crews and personnel ensured that they performed toward the long-deserved objective of a Championship for Mikkola, for above all else. The 41-year-old Finn led two of the five legs in the lengthy 2944 mile event, losing his opening leg lead in the second section return to Yamoussoukro when he touched down on some logs. A 25 minute delay included replacing two punctured tyres and rebuilding the battered front suspension with the help of Buffum and company, but the Quattro still had a bent subframe and bottom wishbones; it was felt that it was safer to leave them on than risk new components that would not fit the contours of the tortured underbody.

The third leg put Mikkola back ahead of Waldegard by 12 minutes, the Toyota losing a wheel, which went on to tragically take the life of a child spectator. Waldegard counter-attacked in the next 380 mile leg, but Mikkola was content at having lost only a minute or so until a number of near head-on crashes with timber lorries and an off reduced his lead to seven minutes and the Safari specification Quattro (around 340bhp at 1.7 bar boost) to an example of how high tech 1990 Stock Cars will look! This time the back wheels were knocked out of alignment, but with less than 400 miles to complete the event, that was a handling problem Hannu would live with happily, if only he could grab those Championship points . . .

The final dash to Abidjan held all the drama that could be generated by three serious contestants. Audi and Toyota continuing their quarrels over following in each other's dirty wake, a problem initially compounded by chase cars following Mikkola and blinding the eventual third-placed Toyota of Eklund. Yet the rally was decided by Mikkola losing 10 minutes in another excursion – which required further rear suspension repairs and a driveshaft.

Waldegard eventually ran out an 8 minute winner over Mikkola, but the Finn was World Champion in all but officially confirmed status from this point on. That was because neither Alen nor Rohrl did contest the RAC Rally, although there was apparently serious talk of Alen getting an Audi, this after Lancar in Britain were unable to come up with the £25,000 needed to run Alen against Mikkola on the RAC in a works Lancia Rally.

Thus the British Championship finale was robbed of any chance to provide a fitting finish (Finnish?) to the 1983 title fight. However, for the Quattro fan there were squads of the ingenious Ingolstadters to be seen at the Bath start – and there were almost as many at the end, with four in the top ten and a 1-2 result.

New factory Quattro A2s were constructed for Stig Blomqvist (44 CMN) and Hannu Mikkola, Michele Mouton acquiring Blomqvist's Sanremo mount. The Blomqvist car was built by David Sutton mechanics at Ingolstadt to the official 360bhp minimum and was converted prior to the start to the electro-hydraulic clutch operation favoured on the factory forest cars.

The works team of Mouton and Mikkola were separated from Sutton's equipe and also ran different tyres, as Pirelli equipped Blomqvist's Quattro and Michelin the Ingolstadt pair. Altogether there were 24 support vehicles for the trio – including Gumpert's delectable A1-bodied road Quattro in red – and a small plane to co-ordinate them.

In older Quattros, with varying degrees of support, were John Buffum/Neil Wilson (BF Goodrich A1, shipped back to the USA after the event); Antero Laine/Pekka Hokkanen (private German-registered A1, damaged by both fire and road accident, rendering it a non-finisher); Darryl Weidner/Rob Arther (in the Quattro A1-bodied machine that had helped grasp two national titles) and Lasse Lampi/Pentti Kukkala (in the ex-Sutton LYV 5X). Whilst both Weidner and Laine retired after fires, neither had anything to do with the factory's earlier infernos, or anything in common. Laine's Quattro smashed the rear oil cooler spilling hot lubricant that was soon ignited by the exhaust. It took the assistance of 12 crews to quench the rear end blaze. By contrast the Weidner trouble was traced to a cracked turbo piping connection, the problem had intruded on a consistent top ten placing before the crew eventually decided their nerves would not stand a further minor outbreak of underbonnet fire, having entertained the spectators with some forest-warming ''flame-outs'' *en route*.

Of the privateer Quattros that made it, Lampi was the highest placed in fourth — beaten by only one 2-WD car, the Manta of Jimmy McRae. Buffum was the most spectacular, taking his battered (but hardly scratched by his 1982 standards!) coupe to sixth.

Of the factory cars it could be said that there was the usual early drama. On a sunny Sunday morning in the Midlands Crest Motel you could watch Mouton desperately churning the starter of her Quattro, whilst Gumpert supervised the pumping of gallons of water-laden petrol around the forecourt. Yes, a mechanic had grabbed the wrong can and tipped 5 to 20 litres (it depended who you spoke to) of water into the tank at the previous service point.

After a quarter of an hour or so of demonstrating what a powerful starter motor and fuel injection pumps can do to rid themselves of a watery layer, Mouton was on her way through the suburban Sunday mimsers, Gallic oaths rampant. That night in Yorkshire she finally tossed the machine off the road sufficiently thoroughly to make her further participation pointless.

Some people will do anything to get in a BHP film...

Christmas card from Barrie Hinchcliffe Productions, the film equipe who bring Championship rallying in Britain and abroad to UK screens, shows how famous the RAC incident that befell Mikkola has become. The draughtsmanship is by Jim Bamber, whose work will be well known to those who have seen his attractive cutaway car drawings in *Rallycourse*.

Mikkola was not outdone, for he had two small accidents on the stately home two day preliminaries, the most important being the eleventh stage Knowsley incident that cost him six minutes and dropped the coupe back to 26th. Hannu confessed the team could not believe such a minor encounter with an upturned log on the inside of a corner (tapped into the ground to prevent corner cutting!) could whip the strut from its mounting, forcing Hannu and Arne to remove the jammed wheel and tyre from beneath the front wheel arch. That task completed, Hertz climbed aboard the Quattro's ''tailplane'' and the Quattro tricycled

quattro

Stig Blomqvist was unmatched on the 1983 RAC Rally of Great Britain, this despite the incident on the longest Dalby stage that led to the need for that temporary rear panel in sheet metal.

uncertainly out of the stage. Mikkola told me subsequently, "I just couldn't believe the car had lost a wheel. We didn't feel a thing in the corner − and you can see the body is not damaged at all."

That incident cost Mikkola any chance of a genuine scrap for the lead of Lombard's 1983 RAC Rally, but that is not to diminish Stig Blomqvist's dominant run to a 9m 53s victory. The Swede was brilliant, totally unfazed by early minor problems created by the injection wiring and the alternator, and surviving a substantial swipe at the scenery around the longest (41 mile) Dalby stage in Yorkshire. That incident left the Quattro with rumpled hindquarters; subsequently the indecently exposed inner wheel arch was clothed with a riveted steel panel that gained paintwork and stickers during the remaining three days of the event.

There had been no question of Mikkola catching up lost ground on the Swedish-crewed Quattro either, for even on Dalby, Stig arrived beneath the lights of the time card hand-in point having covered the longest RAC special stage 1m 20s *faster* than Mikkola, including the accident! Even the bent metal was not really Blomqvist's fault as the mud-splattered front of his Quattro testified to following Henri Toivonen's Opel, to the detriment of the Quattro's lighting. An eventual opportunity to pass allowed Stig the chance to plunge into the gloom, and a mixed surface right-hander, with panel-bending panache!

Of 57 stage times that went to provide the competition mileage on the 1983 RAC, Blomqvist was quickest on 34 and Mikkola fastest on 16. So there was no doubt at all that it was a fine victory, but more surprise that it was Blomqvist's first of 1983 in the world series, until one remembered that the factory had pledged to do their utmost for Mikkola to make the title his, and they honoured that undertaking.

He did it his way. Hannu Mikkola, 1983 World Champion and victor of more Championship rounds than any other driver (16).

A new A2 Quattro was built in Ingolstadt for Blomqvist to use on the 1983 RAC — which he won by 9m 53s — and for use in the 1984 British Open series by Hannu Mikkola.

In 1984 Blomqvist would be the one tackling a full Championship assault whilst Mikkola and Mouton planned a half dozen events, with Rohrl expected to also pick and choose World Championship rallies carefully. Walter had certainly got off to a tumultuous start in his Quattro relationship, for he had already rolled the car in public before the close of 1983, whilst acting as a course car in Germany . . !

Appendix I

1984 Quattro action

For their first major season-long sponsorship deal, Audi waited until 1984 and settled for a West German cigarette company after previous approaches from Marlboro and Rothmans. The HB livery was a lot luckier for Audi than it had been for Suzuki in World Championship motorcycling during 1983. Here is a practice car before the 1984 Monte wearing Blomqvist's identification, although it was not to be Blomqvist's on the event.

Twice World Champion, four times a winner in Monte Carlo and very much the hero of Regensberg and nearby Ingolstadt: Walter Rohrl. Leaving Lancia for Audi, after the Italians had snatched the 1983 manufacturer's title from the German team did not look sensible at the time; particularly with a completely new car-driving technique to master, but Rohrl won his first World Championship rally with Audi. After that 1984 Monte win, the 36-year-old Bavarian had scored 13 Championship victories, only three less than Mikkola, with all but one of Rohrl's wins recorded since 1978.

"Don't go by air, fly with Walter," said the German script on this beautifully executed HB-Audi poster spotted on the 1984 Monte.

quattro

Walter Rohrl, Christian Geistdorfer and a new A2 Quattro were enough to seize Monaco victory. The crew first won Monte in 1980 with a Fiat, 1982 with Opel's debutante Ascona 400, and 1983's win was for the Lancia Rally.

Stig Blomqvist drove his heart out in the early stages of the first snowy Monte for several seasons, but was delayed by backmarkers and gear selection troubles sufficiently that he had to accept team orders to stay second in the later stages, eventually finishing over a minute behind Rohrl. Although Blomqvist did drive as well as many pundits predicted, Rohrl was better. Walter set 15 fastest times to the 9 of the Swede; there were none from Mikkola.

quattro

Mikkola brought his second place 1983 RAC Rally Quattro into third place on the 1984 Monte, hampered by a lack of pre-event tyre testing and therefore suffering some gross errors in selecting the right rubber for prevalent stage conditions. The A2 Quattros started 1984 wearing the new HB colours and a wider, larger diameter, choice of five spoke alloy wheels, but were now conservatively rated at a minimum 380bhp officially

Audi's top trio on 1984 Monte: Mikkola, Rohrl and Blomqvist. Michele Mouton had never had an Audi finish on the event and was missed out. Only Blomqvist was expected to compete in all 1984 World Championship rounds

quattro

Bernard Darniche had poor Audi luck prior to the 1984 Monte – shattering his heel on 1983 practice for Corsica and finishing well down the order on 1983's Sanremo. For the new year the ex-Swedish Rally works Quattro racked up a convincing Group A win in Bernard's capable hands and finished seventh overall – ahead of Markku Alen's dramatic Lancia Rally!

Appendix 2

Mechanical specifications

1980 Audi Quattro coupe

Type: European LHD, two-door, road car.

Engine: Inline five-cylinder, SOHC, two valves per cylinder, alloy head, iron cylinder block tilted 27.5° from vertical. Bore × stroke, 79.5 × 86.4mm (2144cc) with 7:1cr. Bosch K-Jetronic injection, air intercooler, KKK-K26 turbocharger with 0.85 bar/12.09psi max boost wastegate limitation. Transistorised Bosch ignition with Bosch W200 T30 spark plugs. Forged steel crankshaft, six main bearings and belt drive for SOHC. Wet sump lubrication, 4 litres oil.

Output: 147kW/200PS DIN bhp at 5500rpm. 29.1mkp/210.5lb. ft at 3500 rpm.

Transmission: Permanent 4-WD with dual cable operation for centre and rear differential locks individually. Single plate clutch and 3.889:1 final drive. Gearbox ratios: first, 3.600; second, 2.125; third, 1.360; fourth, 0.967; fifth, 0.778.

Body: Unitary steel basic construction. Plastics used for front and rear under-bumper spoilers, tail spoiler, bumper covering and tailgate. Steel wheelarch extensions. Four standard colours with Mocca trim to seats, door interiors, headliner and carpeting. Fuel tank of 92 litres/20.2 Imp. gallons over rear axle. Standard German equipment included: bronze tinted glass all round with laminated windscreen carrying green anti-dazzle strip; stainless steel exhaust with twin tailpipes; two tone horns; twin exterior mirrors with electric heating and power adjust; twin rectangular headlamps with Halogen bulbs, H4 low beam and H1 high; headlight washers; front foglights; choice three metallic paints (Saturn, Helios and Silver Diamond) or Venus red solid colour; alloy wheels and low profile tyres. German market options (Spring 1980): cruise control, central locking, sunroof, power windows, rear window wiper/washer,

7J × 15 alloy wheels, electric heat for front seats; green-tinted heat insulating glass all round, vanity mirror plus light and audio equipment.

Dimensions: Wheelbase, 99.4in/2524mm; overall length, 173.4in/4404mm; overall width, 67.8in/1723mm; height, 52.9in/1344mm; front track, 55.9in/1421mm; rear track, 57.4in/1458mm.

Weight: 2838lb/1290kg.

Suspension: MacPherson strut front with coil spring and wishbone lower arms. Same system at rear, turned through 180° and utilising transverse fixed links instead of steering arms. Front and rear anti-roll bars. Hydraulic strut damping, ex-Audi 80 and 100 models.

Brakes: Hydraulic assistance from central pump, twin circuit with pressure regulator with 11.02in/280mm ventilated front discs and 9.65in/245mm solid back discs.

Wheels & tyres: 6J × 15 Ronal with 205/60 HR Goodyear and Fulda common fitment.

Steering: Power assistance shared with hydraulic brake system, rack and pinion. Turning circle, 44.5ft/11.3 metres.

Electrics: Alternator, 75 Amp, battery 12v/63 Ah. Electronic ignition with air mixture temperature and engine load sensors.

Economy (Audi DIN figures): Urban, 17.99mpg (15.7L/100km) at 56mph/90kph; 35.76mpg (7.9L/100km) at 75mph/120kph; 27.16mpg (10.4L/100km).

Performance (Audi figures): "over 220kph" (136.5mph); 0-50mph, 4.9s; 0-62mph, 7.1s. (*Autocar* 1981 LHD test): 135mph, 0-60mph in 7.3s and 19.1mpg overall, including performance tests.

1981 Group 4 Quattro coupe

Type: Internationally recognised Gp4 competition car.

Engine: Inline five-cylinder, SOHC, two valves per cylinder, alloy head, iron cylinder block. Bore × stroke, 79.5mm × 86.4mm (2144cc) with 6.3:1cr. Pierburg DVG mechanical fuel-injection with single KKK turbocharger in a number of alternative casings. Enlarged air-to-air intercooler with 1.6 bar/22.77psi wastegate-controlled maximum boost. Extra heat treatment of forged steel crankshaft; six main bearings; dry sump lubrication via boot-mounted tank, Castrol contract. Hitachi ignition, Bosch plugs. Oil system modifications in 1981 to enlarge rear cooler (and with it the back spoiler) and replace original dry sump tank with round tank design aimed at eliminating aeration. Inlet valve size up from production 38.2mm to 41.1mm; exhaust valve head diameter increased from 33.3mm to 35.2mm. Bosch ignition replaced original Hitachi.

Output: Minimum 237kW/320PS/DIN bhp at 6500rpm: over 300bhp between 5500 and 7000rpm. Max torque: 42mkp/304lb. ft at 3250rpm.

Transmission: Permanent 4-WD with limited slip differential rear ZF, 75 per cent. Solid shaft centre differential. Fichtel and Sachs competition single plate clutch. Homologated close gear ratios: first, 3.00; second, 2.00; third, 1.50; fourth, 1.217; fifth, 1.040. Choice of three final drive ratios: 4.11, 4.55 and 4.87:1.

Body: Basic steel construction modified and strengthened by Matter & Obermoser GmbH, Graben-Neudorf, including welded aluminium roll cage with tubes extended to cover front strut mountings and extra transverse strength behind front grille, plus extension to rear suspension top-mountings. Aluminium bonnet, front wings and quick-release fascia; polyester plastic bootlid with enlarged spoiler from Sanremo 1981. Wheelarch extension "eyebrows" added and enlarged by Tour de Corse, 1981, together with front spoiler. Extended two-headlamp grille homologated after Acropolis disqualification. Fire-protected Kleber safety fuel tank, 120L/26.4 Imp. gallons, in boot with dry sump tank. Two underbody guards in aluminium, later replaced by Kevlar components in 1982.

Interior: Momo/Personal steering wheel, four point harness, Recaro seating, seven dial instrumentation included: 200km/h speedo, fuel, oil and boost pressures, 10,000rpm tachometer, oil and water temperature dials (150°C scale max). All by VDO, plus various electrical monitoring dials (volts, etc).

Dimensions: Wheelbase, 99.4in/2524mm; overall length 173.4in/4404mm (without auxiliary lamps); overall width 68.23in/1733mm (up an average 10mm according to extension fitted); height, 52.9in/1344mm (lower on tarmac); front track, 57.68in/1465mm (up an average 44mm); rear track, 59.13in/1502mm (up an average 48mm over standard).

Weight: 2618lb/1190kg to 2728lb/1240kg. Regulations asked for 1005kg minimum and Audi claimed "around 1100kg" at 1981 Monte for Mouton's car.

Suspension: Based on Audi MacPherson strut system with strengthened wishbones (length optimised by computer during 1981) and reinforced steering arms. Competition anti-roll bar alternatives front and rear, plus Boge strut damping and alternative coil springs.

Brakes: Four wheel ventilated discs of 280mm/11.02in F&R, alloy calipers and twin master cylinders. No servo-assistance. Adjustable front rear braking bias. Rear wheel hydraulic handbrake.

Wheels & tyres: Mainly Fuchs forged alloy five-spoke, 6 or 7J loose, up to 10in rims for tarmac, all 15in diameter. Tyres, Kleber factory contract 1981-82, from 165 section loose to 11/25 × 15 CS slicks.

Steering: Power-assisted rack and pinion with camshaft drive for hydraulic assistance.

Electrics: High output alternator, rear battery, Carello (×4 or ×6) auxiliary lights (Bosch, 1982 Gp4) for factory cars which had ×4 headlamps early 1981, and ×2 homologated July 1, 1981.

Economy: Circa 6mpg/47L per 100km in competition use.

Performance: Audi quoted top speeds from 108 to 158mph, according to ratios. From 0-62mph in 4.9 to 5.2s and 12.8 to 13.5s for 0-100mph. *Autocar*'s test of David Sutton's similar Gp4 Quattro in September 1982: 0-60mph, 4.9s and 0-100mph, 13.7s (the latter also the quarter mile results) and tested up to 110mph. It weighed 2778lb/1263kg.

1982 Audi 80 Quattro saloon

Type: German market LHD, 4-door, road car.

Engine: Inline five cylinder, SOHC, two valves per cylinder, alloy head, iron cylinder block tilted at 27.5° from vertical. Bore × stroke, 79.5 × 86.4mm (2144cc) with 9.3:1cr. Forged steel crankshaft, six main bearings and belt drive SOHC. Bosch K-Jetronic injection. Transistorised ignition with Bosch W6D spark plugs. Wet sump lubrication, 5 litres oil.

Output: 100kW (136 PS/DIN bhp) at 5900rpm. 17.9mkp/129.5lb. ft at 4500rpm.

Transmission: Permanent 4-WD with vacuum single knob switchgear operating centre or centre and rear differential locks. Single plate clutch with 4.111:1 final drive (32.2km/h per 1000rpm, 19.99mph). Gearbox ratios: first, 3.600; second, 2.125; third, 1.458; fourth, 1.071; fifth, 0.829.

Body: Unitary steel construction with deformable plastics for front and bootlid spoilers, plus underboot rear. Basically an Audi 80 with Quattro 4-WD floorpan (larger centre tunnel, plus rear pick up points). Enlarged 70 litre/15.4 Imp. gallon fuel tank. Standard equipment: leather rim, four spoke sports wheel of 380mm/14.96in; laminated windscreen; sports front seats; enlarged × 4 halogen headlamps; power steering; lockable fuel filler cap. On 1983 UK spec standard features: RHD, central locking, power windows (front), driver's seat height adjustment, front and rear seatbelts and foglamps. German/UK options: leather upholstery, heat insulating glass, light alloy 6J × 14 wheels with 195/60 HR radials, electric heat and operation of door mirrors; manual steel or electric sliding sunroof. In UK radio × 4 speakers and aerial supplied, but not in-car radio/tape unit.

Dimensions: Wheelbase, 99.5in/2525mm; length, 172.56in/4383mm; width, 66.22in/1628mm; height, 54.17in/1376mm; front track, 55.24in/1403mm; rear track, 55.39in/1407mm.

Kerb weight: 2618lb/1190 kg.

Suspension: All independent on MacPherson strut principles with 1982 modifications shared by Quattro (chapter 11) and lighter front springs to suit non-turbo engine weight. No rear anti-roll bar.

Brakes: Vacuum servo-assisted, tandem brake master cylinder, twin circuit with Audi 100 front calipers and Quattro coupe calipers, rear. Pressure regulator on servo for rear discs with failsafe. Four wheel discs, ventilated front, sizes as for Quattro coupe: 280mm/11.02in front and 245mm/9.65in rear.

Wheels & tyres: Standard with 5½J × 14 steels wearing Audi 100 aero hubcaps and 175/70 HR Good Year Allweather. See options.

Steering: Coupe 2-WD Geometry, Quattro hydraulically-assisted rack and pinion. Turning circle, 41.34ft/10.5 metres.

Electrics: Alternator, 65 Amp; battery, 12v/63 A/hr; electronic ignition with induction regulator solenoid.

Economy (Audi Germany figures): Urban, 20.8mpg (13.6L/100km); at 56mph, 38.7mpg (7.3L/100km); at 75mph, 31mpg (9.1L/100km).

Performance: Audi figures: 193km/h (119.8mph); 0-50mph, 6.2s; 0-62mph, 9.1s. *Auto motor und sport:* 196km/h (122mph), 0-62mph, 10.4s, 21.73mpg overall. See also Chapter 11 for UK test results.

Price: As at September 1983 German mkt 80 Quattro was 33,045Dm, equivalent to £8473. Equivalent UK price, £11,269.

1983 Group A Audi 80 Quattro

Type: International GpA competition saloon.

Engine: Inline five-cylinder, SOHC, two-valves per cylinder, alloy head, iron cylinder block, 27.5 degree tilt. Bore × stroke, 79.5 × 86.4mm (2144cc) with allowance for 2178cc from 80.11mm max bore and standard stroke. Average rally cr, 10.5:1. Modified settings for Bosch K-Jetronic injection, maximum valve sizes 38.2mm (inlet) and 33.3mm (exhaust) with production alloy and cast iron intake/exhaust manifolding. Valve lift max, 10.8mm. Forged steel

quattro

crankshaft, six main bearings, belt-drive sohc, modified wet sump lubrication to prevent surge, including baffled sump, but standard oil pump pressure.

Output: 185 to 190bhp at 7500rpm.

Transmission: Permanent 4-WD as per production car but with centre differential lock and competition fitment of limited slip back differential. Stronger driveshafts. Single plate clutch with choice of standard 4.111 final drive, or 4.875 and 4.571 options. Standard gearbox or new casing and closer ratios: first, 3.00; second, 2.00; third, 1.50; fourth 1.217; fifth, 1.040; as per Group 4 and original Group B ratios.

Body: Steel construction with plastic ancillaries on exterior, as per production. Interior has choice of 16kg/35.2lb or 26kg/57.2lb roll cages by Matter & Obermoser, both in aluminium with heavier one featuring more comprehensive cockpit protection, including side crash bars across door openings and rear shelf cross-brace. Examples constructed by Audi Sport, David Sutton Cars had similar seating, safety harness and navigational aids as works turbo coupes. For 1984 Sutton Cars constructed a special 80 for use in the British National Championship by Darryl Weidner that married a turbocharged Quattro five with Kevlar-panelled exterior. This had nothing to do with Group A . . .!

Dimensions (Homologated figures): Wheelbase, 2525mm/99.5in; length, 4392mm/172.91in; width, 1698mm/66.85in; no height given; body width, F&R, 1692mm/66.61in.

The 80 Quattro was a popular sight on 1983 British Open Championship rounds, Harald Demuth driving as spectacularly as ever.

Weight: Circa 1260kg/2772lb.

Suspension: Standard strut principles with replacement reinforced wishbones using uniball joints, strengthened strut casings with threaded spring height adjustment, shorter and stronger steering arms, trackrods with uniball joints and alloy hubs with five-point mounting and centre wheel lock. Boge strut dampers.

Brakes: Eight front disc options listed with two specific rears, both latter close to standard 245mm diameter (239 and 239.4mm respectively). Front from standard 280mm diameter to 304mm (with thickness increased to 28mm in some cases from standard 20mm). Rear's 10mm thickness has one 19mm homologated option. Factory specification included adjustable balance, deleted servo-assistance and provided an hydraulic handbrake. Homologated 4-piston alloy calipers.

Wheels & tyres: In 1983 factory ran Fuchs + Michelin, Sutton Cars BBS + Pirelli.

Steering: Production power-assisted rack with either standard 17.3:1 ratio or homologated 16.7:1 steering ratio.

Electrics: Uprated alternator and battery with Bosch auxiliary lighting for factory and Hella on Sutton Cars 80.

Economy & performance: 7-10mpg, no performance figures available.

January 1, 1983, Audi Quattro-A1

Type: Internationally recognised Group B competition car.

Engine: Inline five-cylinder, SOHC, two valves per cylinder, aluminium head and cylinder block with cast iron dry liners and set 27.5 degrees from vertical. Bore × stroke, 79.51 × 86.4mm (2145cc), 2178cc available from maximum bore of 80.11mm; 6.3:1cr. Turbo multiplied capacity, minimum 3003cc, max 3048cc. Pierburg-Bosch sports mechanical fuel-injection, air intercooler. Group B spec, KKK-K26 turbocharger, evolution A1 allowed K27, both air intercooled. Wastegate boost maximum 1.9 bar/27psi, usual minimum 1.6 bar/22.8psi. Standard inlet (38.2mm) and exhaust (33.3mm) valves replaced by A1 Evolution 41.1mm inlets and 35.2mm exhaust. Bosch electronic ignition. Forged steel crankshaft with additional heat treatment, six main bearings. Dry sump lubrication, round aluminium tank by Matter in boot. Plastics, Kevlar and carbon fibre weaves used for some engine ancillaries on Evolution A1, eg: electric fan/rad shroud, & cam belt cover.

Output: 340bhp at 6000rpm & 1.7 bar boost. Over 305lb. ft torque at 3600rpm.

Transmission: Permanent 4-WD with limited slip rear differential and solid shaft "locked" centre differential. Replacement stronger driveshafts F&R; homologated single piece plastic front to rear propshaft. Final drive ratios, 4.111, 4.571 and 4.625. Usual Audi competition close ratios: first, 3.00; second, 2.00; third, 1.50; fourth, 1.217; fifth, 1.040.

Body: Basic internal construction in steel modified by Matter with choice of three aluminium welded roll cage layouts and one in steel also by Matter & Obermoser: normal alloy cage with forward legs and comprehensive side and rear protection weighed 25kg/55lb. External bolt on panels including large wheelarch extensions in Kevlar with plastics homologated for the bonnet and boot, plus aluminium doors and plastic panes for side and rear windows. Laminated glass front screen with integral heating/demister element. Plastic fire-protected fuel tank by Seger & Hoffman (Premier, UK) of 120 litres/26 Imp. galls.

Interior: Audi Momo three spoke steering wheel, Recaro seats, Sabelt safety harness. Nine-dial instrumentation: 200km/h speedo; 10,000rpm tachometer with telltale; fuel, oil and boost pressure; oil and water temperature, fuel contents; voltmeter.

Dimensions: (Homologated figures). Wheelbase, 2524mm/99.4in; length, 4404mm/173.4in; width, 1733mm/67.5in of Group B multiplied by 6% Evolution allowance = 1837mm/72.32in F&R bodywork.

Weight: 1130kg/2486lb to 1140kg/2508lb.

Suspension: MacPherson strut principles with wishbone lower arms additionally located by forward links, front and rear, plus anti-roll bars. A1 homologation included choice of nine itemised lower wishbone layouts including these constructed in steel, plastic (heavily cross-triangulated and braced), titanium and aluminium as well as wishbones with uniball joints and castor offset variation. New mounting points for wishbones and location links were also specified and photographed. Titanium and aluminium strut variations also offered along with appropriate springs and Boge dampers.

Brakes: Standard twin circuit 280/245mm rear disc layout. Evoluted A1 with choice of three competition calipers, no servo assistance and three ventilated disc choices: 280mm × 25.5mm; 295mm × 28mm and 305mm × 28mm. Discs cross-drilled for extra efficiency. Adjustable bias, pressure relief valve for rear brakes in cockpit and hydraulic handbrake.

Wheels & tyres: Ronal alloys on road cars for homologation. Fuchs/BBS to suit Michelin (factory) and Pirelli (Sutton Cars). From 6 to 7in on loose with up to 12in rims permitted; normal maximum 10in × 15 diameter.

Steering: Power assisted rack & pinion with 22.4:1 ratio; A1 offered replacement trackrods and stronger mounting plate on steering assembly.

Electrics: Competition Bosch alternator, battery in boot, Bosch auxiliary lamps (factory), Hella (GB). Special mounting for alternator above lightweight alloy rocker cover, designed to cure cracking problem on mount: alternator, direct belt-drive from crankshaft.

Economy & performance: 5-6mpg in competition. Typically geared for 115mph loose surface maximum with 0-60mph in 4.5s.

Price: UK quotation for Sutton Cars replica, 1983: "about £75,000".

May 1, 1983, Audi Quattro-A2

Type: Internationally recognised Group B competition car.

Engine: Inline five-cylinder, SOHC, two valves per cylinder, aluminium head and cylinder block with cast iron dry liners and set 27.5 degrees from vertical. Bore × stroke, 79.3 × 86.4mm (2133cc) for basic homologation vehicle, but competition A2s appeared with 80.11mm max bore size allied to 85.0mm stroke, or minimum 79.51mm bores. Homologated A2 capacity, 2110cc multiplied by 1.4 turbo factor = 2954cc; maximum allowable, 2142cc × 1.4 = 2999cc. Bosch electronically managed fuel-injection with some Pierburg-branded components, four (two ignition, two injection) electronic control boxes in cockpit. Air intercooler, Group B prod cars had KKK-K26 turbocharger, evolution A2 equipped with enlarged KKK-K27. Improved exhaust manifolding, plus sliding plate downpipe control (see chapter 11). Compression ratio, 6.5:1. Max boost 1.9 bar/27psi, up to 400bhp at 7000rpm

with 362lb. ft torque at 4000rpm. Evolution valve sizes, 41.1mm (inlet) and 35.2mm (exhaust), as per A1. Competition 85mm stroke steel crankshaft safe to over 8000rpm with six main bearings and dry sump lubrication. Kevlar and carbon fibre composites used for engine ancillaries such as cam belt drive cover, fan shroud, air induction pipe with filter.

Output (Audi PR at Corsican debut): 360bhp at 7000rpm. 450Nm/331lb. ft at 4000rpm.

Transmission: Permanent 4-WD with limited slip rear differential. No centre differential, shorter and lighter homologated gearbox and electro-hydraulic clutch with stronger replacement driveshafts. Two sets of evolution gear ratios, first set as per A1 etc with second set in brackets offering revised fourth and fifth: first, 3.00 (3.00); second, 2.00 (2.00); third, 1.50 (1.50); fourth, 1.217 (1.174); fifth, 1.040 (0.962). Final drives, 4.375 standard, plus 4.286, 4.571, and 4.857.

Body: Basic internal steel construction prepared by Matter or Gartrac with a choice of 16kg or 25kg roll cages from Matter homologated. External bolt-on Kevlar wings with double ducting on rears for brakes and differential replacing A1 single ducts. Plastics homologated for bootlid, bonnet, doors and side/rear windows (bonded) or sliding fronts. Laminated glass front screen, safety fuel tank. Revised wishbone mounting points. Modified transmission tunnel for new short gearbox and front axle subframe rewelded without gearbox mounting brackets, rear axle subframe without differential carrier. Revised front spoiler with multiple grille inlets.

Interior: In competition trim, as per A1. (See chapter 11 also.)

Dimensions: As A1 extended figures — standard 2524mm/99.4in wheelbase, length 4404mm/173.4in; width 1837mm/72.32in.

Weight: 1000kg/2200lb (Corsica) to 1100kg/2420lb forest use.

Suspension: Simplified over A1 options, still MacPherson strut with additional leading link location F&R, plus anti-roll bars. Steel alloy and titanium wishbones homologated with castor offset uniball option for wishbones and track rods. Alloy struts with titanium also homologated, also heavy duty strut for smaller spring diameters with threaded seat. Boge strut damping.

Brakes: As per A1 with three caliper and three disc diameter/thickness of cross-drilled disc layouts listed from 280mm to 305mm. Adjustable balance, hydraulic handbrake, twin master cylinders and pressure relief valve for rear brakes in cockpit.

Wheels & tyres: As per A1, save 11in max allowed rim width, 6J minimum, 15in diameters from Fuchs/BBS with Michelin factory tyre contract.

Steering: Power assisted rack and pinion, 22.4:1 ratio.

Electrics: As for A1.

Economy and performance: 6-8mpg in competition.

Price: Not revealed.

1983 Audi Quattro coupe (USA)

Type: Coupe Quattro road car, October 1983.

Engine: Inline five-cylinder, SOHC, two valves per cylinder, alloy head, iron cylinder block. Bore × stroke, 79.5 × 86.4mm (2144cc) with 7:1cr. Catalytic convertor, oxygen sensor, Bosch electronic injection and digital ignition to suit emission engine running unleaded premium petrol. Usual forged steel

crankshaft with six main bearings. KKK turbocharger and intake charge intercooling.

Output: 160bhp at 5500rpm. 170lb. ft at 3000rpm. Both SAE Net figures.

Transmission: Permanent 4-WD with centre and/or rear differential locking. Single plate clutch and 3.89 final drive. Gearbox ratios: first, 3.60; second, 2.13; third, 1.46; fourth, 1.07; fifth, 0.78.

Body: Federal version with extended bumpers, USA quad headlamps, American instrumentation and narrow neck unleaded fuel-filler neck. Standard equipment included leather seats, air-conditioning, power windows, central locking, tilt/removable sunroof, cruise control, driver's seat height adjustment, tinted glass, AM/FM stereo cassette, rear window wiper, heated electric mirrors and 23.8 US gallon fuel tank. Optional heated seats.

Dimensions: Wheelbase, 99.5in; overall length, 178.2in; overall width, 67.9in; unloaded height, 52in; front track, 56in; rear track, 57.4in.

Weight: 1352kg/2974lb.

Suspension: Front, MacPherson strut with anti-roll bar. Rear, independent coil-sprung struts.

Brakes: Hydraulic power assistance, pressure regulator, dual circuit with 280mm/11.02in vented front discs and 240mm/9.45in solid back discs.

Wheels & tyres: 6J × 15 Ronal alloy with 205/60 HR Goodyear NCT tyres catalogued.

Steering: Power-assisted rack & pinion, 3.4 turns lock-to-lock.

Electrics: Alternator, 90 Amp, battery 12v/63 Amp/hr, digital ignition.

Economy (US figures): City, 17mpg; Highway, 28mpg.

Performance (US catalogue figures − see relevant chapter for independent figures): Top speed, fourth gear, 128mph; 0-50mph, 5.3s; 0-60mph, 7.5s.

Price: $35,000 (£24,823 at December 1983 rate of $1.41).

September 1983 Audi Quattro Sport

Type: Short wheelbase Quattro road coupe.

Engine: Inline five-cylinder, DOHC, four valves per cylinder, alloy head and cylinder block. Bore × stroke, 79.3 × 86.4mm (2133cc) with 8.0:1±0.3cr. Air intercooler by Langerer & Reich, Bosch LH-Jetronic fuel-injection, KKK-K27 turbocharger boosting 98 RON petrol mixture to a maximum 1.2 bar/17psi with wastegate boost control and Bosch all-electronic microprocessor with flywheel sensor pick-up. Over-run injection fuel cut-off system. Alloy pan wet sump lubrication. Quoted engine weights, 145 to 150kg/319 to 330lb.

Output: 220kW/300 PS-DIN bhp at 6500rpm. Peak torque, 330Nm/243lb. ft at 4500rpm.

Transmission: Permanent 4-WD with pneumatic two-stage knob to engage either centre differential lock, or centre plus rear differential lock. Single plate clutch and 3.875:1 final drive (37.3kph/23.16mph per 1000rpm). Gearbox ratios: first, 3.500; second, 2.083; third, 1.368; fourth, 0.962; fifth, 0.759.

Body: Unitary steel inner panel construction with shortened (minus 320mm/12.6in) and modified Audi 80/Quattro floorpan and cockpit.

External panels − bumpers, roof, front and rear aprons − in laminated glass and Kevlar fibre composites. Bootlid and bonnet in polyester resin reinforced glassfibre. Engine bay intake air pipes in carbon fibre with radiator cowlings in Kevlar/carbon fibre hybrid weave. Many of these panels directly from 1983 rally programme A1/A2 source. Fuel tank under rear boot floor, 90 litres/15.4 Imp. gallons. Wet sump lubrication system with filter.

Interior: Fully equipped show car had leather interior, full harness Sabelt seatbelts and four spoke steering wheel. Instrumentation comprised 300km/h speedometer, 0-9000rpm tachometer, centre boost gauge (2 bar absolute/1 bar above atmospheric), 0-120°C water temperature and 0-170°C oil plus and oil pressure gauge reading to 5 bar max.

Dimensions: Wheelbase, 2204mm/86.77in; length, 4164mm/163.94in; width, 1803mm/70.98in; height, 1345mm/52.95in; front track, 1515mm/59.68in; rear track, 1491mm/58.74in.

Weight: Approx 1000kg/2200lb.

Suspension: Competition-derived MacPherson strut and lower wishbone system with leading links and Boge dampers, front roll bar.

Brakes: Twin circuit based on four wheel ventilated discs of 295mm/11.6in × 28mm/1.1in. Fixed four piston calipers, handbrake operated via separate rear calipers. ABS anti-lock braking from 2.75kph onward, non-operational when the differentials are engaged on lock-up — and can be manually overridden by cockpit switch.

Wheels & tyres: Ronal 9J × 15 with 235/45 VR Michelin on debut.

Steering: Audi variable power assistance, rack and pinion.

Electrics: Electronic ignition and injection management with 12v/63 A/hr battery and 90 Amp alternator. Twin headlamp rather than quad Quattro coupe layout.

Economy: Not available.

Performance (Audi pre-production figures): 155mph maximum; 0-62mph in 4.5s.

Price: Estimated at 200,000Dm (£51,282) at announcement time.

Appendix 3

Production & sales

Audi factory comment that 1981 saw sales of 1729 Quattro coupes, and 1690 in 1982. They exported 42% in those years, or 56% including American market of 1982. Between January and April 1983 they made 668 Quattro coupes and 5125 Quattro 80 saloons; between January and October of the same year they produced a total of 1127 Quattro coupes and an impressive 13,403 Quattro 80 saloons. As at January 1984 of 5130 Quattro Coupes made, 2400 had been sold in Germany, and the rest exported.

Ingolstadt production: 1980-83

Quattro coupe
1980	292
1981	1956
1982	1935
1983	—

Quattro 80 saloon
| 1982 | 527 |
| 1983 | — |

Sales: United Kingdom

1981	95
1982	154
1983	329

Quattro 80 saloon
| 1983 (Aug –) | 281 |

Sales: United States

| 1982 | 154 |
| 1983 (to September) | 235 |

Quattro 80
Not on sale USA.

Sales: West Germany

1980	143
1981	938
1982	617
1983	503

Quattro 80
1982 Not sold until January 1983
| 1983 | 5240 – |

Appendix 4

World championship rally record: 1981-83 seasons

Indicates a rally counted only for Driver's Championship, otherwise events counted for both Drivers' and Manufacturers' titles. NB: ''ss'' refers to special stage.

1981

EVENT	CREWS	QUATTRO TYPE	RESULT	COMMENT
Monte Carlo, Monaco January 24-30	Mikkola/Hertz Mouton/Pons	Gp4 coupe Gp4 coupe	91st DNF	Led initially. 8 ss fastest. No stages, fuel system fails.
International Swedish* February 13-15	Mikkola/Hertz	Gp4 coupe	1st	Led all 25 stages. Fastest, 15 stages.
Rally de Portugal March 4-7	Mikkola/Hertz Mouton/Pons	Gp4 coupe Gp4 coupe	DNF 4th	Engine, led 25 of 46 stages; fastest on 16 ss. Fastest, 7 stages.
Tour de Corse, Corsica April 30-May 2	Mikkola/Hertz Mouton/Pons	Gp4 coupe Gp4 coupe	DNF DNF	Engine, 6 stages. Engine 8 stages. In top 6. for 6 stages.
Acropolis Rally, Greece June 1-4	Mikkola/Hertz Mouton/Pons Wittman/Nestinger	Gp4 coupe Gp4 coupe Gp4 coupe	DSQ DSQ DSQ	Led 33 of 34 ss. Led ss 1; 5 fastest times. Also disqualified.
Rally of the 1000 Lakes, Finland August 28-30	Mikkola/Hertz Mouton/Pons Wittman/Nestinger	Gp4 coupe Gp4 coupe Gp4 coupe	3rd 13th Withdrawn	Led, 1-21; 29 of 46 ss, fastest. First visit. Spectator death.
Rallye Sanremo, Italy October 5-10	Mikkola/Hertz Mouton/Pons Cinotto/Radaelli	Gp4 coupe Gp4 coupe Gp4 coupe	4th 1st DNF	30 fastest times. Historic win! 7 fastest times. Led before off.
Lombard RAC Rally, UK November 22-25	Mikkola/Hertz Mouton/Pons	Gp4 coupe Gp4 coupe	1st DNF	Over 10m lead! Off, 56 of 65 ss. Fastest, 6 times.

Hannu Mikkola was third in the 1981 World Championship of drivers, with 62 points to the 89 of Guy Frequelin and the 96 of Ari Vatanen. Michele Mouton was 8th with 30 points.
Audi were 5th in the 1981 World Championship of Makes, with 63 points to the 117 of winners Talbot. Audi Sport did not enter three rounds.

quattro

1982

EVENT	CREWS	QUATTRO TYPE	RESULT	COMMENT
Monte Carlo,	Mikkola/Hertz	Gp4 coupe	2nd	10 ss fastest v 13 of winner . . .
Monaco	Mouton/Pons	Gp4 coupe	DNF	Off, 11 ss – 9 top 5 stage times.
January 16-22				
Swedish	Mikkola/Hertz	Gp4 coupe	16th	Off 29 minutes.
International*	Blomqvist/Cederberg	Gp4 coupe	1st	Fastest 16 of 25 ss.
February 12-14	Mouton/Pons	Gp4 coupe	5th	15 top 5 times
Rally de Portugal	Mikkola/Hertz	Gp4 coupe	DNF	Off, 11 stages
	Mouton/Pons	Gp4 coupe	1st	Fastest 18 of 40 ss
March 3-6	Wittman/Diekmann	Gp4 coupe	3rd	22 top 5 times.
Tour de Corse,	Mikkola/Hertz	Gp4 coupe	DNF	1 ss, gearbox.
Corsica	Mouton/Pons	Gp4 coupe	7th	Only 2 top 5 times.
May 6-8	Wittman/Diekmann	Gp4 coupe	DNF	10 ss, head gasket.
Acropolis Rally,	Mikkola/Hertz	Gp4 coupe	DNF	3-wheeler!
Greece	Mouton/Pons	Gp4 coupe	1st	Led 50 of 57 ss.
May 31/June 4	Wittman/Diekmann	Gp4 coupe	DNF	Deranged steering.
	Cinotto/Radaelli	Gp4 coupe	DNF	9 ss, electrical.
Motogard Rally,	Mikkola/Hertz	Gp4 coupe	DNF	24 ss, 3-wheeler! Fastest 16 ss.
New Zealand	Mouton/Pons	Gp4 coupe	DNF	14 ss, lube loss. 14 top 5 times.
June 26/29				
Rally Marlboro	Mikkola/Hertz	Gp4 coupe	DNF	4 stages, off.
do Brasil	Mouton/Pons	Gp4 coupe	1st	Fastest 18 of 29 ss.
August 10-15				
1000 Lakes Rally,	Mikkola/Hertz	Gp4 coupe	1st	Win by 28s!
Finland	Blomqvist/Cederberg	Gp4 coupe	2nd	Fastest 21 ss v 12 of winner . . .
August 27-29	Mouton/Pons	Gp4 coupe	DNF	Off, 17 stages.
Rallye Sanremo,	Mikkola/Hertz	Gp4 coupe	2nd	Fastest, 18 ss.
Italy	Blomqvist/Cederberg	Gp4 coupe	1st	Fastest, 18 ss!
October 3-9	Mouton/Pons	Gp4 coupe	4th	Fastest 9 ss.
Marlboro Rallye,	Mikkola/Gumpert	Gp4 coupe	DNF	Chase/service.
Cote d'Ivoire	Mouton/Pons	Gp4 Coupe	DNF	45ss, accident. Cost title!
Oct 27-Nov 1				
Lombard RAC	Mikkola/Hertz	Gp4 coupe	1st	5m 43s win. Fastest, 27 ss.
Rally, UK	Mouton/Pons	Gp4 coupe	2nd	Fastest, 16 ss.
November 21-25	Demuth/Daniels	Gp4 coupe	5th	Fastest 7 ss.
	Wilson/Greasley	Gp4 coupe	10th	Fastest 4 ss.
	Buffum/Wilson	Gp4 coupe	12th	Fastest 3 ss.
	Lampi/Kuukkala	Gp4 coupe	DNF	Fastest 1 ss.

Michele Mouton finished second in 1982 World Championship of Drivers, with 93 points to the 109 of Walter Rohrl. Hannu Mikkola was third, with 70 points. Blomqvist 4th, with 58 points – some via Talbot.
Audi won the 1982 World Championship of Makes, with 116 points to the 104 of Opel.

1983

EVENT	CREWS	QUATTRO TYPE	RESULT	COMMENT
Monte Carlo, Monaco January 23-28	Mikkola/Hertz	Gp B-A1	4th	14 top 6 times.
	Blomqvist/Cederberg	Gp B-A1	3rd	16 top 6 times.
	Mouton/Pons	Gp B-A1	DNF	Accident, 12 ss.
International Swedish* February 11-13	Mikkola/Hertz	Gp B-A1	1st	Fastest, 9 ss.
	Blomqvist/Cederberg	Gp B-80 saloon (A proto spec)	2nd	Fastest 7 ss.
	Mouton/Pons	Gp B-A1	4th	Fastest 5 ss.
	Lampi/Kuukkala	Group B coupe	3rd	Fastest 2 ss.
Port Wine Rally of Portugal March 1-6	Mikkola/Hertz	Gp B-A1	1st	Fastest 10 ss.
	Mouton/Pons	Gp B-A1	2nd	Fastest 14 ss.
	Blomqvist/Cederberg	Gp B-A1	DNF	26 ss, F/trans.
	Wittman/Diekmann	Group B coupe	7th	9 top 6 times.
Marlboro Safari, Kenya March 31-April 4	Mikkola/Hertz	Gp B-A1	2nd	Audi's 1st visit.
	Mouton/Pons	Gp B-A1	3rd	Survives 3-wheeler spells!
Tour de Corse, Corsica May 5-7	Mikkola/Hertz	Gp B-A2	DNF	Accident, 24 ss.
	Mouton/Pons	Gp B-A2	DNF	Motor, 27 ss.
	Darniche	Gp B-A2	—	Withdrawn, practice injury.
Acropolis Rally, Greece May 30/June 2	Mikkola/Hertz	Gp B-A2	DNF	Oil loss, 37 ss.
	Mouton/Pons	Gp B-A2	DNF	Accident, 0 ss.
	Blomqvist/Cederberg	Gp B-A2	3rd	Fastest, 18 ss.
	Wittman/Nestinger	Group B coupe	7th	—
Sanyo Rally of New Zealand June 25/28	Mikkola/Hertz	Gp B-A1/2	DNF	Injection, 19 ss. Old body, but Small engine
	Mouton/Pons	Gp B-A1/2	DNF	Engine, 27 ss.
	Blomqvist/Cederberg	Gp B-A1/2	DSQ	Late entry, 8 ss.
Marlboro Rally of Argentina August 1-6	Mikkola/Hertz	Gp B-A2	1st	Fastest, 3 ss.
	Blomqvist/Cederberg	Gp B-A2	2nd	Fastest, 7 ss.
	Mouton/Pons	Gp B-A2	3rd	Fastest 3 ss.
	Mehta/Mehta	Gp B coupe	4th	Fastest 3 ss.
	Wurz/Stohl	Gp A-80 saloon	6th	—
	Di Palma/—	Gp B coupe	DNF	Rolled, 4 ss.
Rally of the 1000 Lakes, Finland August 26-28	Mikkola/Hertz	Gp B-A2	1st	Fastest, 28 ss.
	Blomqvist/Cederberg	Gp B-A2	2nd	Fastest 10 ss.
	Mouton/Pons	Gp B-A2	—	Frequent fires!
	Eklund/Spjuth	Gp B, A2 body	4th	Per's 1st run. Ex-training car.
	Lampi/Kuukkala	Gp B, A2 body	7th	Car, as for Per.
Sanremo Rally, Italy October 2-8	Mikkola/Hertz	Gp B-A2	DNF	Burned out, 27 ss. No quickest times.
	Blomqvist/Cederberg	Gp B-A2	DNF	Accident, 53 ss. Fastest, 22 ss.
	Mouton/Pons	Gp B-A2	7th	Fastest, 2 ss.
	Darniche/Mahe	Gp B-A2	9th	No quickest times.
Marlboro Cote d'Ivoire* October 25-30	Mikkola/Hertz	Gp B-A2	2nd	At least 3 offs.
	Lampi/Harsch	Gp B-3 seater	—	Withdrawn; on event chase car for Mikkola.
Lombard RAC Rally, UK November 19-23	Blomqvist/Cederberg	Gp B-A2	1st	Led all but 4 ss.
	Mikkola/Hertz	Gp B-A2	2nd	3-wheel delay!
	Lampi/Kuukkala	Gp B-A1	4th	Smooth performer.
	Laine/Hokkanen	Group B coupe	DNF	Fire.
	Buffum/Wilson	Gp B-A1	6th	Bravery paid.
	Weidner/Arthur	Gp B-A1	DNF	Small fires.

Hannu Mikkola in the factory Quattros won the 1983 World Championship for Drivers, with 125 points to the 102 of Walter Rohrl. Stig Blomqvist was fourth (89) and Mouton fifth (53). Equal eighth-placed Shekhar Mehta and Lasse Lampi also used Quattros, Lampi regularly and Mehta only for Argentina. Tenth placed Championship runner, Eklund, also used a Quattro once (1000 Lakes).

In the 1983 World Championship of Makes Audi were second to Lancia with 116 points to 118.

A superb study of what Quattro traction means, each of four tyre tracks telling a gripping story. We leave Audi and Walter Rohrl winning at the beginning of 1984, but look forward to new chapters in the saga of Audi's road and rally search for *True Grip* . . .

quattro

April 1984 and we are allowed a few Bavarian track laps with the 300 bhp SWB Quattro Sport. We start alongside Walter Rohrl and then drive the Maestro ourselves, after experiencing the extraordinary Quattro stability, which is apparently unimpaired by a wheel base shorter than that of a Metro! The production Quattro Sport, homologated for May 1 and that month's Corsican Rally début, swept towards 140 mph of its 155 maximum with a Ferrari's ferocity from 4,000 to 7,200 rpm, reaching 60 mph from rest in some 5 seconds. Complete with stiffer suspension, set up with more rear end firmness as for a sporting front drive, and Michelin 235/45 VR radials on 9J wide wheels, the ultimate road Quattro cornered without apparent limit to its enormous capability – and with little visible roll. Priced beyond £52,000 in Germany, Audi expected to make several hundred more than the initial 1984 batch of 220. Just 18 were ear-marked for Britain with some cash deposits taken before the German press launch!

Index